D1257916

Reimagining Businesses with AI

Reimagining Businesses with AI

SUDHI SINHA
KHALED AL HURAIMEL

WILEY

Library of Congress Cataloging-in-Publication Data:

Names: Sinha, Sudhi, 1975- author. | Huraimel, Khaled Al, 1974- author.
Title: Reimagining businesses with AI / Sudhi Sinha, Khaled Al Huraimel.
Description: First Edition. | Hoboken : Wiley, 2020. | Includes index.
Identifiers: LCCN 2020028779 (print) | LCCN 2020028780 (ebook) | ISBN
   9781119709152 (cloth) | ISBN 9781119709176 (adobe pdf) | ISBN
   9781119709169 (epub)
Subjects: LCSH: Artificial intelligence—Economic aspects. | Information
   technology—Management. | Organizational learning. | Organizational
   change.
Classification: LCC HC79.I55 S565 2020 (print) | LCC HC79.I55 (ebook) |
   DDC 658/.0563—dc23
LC record available at https://lccn.loc.gov/2020028779
LC ebook record available at https://lccn.loc.gov/2020028780

Cover Design: Wiley
Cover Image: © vs148/Shutterstock

I dedicate this book to my astounding better half, Ms. Sohini Sengupta, who has been the bedrock of love and support in a tumultuous 2020. She motivated me every day to complete this book so that I can share my learnings, experiences, and ideas with the rest of humanity. The year 2020 is one that history will remember as a turning point due to the COVID-19 crisis; 2020 will also be remembered as the main pivot point when the world is reimagined with AI and digital technologies. This book will hopefully play a small part in helping people traverse that journey.

—Sudhi

I dedicate this book to my parents with love and gratitude. You are the greatest factor contributing to my pursuit of knowledge and giving.

—Khaled

Contents

Acknowledgments

WRITING THIS BOOK HAS been an exhilarating experience. The world is going through an important and interesting transition in which AI and digital technologies are redefining how we live and how we work. This book intends to help business executives, policymakers, technology leaders, and academia reimagine the new world. This journey would not have been possible without the contribution of many.

We would first like to thank Mr. Bill Jackson, President of Chicago Associates, and Head of The Discovery Partners Institute. Bill has always inspired us, taught us to be thoughtful and bold, and encouraged us to "pull the future forward." You make everybody who comes in contact with you a better person and professional. We would also like to thank Dr. Youngchoon Park and Dr. Young M. Lee, two treasured colleagues who have opened our eyes to the possibilities of AI and helped us reimagine a world with AI. Vikram Chowdhary, Mandar Agaskar, and Sachin Patil have been immensely helpful in creating the various visualizations for the book. We salute their amazing creativity and contribution in making many of the ideas visually memorable. We would also like to thank Samuel Freeman and Michael Beck, who have been instrumental in helping us create the frameworks for defining and quantifying value. Next we would like to thank Dr. Jignesh Patel, serial entrepreneur, Professor at UW Madison, and CEO of DataChat, as being a thought partner in our journey. We thank Sujith Ebenezer, Karl Reichenberger, Subrata Bhattacharya, Shyam Sunder, Braja Majumder, and Asif Shafi for being great sounding boards and collaborators over the years. We thank Ms. Maria Hurter, Exec Assistant to the Group CEO of Bee'ah for coordinating many of the discussions and exchanges across country borders and time zones for this global collaboration. We express our gratitude to Ms. Nicole Wesch, Chief Communications Officer of the Schindler Group, who helped us organize the participation of Mr. Silvio Napoli, Chairman of the Board of Directors of Schindler. We also thank Ms. Sarah Anderhalten of Henkel for coordinating the participation of Mr. Michael Nilles, CDO of Henkel, for this project. Silvio and Michael have been inspirational leaders in the digital transformation of some of the biggest corporate giants and have helped shape the leadership conversation in this book.

We are also immensely grateful to the trust and support from Mr. Salim Al Owais, Chairman of Bee'ah, who has allowed to push the boundaries to make Bee'ah what it is today and a regional pioneer in digitalization and sustainability.

Last but not least, we thank our Executive Editor, Mr. Sheck Cho, and Managing Editor, Ms. Susan Cerram, of Wiley for their help to bring this project to life. Sheck was one of the first who believed in this effort and mentored us throughout the journey. Susan helped us immensely in managing the publication, giving us valuable inputs, and keeping us on track.

CHAPTER 1

Introduction

"Artificial intelligence will reach human levels by around 2029. Follow that out further to, say, 2045, we will have multiplied the intelligence, the human biological machine intelligence of our civilization a billion-fold."

—*Ray Kurzweil*

Evolution is the story of tension and mutation. A difference between aspirations and available resources creates tension while changing needs and advancing technology drive mutations. Successful mutations thrive until eventually they, too, are replaced by more successful variants. By its very definition and design, evolution is a slow process. However, every once in a while, evolution is known to change pace, resulting in rapid strides that suddenly leave the standard way of life redundant and usher in a new era.

We live in an increasingly digital world – one in which we are inundated by IoT devices, connectivity, data, applications, and new experiences every moment. Our economy and our way of life are rapidly transforming into a digital one for most parts. This change is requiring businesses to rapidly reinvent themselves in this new world order, not only to thrive but sometimes just to survive.

In very recent times, Artificial Intelligence (AI) has taken center stage in the digital space. AI has existed as a discipline for more than 60 years now; its recent rejuvenation is driven by the advances in digital capabilities around IoT, big data management, cloud computing, and communication technologies. As per a recent McKinsey study,[1] by the end of 2030, the impact of AI is expected to be about $13 trillion with over 70% of companies impacted by AI. An Accenture study on the subject talks about a similar impact and interestingly identifies innovation diffusion as a key benefit in addition to productivity-related benefits. A Forbes study quoting a similar influence cites AI as the "new electricity" already driving a $2 trillion impact on the economy. Whichever study we refer to, the effect of AI on the economy and our lives is undeniable. While these numbers are pre-COVID-19 crisis, they still hold. While the timing may shift as the world starts returning to normalcy, there is no doubt about the extent of the impact. As we will see in several later chapters, COVID-19 has increased the need for AI in every aspect of our lives.

The promise of AI was rooted in the desire to simulate human cognition in the machines as they started becoming more pervasive in the first half of the 20th century. While the academic community and selected industry researchers were successful in developing the mathematical and statistical foundation to solve several AI problems, lack of data and computational power limited the practical implementation of AI on a large scale. These recent digital technological advances allow us to now connect to a very large population of people and things to collect huge volumes and varieties of data, manage and process that data inexpensively and effectively, and apply the AI-based algorithmic analytics to create new insights and drive new experiences and outcomes.

Let us first understand why AI even matters. In the last couple of years, we have already moved from an information age to an `algorithmic age`.[2] A few factors have driven this transition:

- Human sensory functions and the human brain have significantly more things to process today. This means that our attention spans are reducing and we also need capabilities to react fast to new inputs and events. We become more effective if along with information we are given more actionable insights. Consequently, we prefer to engage with different types of businesses and services that give us more actionable insights along with the information.
- Similarly, businesses are also flooded with significantly more information than they were ever exposed to and ready to deal with. Information is now coming from the connectivity of their devices and processes, inputs from users, and other types of transactional data that is getting generated every second. On top of that, they are in a complicated competitive environment that is rapidly transforming as technology is reducing the barriers of historical knowledge, access, and infrastructure required by businesses to be successful. Businesses now have to compete for users' attention every second and use that opportunity to demonstrate better value than others. Businesses also need to quickly innovate around their business models and services to avoid being disrupted.

Traditional business practices and underlying technology infrastructure that were based on predefined rules do not allow one to respond to these types of rapid synthesis and reaction scenarios. It is not possible to know every possible scenario and plan for it, so we need more machine-driven cognitive capabilities that require AI to now become more pervasive, hence the transition from the information age to algorithmic age. In his Future of Life Institute article, AI researcher at the University of Louisville Roman Yampolskiy said, "AI makes over 85% of all stock trades, controls operation of power plants, nuclear reactors, electric grid, traffic light coordination and . . . military nuclear response. . . . Complexity and speed required to meaningfully control those sophisticated processes prevent meaningful human control. We are simply not quick enough to respond to ultrafast events such as those in algorithmic trading and . . . in military drones."

While AI brings a lot of new possibilities, it also brings new problems because businesses have to now reinvent themselves in this new world order. Traditional economic models and management practices are being disrupted. Companies that have considered AI as only a technology enabler for incremental improvements have missed the mark and there is increasing realization among business leaders about that. Those who have taken a more holistic transformative approach are emerging as the leaders in their space in this new world order. The largest technology companies of the world like Microsoft and Google are pivoting with more AI centricity; financial services companies like JPMC are using AI to renovate their client engagement; a traditional industrial giant like Schindler is driving rapid growth using digital and AI; a new age environment management company like Bee'ah is basing its future on AI; and small progressive nations like UAE have made AI a national agenda with possibly being the only country with a separate minister of AI.

The recent COVID-19 crisis has amplified the need for us to focus on digitization and AI. Our world rapidly changed in the first three months of 2020. From being highly integrated and interdependent, we moved into an era of isolation, containment, fear, and remote working in no time. A previously vibrant global economy is seeing one of its worst crises ever; many companies will not make it through this crisis. Organizational resilience in being able to meet the challenges of an unpredictable future is key to survival in this environment. Analytics today is a core capability for achieving such resilience. AI has also been incredibly useful in working through the crisis, forecasting the rate and direction of infection spread, and helping with decision support for containment strategy effectiveness and even with research around the vaccine.

While AI did see many springs and winters over the past 70 years of its existence, it is now firmly intertwined with everything we do. Let us begin our journey into the exciting world of AI.

EVOLUTION OF AI

This book is about the future, but we will spend a little time discussing the past because understanding evolution gives us context and helps us appreciate the path to the future. In this section, we have divided the evolution into multiple eras; these are our choices, they are not industry standards.

Since the beginning of civilization, humans have been ruminating about recreating human-like capabilities in machines. Starting with Greek mythology, there are references to machine-men. Fiction literature is littered with examples of artificial intelligence for a couple of hundred years now. Mary Shelley's *Frankenstein* (1818), Samuel Butler's *Darwin Among the Machines* (1863), and Karel Čapek's *R.U.R. Rossum's Universal Robots* (1920) are some examples of publications where concepts of intelligent devices and robots were discussed. Beyond literature, these ideas also showed up in motion pictures and television from the early days. Arguably, the 1927 German science-fiction film *Metropolis* is the first movie to depict a robot. A very popular show from the 1960s in the United States, *The Jetsons*, also very accurately depicted a future world. While the show was set in 2062, a number of the cool technologies shown in that are already part of our daily lives; these include video calls, robotic vacuum cleaners, robotic assistants, tablet computers, smartwatches, drones, holograms, flying cars, flat televisions, jetpacks, and many more. The trend of depicting a technology-enriched future has continued to the present day. We often take inspiration in life from literature and fiction. That can be said to be true for AI as well.

The 1950s – The Nativity Era

The birth of AI as a formal disciple of study and practice happened in the 1950s. Alan Turing, John McCarthy, Marvin Minsky, Allen Newell, Nathaniel Rochester, Claude Shannon, and Herbert A. Simon are considered as the founding fathers of AI. Norbert Wiener laid the foundation for cybernetics, Claude Shannon conceptualized information theory, and Alan Turing described thinking machines. The confluence of these ideas led to the development of AI. The term *artificial intelligence* was first coined by John McCarthy. Dartmouth Summer Research Project on Artificial Intelligence in the summer of 1956 was the event were AI was first formalized. It started as a proposal made several months earlier by McCarthy, Marvin Minsky, Nathaniel Rochester, and Claude Shannon where the term *AI* was first used. The proposal states,

> We propose that a 2-month, 10-man study of artificial intelligence be carried out during the summer of 1956 at Dartmouth College in Hanover, New Hampshire. The study is to proceed based on the conjecture that every aspect of learning or any other feature of intelligence can in principle be so precisely described that a machine can be made to simulate it. An attempt will be made to find how to make machines use language, form abstractions and concepts, solve kinds of problems now reserved for humans, and improve themselves. We think that a significant advance can be made in one or more of these problems if a carefully selected group of scientists work on it together for a summer.[3]

But AI did not originate suddenly because of the academic research from the 1940s and 1950s. The roots of AI lie in formal reasoning, which has a very long history of over 2,000 years. References to formal reasoning can be found in texts from ancient Greece, India, and the Chinese. It is interesting to note that many early mathematicians were also philosophers. German mathematician Gottfried Leibniz was one of the first to suggest that human reason could be explained as mechanical calculations. *Principia Mathematica* by Alfred North Whitehead and Bertrand Russell published in 1910 is one of the seminal works that laid the foundation for modern mathematics and logic. For a very long time, we humans have been making progress in our quest to create intelligence artificially.

Seventy years back, in the decade of the 1950s, hype cycles did not exist and technology took a long time to transition from the academic realm to practical industry implementations. AI faced the same fate. In its decade of birth, the world saw foundational concepts around AI getting established. But there was a lot of optimism generated in this decade because people could now realistically see computers (machines) undertaking tasks, albeit simple ones, that so far only existed in the fiction realm. One important development in that decade was the invention of one of the earliest programming languages, Lisp, by John McCarthy in 1958. Its significance was realized in later decades as it became the mainstay for AI programming for a long time.

The 1960s – The Foundation Era

The optimism and energy of the 1950s led to the development of a lot of fundamental theories in the 1960s that form the basis of AI even today. Many advancements gave AI the legs to move from a theoretical possibility to practical applicability. Here are some of the highlights:

- **Generic systemic and programming approach to solving any problem.** Development of General Problem Solver technique. At the closing of the previous decade, Herbert A. Simon, J. C. Shaw, and Allen Newell wrote the first program for unconstrained problem-solving.
- **Using math to solve AI problems.** The introduction of Bayesian methods for inductive inference and prediction. Ray Solomonoff took the original theorem of Thomas Bayes and improvements to it made by Pierre-Simon Laplace and developed it further to meet the needs of AI.
- **Introduction of robotics.** Unimate was the first industrial robot that worked on a General Motors assembly line to transport die castings from an assembly line and welding these parts on autobodies. This was a complex task, and with the machine doing it, it increased the safety of workers who were routinely injured in executing that task. Toward the end of the decade, Shakey the Robot emerged as the first general-purpose robot that could analyze commands and decompose them into smaller executable components before carrying out the commanded tasks.
- **Mathematically modeling past data to predict the future.** Introduction of Machine Learning (ML). The roots of ML go back more than 200 years when Thomas Bayes created the Bayes Theorem. In the preceding decades, a lot of discovery around ML happened. But this is the decade when it formally started taking structure post the invention of Perceptron, the introduction of Bayesian methods in AI, and the development of other algorithms.
- **Computers were able to understand and process human language.** Introduction of Natural Language Processing (NLP). Joseph Weizenbaum, professor of the MIT Artificial Intelligence Lab, built ELIZA, the first NLP program that could converse about any topic in English.

Buoyed by these developments, the decade ended with further optimism. MIT AI scientist Marvin Minsky predicted that "in from three to eight years we will have a machine with the general intelligence of an average human being." But that was not to be and AI will hit its first major brakes in the next decade.

The 1970s – The First Winter Era

From the mid-1970s to early 1980s is known as the First Winter of AI when the progress was halted by technological challenges, increasing skepticism, lack of funding, and very limited progress in real-world applications.

That era was also the early days of development of computers. There was not enough computing power available for many of the algorithms to work in any meaningful way. For example, the promise of NLP was dampened because the vocabulary could not be expanded beyond 20 words or so. Pattern recognition and image processing could not progress further for similar reasons. The capabilities of robots remained stagnant. While in the previous decade many academics went on celebrating the promise of quick progress in AI, in this decade a different group of academics were very vocal critics of the possibilities of AI and its inability to solve problems at a meaningful scale. Most of the funding for AI research so far was sponsored by government bodies, a number of them associated with the military. Consequent to the lack of progress and ensuing criticism, most of the funding got pulled.

However, this was not a completely lost decade. There was a lot of theoretical research and publishing that happened in this decade around visual perception, natural language processing, and various algorithmic approaches. Three very important things did happen in this decade that had a significant impact in the years to come:

- Herbert A. Simon won the Nobel Prize in Economics for his theory of bounded rationality, one of the cornerstones of AI.
- The concept of schemas and semantic interpretation of data was introduced by Marvin Minsky in 1975.
- The world's first autonomous vehicle, albeit a basic one but fully computer-controlled, was built by Hans Moravec in the Stanford AI Lab.

The pessimism and slowdown in the last few years of the decade helped AI jumpstart in the following decade.

The 1980s – The Resurrection Era

AI got a new lease of life in the 1980s and this decade became crucial for the advancement of many capabilities that will propel AI forward. Progress was seen both on the hardware and algorithmic side. Furthermore, government support for AI research started to flow through again. Here are some of the highlights from this era:

- **Rise of expert systems to solve specific problems.** By mimicking experts in specific domains and using algorithms to solve more well-defined problems, AI again started proving its value.
- **Machine learning got revived.** The introduction of the Backpropagation technique enabled error correction in prediction models.
- **Initiation of the Fifth-Generation Computer Systems project.** The Japanese government effort started the introduction of massively parallel computing to solve AI problems and take the machines closer to human reasoning levels.
- **Computing power–enabled ANN algorithms.** New electronic transistors and very large-scale system integration (VLSI) development for integrated chips allowed the processing power of computers to dramatically rise, enabling processing-intense algorithms like artificial neural networks.
- **Development of knowledge systems.** Starting with Cyc, many advanced knowledge management systems using AI started getting developed; the foundation was laid for future projects like Deep Blue that catapulted AI to the next level.

This decade accomplished many things to give AI the ability to scale in solving complex real-world issues and break out of the academic realm.

The Brief Interlude

The years 1987 to 1993 saw another slowdown of the AI-wave largely driven by the inability of the hardware and computing capabilities to keep up with the algorithmic progress. Consequently, the broader impact was not felt and funding was again cut. However, this did not last for too long. The research community retreated in the background and operated behind the shadows to come back with some impressive accomplishments in the 1990s.

The 1990s and 2000s – The Second Revival

Finally, during this era, AI broke out of the academic world and started becoming more mainstream. This was greatly aided by the improvements in computing power and the development of distributed systems. A lot of the algorithmic development, originally done for AI, finally proliferated the business world for data mining, search (like Google), robotics, medical diagnostics, financial services, and other industrial applications. In the 1990s, there were many other notable games in which AI-powered computer programs won. AI program DART was deployed for military purposes in the First Gulf War. In the first decade of the next century, a lot was achieved in robotics and autonomous driving. Many disciplines of AI like machine learning, intelligent tutoring, case-based reasoning, multi-agent planning, scheduling, uncertain reasoning, data mining, natural language understanding and translation, vision, virtual reality, games, and other topics got an opportunity for real-life demonstrations.

This was the time when the world was first consumed by the Y2K crisis, then by the Internet, and thereafter the massive boom in e-commerce and dot-com companies. So, while AI did not get much publicity, it kept making progress in the background. This helped because there were no inflated expectations to meet, yet researchers were able to contribute to solving business problems. Two very notable things did happen in this era that eventually led to the current hype around AI:

- Deep Blue defeated chess champion Gary Kasparov in 1997 and created a huge buzz around the power of computers and algorithms.
- Multi-agent systems started to mature with new concepts from decision theory to create intelligent agents; we shall discuss multi-agent systems a few times later in the book.

The world celebrated 50 years of AI in 2006. AI gained a lot of ground during its second revival. It took a bit of time, but after its first 50 years of existence, AI started to gain significant traction.

The 2010s – The Renaissance Era

The decade of 2010s will be known as the time when AI took center stage in technology-led transformations. The primacy of AI can be attributed to the gains made by big data, cloud, and IoT in the preceding years as well as the continued development of AI in the background. Advances in big data, cloud, and IoT solved two major issues that had plagued the progress of AI: enabled enough data and ensured enough compute capabilities. Deep learning became feasible and amplified the value of ML and AI more broadly, expanding its utility to many more problem spaces than before. Major technology players like Microsoft, Google, Amazon, and others made AI their main agenda in this period. Since the developments are recent, we will not get into more detail here.

Figure 1.1 depicts the evolution of AI over the past seven decades.

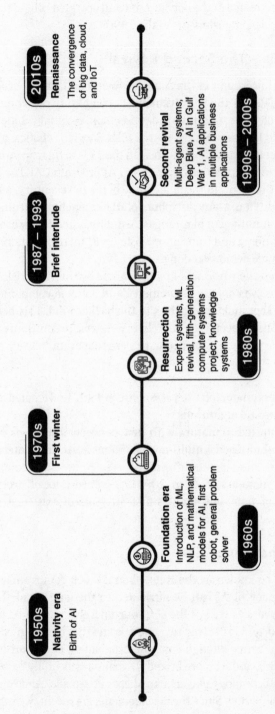

FIGURE 1.1 Evolution of AI

AI AND ITS BRANCHES

Many researchers classify AI techniques as:

a. **Weak AI or Narrow AI.** These are applications directed to a specific problem; currently most of the practical AI implementations in the world fall under this category.
b. **Strong AI or Artificial General Intelligence (AGI).** This is when the machine can interpret the problem just like humans and act on it. Popularly this type of transition into is also known as *singularity*.[4] This is still in the lab environment and may take several decades before any meaningful application comes to life. There are many ethical issues involved with AGI, too.
c. **Superintelligence.** This is when the machines overtake the capacity and capabilities of the human mind, going further beyond the state of singularity; this is still in early research stages.

AI deals with a variety of problem types. There are different methods to solve these different types of problems. The differences in methods lead to the different branches or disciplines within AI. Let us start with the problem types at the topmost level and their corresponding methods (hence branches) of AI:

a. Predict a future state based on past data – **machine learning**
b. Process human language either as text and/or voice – **natural language processing**
c. Understand and interpret images – **image perception**
d. Infer insights – **reasoning systems**
e. Organize knowledge and use it to solve complex problems – **knowledge-based systems**
f. Mimic human-like capabilities using machines – **robotics**
g. Plan and execute complex tasks in an unknown environment – **planning**

These AI methods are not uniquely distinctive and are often used in conjunction to solve problems. However, there is enough specificity for them to qualify as separate branches of AI.

The discipline of machine learning has been extensively talked about. Within machine learning, there are many approaches like:

■ **Supervised learning.** This technique is applied when there are very specific well-labeled datasets available for the program to learn the pattern and predict the output. Regression, decision tree, nearest neighbor, and support vector machines are some of the popular supervised learning algorithms.
■ **Unsupervised learning.** This technique is applied when data is not properly labeled and very little human input is available but the program has to find the most probable pattern and outcome. Clustering, anomaly detection, and neural network algorithms are frequently employed for unsupervised learning.
■ **Reinforcement learning.** This technique is applied when there is quite a bit of variability and ambiguity around the data, a lot more than for using supervised and unsupervised learning. In this method, the program takes feedback intermittently during the execution of the program and adapts its logic. This technique is the most popular one for designing multi-agent systems and applications like autonomous driving. Most AI techniques with the

data scientist start with a model; in reinforcement learning, one does not have to start with a model, and the model can emerge during the analysis.

The diagram in Figure 1.2 is a handy depiction of the various branches of AI.

For the last several years, deep learning has been very talked-about in the AI scene. It is one of the more popular reinforcement learning techniques today. Companies like DeepMind have contributed a lot to the popularity of deep learning. Deep learning uses artificial neural networks and convolutional neural networks. Deep learning is inspired by how biological systems learn. It works in layers and through multiple passes of the learning algorithms over the data. With each layer of analysis and learning, there is a higher level of abstraction of the raw input data to create new insights. This way the program can find correlations between actions by interpreting the corresponding data. This approach allows deep learning to work without predefined constraints and find new boundary conditions of optimal performance or achieving an objective. In rule-based systems, we create the rules based on history or understanding; deep learning helps us explore the unknown possibilities. For example, in the famous example of DeepMind optimizing HVAC systems using deep learning, they were able to find new ways of substantially reducing energy consumption by changing the sequence of operations and flow of chilled water using rules that were identified by the AI programs instead of being preset by humans. Deep learning is emerging as one of the more popular AI techniques in tackling complex problems that are not fully understood. There are many different types of deep learning algorithms like multilayer perceptron, convolutional neural networks, recurrent neural networks, autoencoder, long-short-term memory, deep belief networks, etc. Deep learning techniques have also been employed to enrich supervised and unsupervised learning in addition to being one of the most popular reinforcement learning techniques.

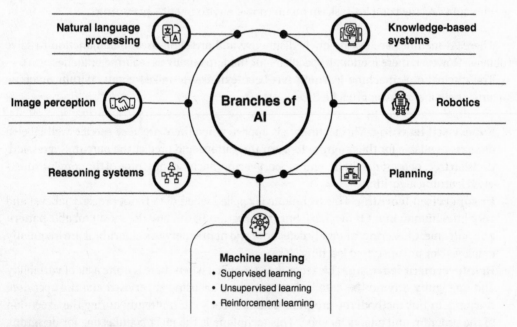

FIGURE 1.2   Branches of AI

A BIT ABOUT ALGORITHMS

Let us now clarify a few things about algorithms. The myriad techniques and algorithms can get very confusing for the uninitiated. Simply put, algorithms are the mathematical expressions that capture the process and logic chain for decision making. AI techniques, like the ones described above, take those algorithms, use data, and create insights from the decision-making process. Algorithms are the tools while data provides the fuel for the vehicle of AI to function.

Here are the top-nine things to keep in mind about algorithms:

1. **The same algorithm can be used in multiple AI techniques.** For example, the Convolutional Neural Network (CNN) algorithm can be used for both classifying and recognizing images as well as predicting the future value of something. So, the same algorithm can be applied differently for finding out which is the picture of a cat, a dog, and a traffic light, and at the same time predict how much energy your home will most likely consume tomorrow.

2. **Multiple algorithms can be applied to solve the same problem class.** For example, two different algorithms, like random forest and support vector machines, have been applied successfully to predict equipment failure. However, rarely are multiple algorithms applied to the same problem set simultaneously.

3. **Certain algorithms are better suited for specific problems.** For example, the CNN algorithm from point 1 above is better suited for energy prediction modeling as opposed to the image recognition problem.

4. **Each algorithm has a general method and a specific architecture as it gets applied to solve specific problems.** Every algorithm has a standard mathematical analysis process. However, during that analysis, it can use different variables and computations in different sequences, changing its architecture.

5. **The same algorithm can have different architectures.** Therefore it can be adapted to be applied differently for different problem classes using different techniques.

6. **Effectiveness in selecting the best algorithm for a problem comes from experience.** Data scientists with years of experience and exposure to a variety of problems can intuitively figure out the best approach. Some tools can help you navigate that, but most of them are still in their infancy.

7. **Algorithmic development is an iterative process.** Even the most experienced data scientists will refrain from claiming success at the first pass. They will experiment with multiple techniques, multiple algorithms, different architectures, and different cuts of the dataset before they finally work on a solution. This is also a very effective way of approaching this space because there are multiple choices.

8. **The algorithmic process starts with feature engineering.** This is the process of determining which variables among all available in a dataset have more relevance and better-quality data for the analysis and desired outcome. Some of the algorithms, like the deep learning algorithm LSTM, self-determine which variables are more important and relevant for the algorithm architecture.

9. **Usually, the quality of data from variables determined at the feature engineering stage is more important for most algorithms and most techniques.** However, for

certain techniques like deep learning, getting access to large volumes of data collected over time is equally important. Compared to classical algorithms like decision-tree or regression models that require sample data in tens of thousands, LSTM-type algorithms used in deep learning need samples to the tune of tens of millions.

Unless you have a strong background in statistics, understanding algorithms and the techniques can be challenging, and that is why we have data scientists. But it is important for every business and technology leader to have a basic grounding in the subject to engage intelligently with their data sciences teams.

CRITICAL SUCCESS FACTORS FOR AI INITIATIVES

Even though the discipline of AI is more than 70 years old, its broad application in the business world is more recent. There are hundreds of examples of successful AI projects, but there are precious few that are enterprise-wide and have made a big impact on a company. We do see a lot of great success stories in the government and smart city space, especially with surveillance. For example, China has one of the most incredible surveillance networks with hundreds of millions of cameras across the country and can not only monitor people but also predict potential problems. Similarly, there are many successful case studies in space research, defense, and scientific exploration.

Here are some examples from the business world where AI is at the heart of the present and future success of the enterprise:

- **Uber.** All routing, pricing, and time estimation functions in the app are now made by AI.
- **Amazon.** The entire shopping experience, dynamic pricing decisions, and recommendation engine that drives the massive amount of cross-selling are based on AI. Amazon.com is probably the biggest power user of AI in the world.
- **Tesla.** The majority of the driving features of Tesla today are based on AI and the future self-driving cars from Tesla will be fully run by AI. They are one of the most sophisticated users of computer vision, robotics, and machine learning.
- **Facebook.** All the recommendations on Facebook, whether it be for new potential friends or people to follow or ads for products and services or travel recommendations or even posts, are all determined by AI.
- **JPMC.** The bank has completely changed its customer service function and many of its internal operational processes by using AI techniques. We will talk more about this in a subsequent chapter on how AI will transform financial services.

In the last few years, the phrase *digital transformation* has been thrown around a lot. Now, this is being used more frequently with AI. We talk about that a bit in this book, too. While there is no universally accepted definition of digital transformation, here we define it as the integration of products, processes, and strategies within an organization by leveraging digital technologies such as the cloud, the edge, IoT, digital twinning, AI, and more. When AI is the backbone to make businesses more intelligent by way of accessing technology to make smart decisions, we call it AI-led digital transformation. This includes creating a data-enabled environment and analyzing captured data to make meaningful predictions and choices. The Uber example from above is a perfect example of such a transformation.

We have studied hundreds of projects and scores of companies implementing AI. Through this exercise, we have found some best practices that lead to a higher probability of success with the AI initiatives, and missing them usually leads to disappointing results. Here are some of the key ones:

a. The problem should be big but well-defined.
b. First figure out the business value of solving the problem before you unleash the data scientists.
c. Choosing the right algorithm matters a lot.
d. Involve partners, but keep control over the data and algorithms.
e. Change management is critical.

As we go through the different chapters in the book, we will be talking more about each of these best practices.

One thing that we have learned through the evolution of AI is that while science and math have always been extremely competent, other impediments limit the impact of AI. So, it is important to have realistic expectations and be thoughtful about the implementation.

PURPOSE AND STRUCTURE OF THE BOOK

Most organizations are making AI a part of their core agenda for their survival and success in the future. But sometimes their leaders struggle with developing a roadmap for how to reimagine their world with AI. This book is intended to help both business and technology leaders navigate the complex world of AI with its myriad dimensions in several ways:

- Understand the opportunity landscape.
- Develop a framework for business transformation.
- Investigate the possibilities across multiple industries.
- Build a technology foundation and the enabling ecosystems.
- Address broader societal concerns around ethics, privacy, and security.
- Manage the change.

This book has two types of chapters – one focused on how AI will transform specific industries and the other type focused on deployment aspects of AI across many industries.

After this introductory chapter, in Chapter 2 we will discuss how to build a framework for applying AI to any business domain.

Then we will dedicate the next eight chapters to how AI will transform eight specific industry verticals:

1. Healthcare
2. Education

3. Transportation
4. Retail
5. Financial services
6. Built environment
7. Smart cities
8. Smart government and citizen services

We chose these eight because they impact our individual lives and businesses more than others and are also the biggest contributors to a nation's GDP and future prosperity. We started this book before the COVID-19 crisis hit us, but as we kept writing we realized that the industries we had selected are also the ones that are most relevant in this current scenario.

Chapters 11 and 12 are the only technology-oriented chapters in this book, but they are not very deep into the technology or algorithms. Chapter 11 focuses on how to build a technology landscape while Chapter 12 goes into the nuances of ethics, privacy, and cybersecurity. Our goal is not to make you a technology expert; it is to give you enough orientation and tools for a holistic perspective.

Chapters 13, 14, and 15 focus on helping you get organized around your AI initiatives and manage change. Change management is an extremely critical part of the success of any AI initiative.

We believe there are a few unique aspects of this book:

■ This is possibly the first and only book that tackles the topic of AI from a holistic business transformation perspective and focuses on multiple industries.
■ This is a how-to book that contains some fundamental research and thinking into the various topics influencing and being impacted by AI.
■ This book is peppered with a lot of practical examples and innovations as observed in this evolving landscape.
■ This book will demystify the technical intricacies involved with AI for the readers and show them a path to success.
■ This book requires rudimentary technical understanding and basic management orientation to navigate the space of AI effectively.

As you will see, there are several areas of overlap between the different industries and technology choices, which further proves the point that AI will morph the way we live and work.

We hope you share our excitement and find this journey with us to be useful.

 ## REFERENCES

(1) *Modeling the Impact of AI on the World Economy*; McKinsey Global Institute; September 2018.
(2) *Dawn of The Age of Algorithms*; Sudhi Ranjan Sinha; January 2018.
(3) *A Proposal for the Dartmouth Summer Research Project on Artificial Intelligence*; John McCarthy, Marvin Minsky, Nathaniel Rochester, and Claude Shannon; August 1955.
(4) *The Coming Technological Singularity: How to Survive in the Post-Human Era*; Verner Vinge, Winter 1993.

CHAPTER 2

Building a Framework for Applying AI

"You don't have to be a genius or a visionary or even a college graduate to be successful. You just need a framework and a dream."

—Michael Dell

 INTRODUCTION

Artificial Intelligence (AI) as a subject is very vast and its applications very wide. In the first chapter, we explored the various branches and flavors of AI. As mentioned in the introduction, as per a recent McKinsey study,[1] by the end of 2030, the impact of AI is expected to be about $13 trillion with over 70% of companies impacted by AI. This means that nobody will be left untouched by the implications of AI. Most businesses and business leaders feel compelled to do something about AI as they have in the past with every new technology hype. They are motivated by the risk of being left out, so they do something. Often these AI initiatives are delegated to the CIO or CDO or other senior technology leaders. If AI is used for its new analytical capabilities to improve some aspects of internal operations or product performance, their impact is limited and the transformational goals are not achieved. To make a bigger impact, business leaders and the C-suite need to sponsor and monitor the efforts themselves. They also need to think in terms of a framework to drive these initiatives and capture the value. The COVID-19 crisis has ensured that digitization is on top of every business leader's agenda and that they are actively exploring advanced analytical techniques like AI to ensure that their businesses survive today and eventually thrive tomorrow.

A framework is a structure for success; it contains all the components that are required for success in this transformation effort, their interrelationships, and the flow of action and effects throughout the ecosystem.

The notion of frameworks has been around for a very long time. Frameworks have been used from theology to computer programming. Several reputed analysts and consulting firms have created frameworks to use in business value modeling. We have seen the Gartner model and the Accenture model as good starting points.

The Gartner Business Value Model examines the Business Aspect, the Aggregates, and the Primes. The Business Aspect is a broad functional area like demand management. The Aggregates are the topical areas within the broad functional area. Under demand management, Aggregates are topics like market responsiveness, sales effectiveness, and product development effectiveness. The Primes are a layer of further decomposition going into specific metrics that collectively represent the state of the Aggregate. For example, sales effectiveness Aggregate has many Primes like Sales Cycle Index, Sales Close Index, Sales Price Index, etc. There are many advantages of the Gartner model – it combines the essence of many models like Balanced Score Card and Economic Value Added, it is very detailed and has precise definitions, and it touches nearly every functional dimension of the organization. This model, however, is not tied to AI-driven analytics nor takes a view beyond the functional considerations.

The Accenture model, on the other hand, is more AI-oriented and has more of a flavor of outcome-oriented business value beyond the functional consideration. This model looks at four different solutions activities – efficiency model, expert model, effectiveness model, and innovation model. The efficiency model uses AI to make routinized analytics more efficient, repeatable, and low-cost. The expert model introduces the human into the loop. The effectiveness model takes into account more expansive and unstructured organizational aspects. The innovation model focuses on finding new boundaries.

Both of these frameworks are very good and effective when properly used. There are many others and we cannot get into the details of each of them due to limited space and time.

In our opinion, when we are trying to solve serious business problems using advanced analytics, a good framework we use in such cases should have the following guiding principles:

a. **Start with a customer-back approach.** A lot of times we get mired in internal complexities and competitions, often forgetting the purpose of why we exist and how we serve customers. Taking a customer-back approach helps keep the focus on the end goal of being able to serve more customers better, which drives profitable growth – the primary purpose of any business. This approach also avoids any internal conflicts and forms the basis of a prioritization and decision North Star that everybody can rally around.

b. **Be economic value–focused.** In any organization, there are always a lot of activities and processes. Not every activity or decision has the same impact on the outcome of the business. A good framework should capture the ones that create true economic impact and are not just reflective of relative internal significance put on it by an internal function.

c. **Captures all the triggers and catalysts.** Present-day business processes are very complicated and convoluted. They are also interdependent and influenced by many factors, some of which may not be naturally obvious. To capture a business process comprehensively, it is critical to capture all the factors that are a trigger or catalyst to change in the performance of any metric or business outcome. For example, very often the stock market index is influenced by sentiments around sociopolitical events, sometimes even in a different part of the world.

d. **Represents the flow of information, decision interventions, economic impact, and process interfaces.** In other words, the framework is a good representation of how human initiative and intelligence impacts the business. In doing so we have to carefully balance details with the right level of abstraction because we do not want to be lost in the details and lose sight of the purpose, which usually will be to change some specific outcomes.

e. **It is a comprehensive and easily understandable representation of the business for nearly any stakeholder.** The best process frameworks are a single-page snapshot of a business.

Figure 2.1 is a good visual representation of these principles.

While AI offers a lot of promise, there are many examples of failed AI initiatives as well as organizations having less than satisfactory results with their AI efforts. In a survey done by *MIT Sloan Management Review* and Boston Consulting Group and released in October 2019[2] covering over 2,500 executives, it was reported that 70% of the respondents surveyed did not see the expected impact of AI. In the same report, successful companies were identified to have taken business-led AI initiatives instead of just leaving it to IT with minimal business involvement. Focus on customer impact and consequent business impact is paramount to the success of any technology-intensive transformation. So it is critical to have the right business value framework to manage these projects over a long period of execution and impact.

FIGURE 2.1 Guiding Principles of Business Value Framework

In this chapter we shall cover more detailed guidance, frameworks, and best practices on the following topics that will help build the framework for applying AI in your business:

- Identifying the future state
- Building the technology strategy
- Defining the business case
- Creating the solution roadmap
- Identifying AI capabilities
- Establishing a governance process

IDENTIFYING THE FUTURE STATE

Identifying the future state of a business is one of the hardest exercises. It requires a very deep understanding of the business, how it creates value for its customers, in which context of the market and competitors it operates, what are its core capabilities and competitive differentiators, and how these various factors play over time. While doing a deep analysis of a business to understand what contributes to its success now and what will drive success in the future, it is critical to be very objective, dispassionate, and methodical. Each hypothesis must be tested and validated.

When faced with transformative forces like technology, in this case, AI and other digital technologies, businesses have to rethink and redefine their current business model and not just make it an exercise in technology and effort in marketing. Several large companies with a very successful track record of creating impressive technology for internal improvements took those initiatives as a basis for being able to transform the entire market, but they ended up being deficient in changing their internal business practices, creating new business models for the market where they add significant value just beyond technological capabilities and are agile and adaptive over time because both the market and the technology will keep evolving. The biggest risks business leaders need to avoid are the ones emanating from when marketing overtakes the value created by the product.

To define the most likely future state of the business, we recommend a three-step process – start with the customer, know what creates value, and finally model the future state.

Step 1: Create a Customer-Back Engagement Journey Map

Many frameworks take an internal operational view of the capabilities and activities of an organization and most frame them in functional buckets. These approaches are easy to organize work because that is what we are used to on a day-to-day basis. However, such an approach will most likely also end up making the current state slightly more efficient as opposed to exploration for a very different future state. So, we recommend using a customer-back engagement journey map. Since the customer is the final arbitrator of the value created, it is prudent to review from their lens.

We will use an example to explain how to create journey maps. We will start with a simple example of a customer buying a high-value industrial asset and trace it through the major lifecycle events of the asset until it gets replaced. The diagram in Figure 2.2 is a high-level view of this journey, which will last several years.

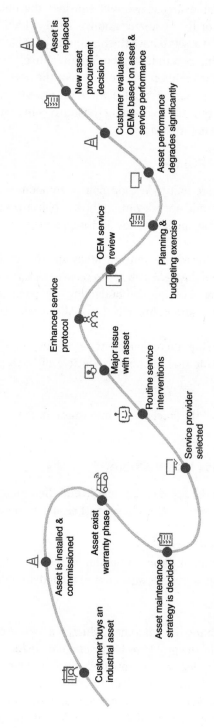

FIGURE 2.2 The Journey Map

While drawing a journey map, it is important to remember the primary objectives of the various stakeholders. In our example, we will consider the objectives of two primary stakeholders – the asset owner or the customer and the OEM, which also provides service in this case. The customer wants the asset to have the maximum possible life, highest reliability of performance, and lowest operating cost that includes maintenance. The OEM wants to help the customer achieve her goal, get the maintenance contract for the asset, maximize any ancillary service opportunities, and be the preferred supplier when the asset is replaced after many years. The objectives are important to consider in drawing the journey map so that the key influences to achieving those objectives are not missed.

Step 2: Identify Decision Points

In any business process, there are many decision points, sometimes hundreds, but there are always a few which matter more and are relevant to the key objectives that have been identified as part of this exercise. So, in our example, the key decision points are:

- When the customer decides the maintenance strategy and the service provider – impacts all the customer's objectives and the OEM's ability to secure the service business
- When the customer is doing planning and budgeting – impacts the customer's operating cost and performance considerations, impacts the OEM's service renewals and pull through service business
- When the customer is choosing the replacement asset – impacts OEM's objective of retaining the customer relationship and customer objective of having the best cost and best performing new asset

Identifying the decision points precisely is important because they have a significant influence on analytics.

Step 3: Build the Business Value-Chain

Knowing the journey-map and the key decision points and their impact helps us build out the business value-chain. A good business value chain must be able to answer three questions:

1. What problems are we trying to solve?
2. Do you have the data or minimally know what data is required to solve those issues?
3. What specific use-case, that is, specific situation of an activity or a product or service will help solve the problems?

We start the process by defining the outcomes, which is a way of capturing the future state of the impact by solving some of the problems in the current customer-back journey map. For each of the defined outcomes, we list one or more objectives, and for each of the objectives, we list one or more use cases. There is always a possibility of a many-to-many relationship between the outcomes, objectives, and use-cases; but it is better to have as much singularity and granularity as possible so that we can synthesize what is most relevant and what is most important.

In our example, Table 2.1 shows how we can capture the outcomes, objectives, and use-cases.

TABLE 2.1 Use-Case Derivation Methodology

Outcome	Objective	Use-Cases
Improve asset management	Optimize performance, reduce operating expenses and asset lifecycle cost	◾ Monitor the asset performance remotely and continuously ◾ Predict future performance and operating cost ◾ Proactively identify performance issues requiring maintenance ◾ Recommend strategies to optimize operations and maintenance ◾ Minimize the impact of asset-degraded performance or maintenance intervention on other operations ◾ Budgeting, forecasting, financial planning ◾ Net present value (NPV) management of assets

Going through the above steps leads to a very thorough understanding of value creation. You can arrive at the quantified value creation and thereby the opportunity landscape by plugging in actual financials based on your particular situation. Now you should have a pretty good view of the future state.

The Efficient Frontier Model

In 1952, Nobel Laureate Harry Markowitz[3] introduced a model for managing portfolios of investments based on risks and returns. We have taken inspiration from the same model and adapted it to frame value creation.

In our adaptation of the model, we consider X-axis as the cost dimensions and Y-axis as the revenue dimensions. The progression of the X-axis shows reducing cost impact and progression of the Y-axis shows increasing revenue impact. Every business operates in an efficient frontier, which is the profit or value creation envelop. The objective of any business is to keep pushing the envelope to the next frontier. (See Figure 2.3a.)

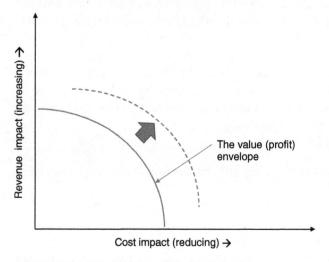

FIGURE 2.3A The Efficient Frontier Model

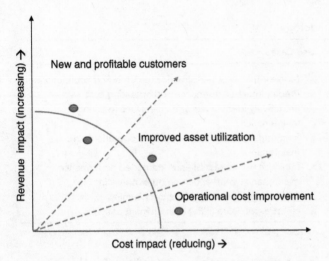

FIGURE 2.3B   The Efficient Frontier Model with Initiatives

The various initiatives can be plotted in this graph based on their financial impact. For example, if you have a set of initiatives that address operational costs of the business, some which address better asset utilization in business and some which go after new growth markets, you can put them in relative placement in the manner shown in Figure 2.3b.

We have found the Efficient Frontier Model framework to be a very useful conceptualization, prioritization, and communication tool to put context to the various initiatives that are part of the transformation.

Design Thinking Model

Design Thinking is a very effective cognitive thinking methodology to solve complex problems, especially if they have a lot of layers and interdependencies, the kind we have to deal with in the AI and analytical world. Design Thinking traces its roots to the 1960s with early efforts to blend science with the art of design. Design firm IDEO and the Stanford Design School made it popular starting in the 1990s. Today this is very widely used and talked about in the business world. You can find dedicated practices in all the major consulting firms as well as boutique firms specializing in Design Thinking. Several universities around the world are offering courses in Design Thinking and there is already a lot of literature around this subject. Our goal is not to recreate or rehash them there; we aim to expose you to the methodologies so that you can apply them in understanding and solving your business problems using analytics.

Broadly, Design Thinking involves five major steps:

1. Empathy – understanding the context, including all behavioral and human elements associated with the business context
2. Define – articulating the problem and the personas involved with the problem
3. Ideate – thinking about possible solutions
4. Prototype – modeling the solution in parts to validate problem and solution hypothesis
5. Test – running short cycle innovations to validate the efficacy and effectiveness of the solution

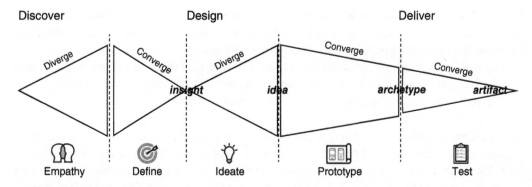

FIGURE 2.4   Design Thinking Model

But Design Thinking is not a linear process; like any other creative process, it is iterative and enriched by different types of background and thinking of the participants.

Some experts believe that the five steps contribute to three outcomes – Discover, Design, and Deliver. They also believe that you have to go through an iterative process of diverging and converging to get the best insights and ideas. Figure 2.4 blends this thinking with the five-step classical process.

BUILDING THE TECHNOLOGY STRATEGY

Once you know the future state reasonably well, the next major activity is to define a technology strategy to effectively assess the feasibility of the ideas and identify the most optimal path to success. To understand the data and analytics needs to inform the technology strategy, three primary questions have to be answered:

1. What capabilities are most exciting?
2. Can we connect the "right" capabilities with their problems?
3. Which scenarios emerge as we connect the dots?

While defining the future state, you have outlined the business process flow and major decision points. In building the technology strategy, similarly, you will have to create the data journey. There are five major steps in any data journey:

1. Collect the data.
2. Assess the data.
3. Interpret the data and provide guidance.
4. Improve performance.
5. Predict needs and events.

These are sequential but cyclical steps, repeating again and again.

Along with the data journey, you need to create a more detailed activity map of the business process or desired outcomes. The purpose of the activity map is to realize the outcomes identified during the use-case definition and provide a more comprehensive view of the future state. Each activity should ideally be classified as value-creating or value-enabling so that we can get more precise on the diagnostics needs and the technology strategy.

Figure 2.5 is a simple pictorial representation of how to map the data journey and activities for the continuing example of improving asset management from earlier in this chapter.

In building the technology, here are a few important things to remember:

a. Avoid the temptation of thinking of platforms and applications to solve your business problems and instantiate the future state. In today's app-based economy, quite frequently our thinking gets conditioned by the plethora of apps that we are exposed to every day. At this stage, you should be exclusively focused on the strategy part, not the technology implementation part; that comes later when you are designing the solution.
b. In thinking through your data journey and activities, do not be constrained by the data you have today or what you can get access to easily. The available options around sensors and data management are enormous and cost structures are also coming down rapidly. You must identify the important data elements and activities you need to solve your problem and create value.
c. Connecting the dots requires a methodical approach and critical thinking. People who have a deep operational understanding of the business process should provide inputs to this exercise. It is better to validate and cross-check every assumption. Often you will end up coming up with completely new paradigms of the business processes that might be disruptive to your organization and even possibly for the market. But that is the whole point of a transformation exercise using analytics – to see beyond the obvious.

As you can see, developing the technology strategy for building out the AI framework is not a technology exercise; it is more of a business thinking and rethinking exercise. So while you should have your technical leadership involved, the exercise must be business-led.

DEFINING THE BUSINESS CASE

Step 3 is to establish a digital business case and gather the calculations needed to arrive at the ROI of the digital transformation journey. When building an AI digital business case, value creation is clearly articulated through financial returns and additional, measurable benefits. We evaluate the state of the current technology stack and identify the most viable systems for implementation that will maximize value and minimize associated costs of the digital transformation. Similar to the other steps, there are some key questions you need to answer for developing the business case and arriving at the ROI calculations:

■ What analytics can and should be built?
■ What is the current state of systems and data?
■ What are the value creation, associated costs, and return?

You start with the capabilities and activities identified in the previous step, and then for each group, you identify the value created and financial impact of the value creation and additional

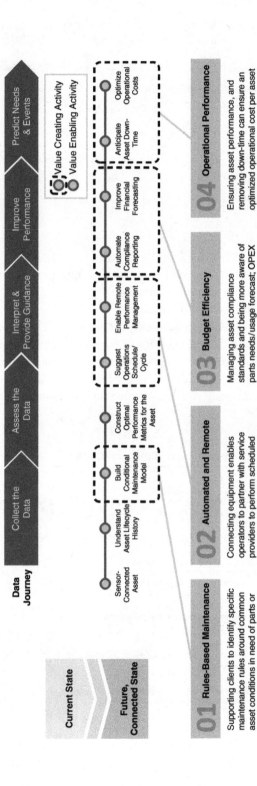

FIGURE 2.5 Technology Strategy: Data Journey and Activity Map

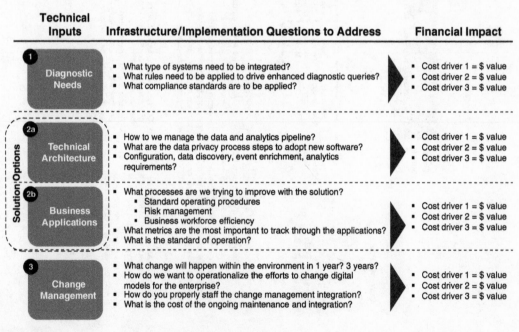

Activity Thread	Value Created	Financial Impact	Additional Benefits
Activity 1 Activity 2	• Value created #1 and how • Value created #2 and how • Value created #3 and how	• $$ value impact for #1 • $$ value impact for #2 • $$ value impact for #3	• Intangible #1 • Intangible #2
Activity 1 Activity 2	• Value created #1 and how • Value created #2 and how • Value created #3 and how	• $$ value impact for #1 • $$ value impact for #2 • $$ value impact for #3	• Intangible #1 • Intangible #2

FIGURE 2.6 Returns Modeling through Analytics

intangible benefits. Sometimes the intangibles can be strategically important, but we do not recommend any major investments only for intangible benefits.

Figure 2.6 illustrates a way to think about this exercise.

To complete the business case, you need to build out the cost base next. The investment may be minimal in terms of collecting new data, or implementing new sensors, or building out new applications. However, in our experience, if you are undertaking a truly transformative exercise, the AI initiative will most likely require broader technical work to be done to fully realize the benefits.

Figure 2.7 provides a framework to help you think through the various cost dimensions that might be involved.

FIGURE 2.7 Cost Modeling for Analytics Initiatives

Now that you have a good idea about what benefits you can get and how much money you might have to end up spending, you can easily build out the business case and decide whether to pursue further or tweak the objectives or approach or just drop the whole idea.

 CREATING THE SOLUTION ROADMAP

The fourth and final step is designing the solution and implementation plan to realize the desired customer outcomes defined in Step 1. We look back to the technology strategy and data collected from the business case to identify what system elements must first be piloted, which datasets will maximize impact for the customer, and what resources are required to implement the plan. Understanding the linkages between outcomes and the delivery process to realize them is how we seamlessly connect the mission of the building to the mission of the business.

In this book we will not get very detailed in the solution roadmapping and design exercise. Technical design and development are very evolved disciplines; literature around these topics is extensive. Analytics initiatives follow a similar pattern and path as most other digital transformation projects. You can also refer to our previous books for frameworks, models, and best practices in solution development around IoT, big data, and analytics.

There is, however, an important distinction when it comes to choosing or building the right data platform for AI as opposed to normal data applications or IoT applications. Table 2.2 captures some of the nuances of the different platforms and highlights what an AI-centric data platform must have.

The differences are important to understand because these are long-lasting and expensive choices that business leaders will have to make.

TABLE 2.2   Platform Comparison

	Normal Data Platform	IoT Platform	AI Platform
Integration	Similar sources of data	A wide array of sensors and sources of data	Any kind of data source giving any format of data
Data Organization	Usually structured	Semi-structured	Structured, semi-structured, unstructured – all possible combinations
Sensor Fusion Support	No	Limited	High
Data Contextualization	No	Limited	Flexible graph-based
Analytics	Data gathering and reporting	Heuristics-based analytics	Learning-based analytics
Autonomous Feedback Loop and Continuous Learning	No – completely human dependent	Limited – expert intervention required extensively	Highly autonomous and learning-driven
App Enablement	Desktop dashboards and mobile apps	Desktop dashboards and mobile apps	NLP apps, immersive apps
Extensibility	To specific dataset outcomes	To specific processing chain outcomes	To enterprise outcomes

IDENTIFYING AI CAPABILITIES

In our experience, it is always helpful to classify the AI capabilities an organization needs into a unified common framework, making it easier for everybody to communicate and rally around. Here is a framework we have built that you can use – the SLOPE framework wherein the AI capabilities are classified for their primary purpose of Sensing, Learning, Optimizing, Predicting, and Entropy. There is a bit of a logical sequence of analytics that we tweaked to create the acronym.

Sense

Sense capabilities enable accessing and collecting data from all sources of data, cleansing it, classifying it, and making it ready for further analytics. The sensing capability includes intelligent mechanisms for automatic detection and removal of outlier data, data cleansing, and imputation of missing data using AI techniques. Correlating different types and formats of data is also a key role in sense algorithms. The data under consideration here include both real-time data and historical data. Examples of sensing include collecting the sensor data of an asset, its operational impact data from other sources like utility consumption data, its design data, data from other systems and assets related to, and external sources of information outside of the information network it is part of, but which is critical to get a complete picture of the asset performance and its impacts such as weather or energy costs.

Learn

Once the data is sensed, the AI solution learns the evolution and patterns of different states in the operational process that generate or engage with the data and what influences the change of states for the data or the operational processes. The AI solution learns how current/future states are influenced by past states, controllable actions, and external disturbances. The learning is performed with various algorithms, and the capability is also referred to as building an "algorithmic digital twin" of various processes and data elements. Learning in the asset example will include learning about how operational parameters change under different conditions, previous failures, triggers for past failures, other conditions when the failure event occurred, what got impacted when the failure happened, how long it took before the asset or the system it is part of became fully functional again, and so on. The learning provides context.

Predict

Once the learning is done, various states in the future can be predicted by AI. The prediction enables making intelligent decisions of changing controllable actions that can help achieve the outcomes desired. For example, if we can predict the future failure possibility of a high-value asset, we can take a lot of remedial steps to either avoid the failure or have a backup plan in the event of a failure. In another example, if we can predict that some events, like a health-scare or major sociopolitical events, might impact people's productivity, steps can be taken to isolate and manage the impact.

Optimize

Post-prediction, an AI system can also optimize or recommend steps to optimize the various controllable variables to reach the outcomes that have been laid out as part of the AI-framework. The optimized AI algorithms work very closely in conjunction with the predictive algorithms. Optimizing is always in the context of a defined objective function of what state the system needs to reach and what constraints the system has to deal with. For example, optimizing the functioning of the asset to either be more cost-efficient or be most performance efficient or be most longevity efficient are different choices the analytics can recommend or execute.

Entropy

Entropy is not a concept that has been used widely so far in AI applications, but AI is best suited to model and forecast highly disruptive events that are outside of normal considerations. We are now in the Black Swan zone. For example, could Arab Spring have been predicted? If we analyze and extrapolate socioeconomic data, growing unrest in the population, and other data streams, we would not have concluded the magnitude of the event. However, when we synthesize a whole variety of data that previously was never considered together, we can start to draw different conclusions. Michael Gordon of Wilson Center wrote a very scholarly article on this topic in February 2018 where you can see that systematically and methodically a lot of the analysis and inferences can be put together. This type of AI application is part science and part art because how do you train the machine or the algorithm on what to look for and where to start?

Figure 2.8 represents the various stages of the SLOPE framework.

 ESTABLISHING A GOVERNANCE PROCESS

Establishing a good governance process around AI initiatives is as important as building a good framework to initiate and manage them. Often a business leader will trigger some AI initiatives and then talented researchers take over. They may end up focusing on very interesting and intellectually challenging problems without a full view of their business impact. Finding good AI talent is difficult and can be very expensive, so it becomes even more critical to ensure that the right focus and prioritization are reviewed periodically.

Here are some recommended best practices for establishing a good governance process around AI:

1. Appoint an AI leader who has a strong sense of the business and is primarily driven by the business outcome.
2. Establish a steering committee comprising business leaders who have a view of the future, understanding of technology and technology curves, appreciation for analytics, and appetite for experimentation. Business leaders should be able to represent both the customer and the product/service. Avoid an overwhelming number of short-term results focused on operational leaders in the steering committee because this is a long-view game. The steering committee should be peppered with a few selected internal and external AI experts,

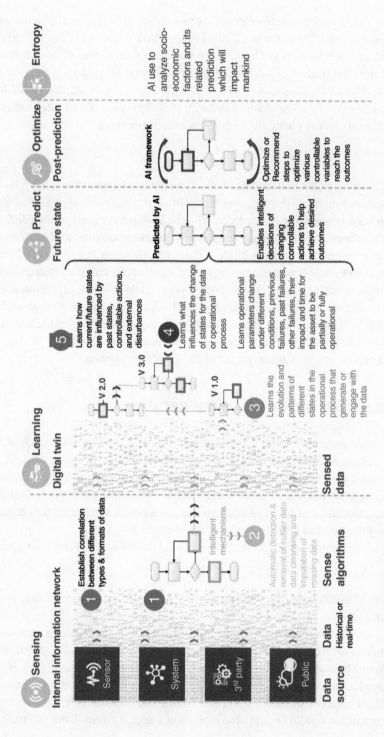

FIGURE 2.8 The SLOPE Framework

including the leader of your AI organization. This will allow a balance between possibilities and practicalities. The steering committee should be empowered with resource allocation and prioritization, it should also be given a 3- to 5-year horizon to operate in with intermittent success measures and deliverables.

3. Create a prioritization matrix and publish it widely for educating the rest of the organization and being transparent with all key stakeholders. The prioritization matrix should be guided by economic desirability from the perspective of customer value creation and capture, technical feasibility, and competitive differentiation. The Efficient Frontier Model is a good one to map the AI initiatives against and see how they rack and stack.

4. Review progress minimally monthly and prioritization minimally quarterly. A lot can change in the business in a short period; new issues may come up and new opportunities present themselves. The AI team should be able to understand and react to them.

5. The review process should be less about status reporting and more focused on learning from analytics and discussing the business impact. These are new areas that a broad swath of business leaders has to get comfortable with and also proficient with. So, the dialogue becomes critical for the learning and internalization process.

6. Usually, specific AI initiatives will be more aligned with an existing product or service business or function. So, it is good to have the data scientists aligned with such groups so that they can draw upon the domain experience of the existing team members. However, it is also critical to have a unified AI team because talented data scientists are usually attracted to other exceptional experts in their field and perform best in a high-performing peer group. Building a critical mass of data scientists in a central pool to drive AI initiatives is found to be an important criterion for success.

7. Conjoin the AI research team and the product or technology development teamwork on common release schedules of capabilities. Disconnected pursuits have led to many good AI efforts languishing for lack of implementation.

8. Make the AI initiative timebound. Today there are enough analytical techniques, computing power, and data that most business problems can be solved in a 3- to 6-month horizon using AI. One may need a bit more time to harden the analytics or the technology and also properly productionize it, but the core development should not take too long. Delays are usually indicative of the wrong approach, inadequate talent, or internal dysfunctions – any of which should be nipped in the bud.

Any governance process must be adequately documented, but more importantly, shared and socialized with all the stakeholders. The effectiveness of the governance process must also be reviewed annually and adapted as appropriate.

SUMMARY

As you embark on your AI journey, you must take a structured approach to avoid getting lost. This chapter has intended to help you with that.

You start by identifying the future state of your business. The future state design is arrived at by synthesizing market trends, competitive actions, new technological possibilities, and most importantly how to create new and improved value for your customers. This process culminates with listing out the various use-cases that will be part of your transformation program. The Efficient Frontier and Design Thinking models are good tools to help you identify the future state.

Once the future state is identified, you then build out the technology strategy and then the business case. It is important to follow that sequence because choices made around technology can have serious implications on both investments and returns. Finally, the solution roadmap gets the transformation going.

Next, we introduced you to the SLOPE framework as an easy tool to help you think through your algorithmic needs.

Finally, we ended the chapter with some of the best practices in managing large-scale AI and digital transformation. Such programs are a huge change management exercise and the significance of culture and capability changes should not be underestimated. We have a whole chapter dedicated to managing change in this book.

Starting in the next chapter we go deeper into the various industry sectors.

REFERENCES

(1) *Modeling the Impact of AI on the World Economy*; McKinsey Global Institute; September 2018.
(2) "Reshaping Business with Artificial Intelligence"; *MIT Sloan Management Review*; October 2019.
(3) *Portfolio Selection*; Harry Markowitz; March 1952.

CHAPTER 3

Transforming Healthcare with AI

"We should think about AI the way we think about patient care – as a continuum, spanning care areas and disease states."

—Dr. Mark Michalaski, clinical data scientist

INTRODUCTION

Healthcare is one of the largest and most important industries globally. The recent COVID-19 crisis has made this the most important industry today and it will continue to occupy the center stage for many years to come. By 2023, the healthcare industry is expected to reach $12 trillion globally.[1] Starting in 2018/19, the growth rate for this industry has been nearly 9%. This has accelerated by over 100 basis points when compared to five years back. This is driven by major macroeconomic shifts around the world that we will discuss in the next section. As big as the industry is, it is also highly fragmented. The top players globally and collectively represent merely a single-digit share in the healthcare economy.

Healthcare is a very multifaceted industry. It has employed a lot of people and has been the cornerstone of many technological advancements that have permeated to other industries as well. However, the growing share of healthcare as a percentage of the nation's GDP drains resources that are required for other aspects of economies. In the United States, national health spending is projected to be nearly 20% of the GDP by 2025, which is just around the corner. In the 1960s, this impact was one-fourth of what it is shaping up to be today. In nearly all developed and developing nations, the story is similar. The rising costs of healthcare are not only drawing from national resources but are also impacting the bottom line of private companies and individuals.

But more importantly, health is directly associated with a nation's economic prosperity and social advancement. In January 2000, the World Health Organization (WHO) established the

Commission on Macroeconomics and Health (CMH) to investigate this topic and make some recommendations.[2] It found many interesting facts such as:

- Increasing life expectancy from 50 to 70 years improves the annual growth rate by 1.4%.
- Ills like malnutrition and infant mortality can negatively impact GDP between 0.23% and >4%.
- A third of several of Latin America's economic growths between 1975 and 1990 can be attributed to improvements in the population's health.
- Research going back 200 years suggests that a third to half of the prosperity of developed nations like England can be attributed to improvements in food consumption and health.

On the flipside, as we have seen with the COVID-19 crisis, a major healthcare event like a global pandemic can destroy the world economy in a very short period.

Healthcare touches all of us around the world every day. There is universal agreement that healthcare is important and critical for the advancement of human society. Technology and a target-rich environment make it ideal for transformation today.

Like every other aspect of our lives and economy, the healthcare industry is also being deeply impacted by the growth of digital technologies. There is a newly emerging segment called Digital Health Market. As per Global Market Insights research, between 2019 and 2025, this segment is expected to experience a growth of nearly 30% and reach a size of over $500 billion.[3] There are many other industry reports which similarly suggest that the healthcare IT industry has already crossed half that mark and the growth is accelerating.

Healthcare is also a very complex ecosystem that is defined and influenced by multiple stakeholders like patients, doctors, hospitals, medical devices, pharmaceuticals, home, environment, and education across several dimensions like research, diagnostics, care, and awareness. Technology influences every aspect of this ecosystem in many ways and makes them more integrated as we shall see subsequently in this chapter. (See Figure 3.1.)

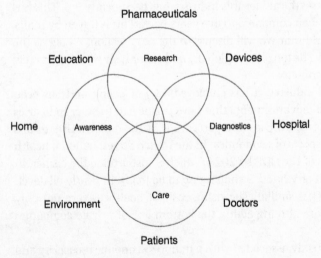

FIGURE 3.1   Healthcare Ecosystem

The healthcare industry is a very data-intensive one. This industry is expected to generate over 2,000 exabytes of data in 2020, which if fully harnessed exceeds the global data center storage capacity. The growth of this data is driven by increased proliferation of IoT, electronic medical records, collection and processing of clinical and research data, and general growth of information in this space. From a data and analytics standpoint, this industry has also very high sensitivity to timeliness, accuracy, trustworthiness, privacy, and variety. The role of AI-driven analytics will focus on solving issues across all of these different dimensions. In 2021, the healthcare and life sciences analytics market is expected to cross $25 billion, making it one of the most important analytical spaces.

However, this industry – be it diagnostics or research – works on averages. Each individual is unique with a unique lifestyle and unique health signature. Our current health and future well-being are impacted by several different parameters like current vital statistics, sleep patterns, food habits, work habits, workout habits, family history, environmental factors at home-work-transit, historical response to certain treatments and allergies, the health of other family members, mental state and pressures, the evolution of physical conditions over time to show a pattern and detect the motion of those emerging patterns, genetic signatures, community signatures, etc. All such information exists, but exists in silos, rarely associated and contextualized, and not considered to the level of depth for appropriate diagnostics or remedial purposes. Similarly, there is new information available around causality, treatments, and medicines every day, a large portion of which is not accessible for individual consumption or contextualization.

This industry also faces the issue of being distributed and disconnected in the various disciplines and dimensions of care. We go through multiple healthcare interventions at different points in time and in different locations. While we are always asked about our health-related histories, and we do our best to share them, there is limited reliability of such information. Often such information is also tainted by the educational background, awareness, societal constraints, and other such factors of the patients or their family.

Healthcare is one aspect of our lives where it becomes most challenging and damaging to react after the fact. In an ideal situation, except for accidental cases, we would like our health to be predicted and remedial measures to be taken.

AI will change the healthcare industry in several ways – enable true personalization of healthcare with much-targeted diagnostics and treatment; anticipate the needs of patients and medical professionals; integrate the full lifecycle of healthcare from home to hospital; and feed the complete ecosystem of healthcare into one harmonized engine. In this chapter, we shall explore how AI and digital technologies will transform the healthcare industry.

UNDERSTANDING THE MACROSCOPIC FACTORS DRIVING SMART CAPABILITIES IN THE FUTURE OF THE HEALTHCARE INDUSTRY

The healthcare industry is today at an inflection point for a transformation. There are four major driving forces behind this transformation – Policy, Economy, Society, and Technology (PEST).

Across many nations, healthcare reforms are a key policy agenda. Policy actions are trying to work on issues related to the inclusiveness of the population in the healthcare system through insurance and affordability interventions, as well as improve the quality of care. Reform policies

include many techniques like monitoring the flow of drugs and their prices, multifactor validation of care provided and costs incurred, tying payments to outcomes instead of being purely
based on services provided, increasing electronic traceability of treatment and the environment in which the treatment or care was provided, remote monitoring of patients and remote
administration of care, and a host of other such innovative programs. Governments are constantly creating incentives to increase inclusiveness and improve affordability, but sometimes
these measures pose serious operational challenges for the hospitals, medical professionals,
pharmaceutical companies, and other ecosystem stakeholders. With the increasing focus on privacy and cybersecurity concerns, there is yet another layer of a compliance framework that
healthcare systems now have to deal with.

In their seminal work, *Getting Health Reform Right: A Guide to Improving Performance and
Equity*, popularly known as the "Control Knobs Theory," Marc Roberts, William Hsiao, Peter Ber-
man, and Michael Reich of the Harvard T. H. Chan School of Public Health have created a very
useful framework to think about such policy interventions in the healthcare space (Figure 3.2).

The economic forces behind healthcare transformation present some interesting challenges
as well. On one hand, we have societies or sections of societies where higher disposable income
is driving a greater focus on health and quality of care. Personal expenditure on healthcare in

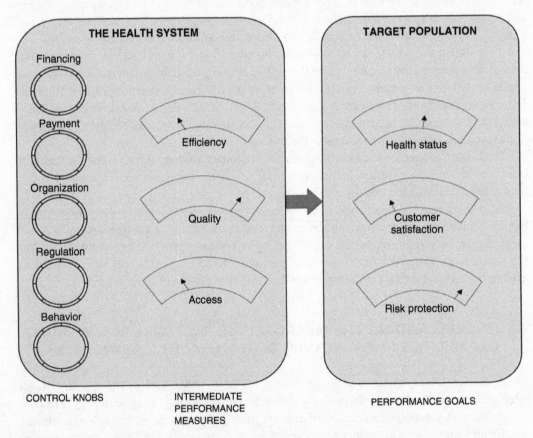

FIGURE 3.2 Control Knobs Theory

many economies like China is nearing 10% of per-capita disposable income. On the other hand, we still have a large population in the world that is economically disadvantaged, has limited access to necessities, which includes healthcare, and consequently creates a drain on the overall economic output of the nation. In both scenarios, there is a need to shift the focus of health-care from treatment to prevention. Better prevention requires policy-driven infrastructure in every aspect of the healthcare ecosystem as well as mass-scale education. Looking at it from the healthcare providers' perspective, better care requires more specialization and more tools, which in turn creates capacity and cost constraints, thereby challenging the goals of affordable, inclusive, personalized, and timely care. The increasing participation of private players or public-private-partnership (PPP) models is also changing the economic dimensions of the healthcare industry because they bring different performance considerations and investment-return time horizons than the completely public-funded systems.

On the societal side, there are many changes as well which are influencing healthcare transformation. We have the growing urban–rural imbalance in healthcare driven by rapid urbanization across most nations. We also have aging populations in most nations, which cre-ates additional pressure on the healthcare systems. Finally, families becoming more nuclear are impacting the individual's ecosystem during times of need. These factors have intensified the supply–demand problems of healthcare. Traditional hospitals are no longer able to meet the growing demand for medical services, and going smart is essential. Chronic diseases are becoming the number-one threat to public health in many growing economies. They exert tre-mendous pressure on both physicians and patients due to factors such as long duration, complex causes, and the need for frequent interactions between physicians and patients. The problem is compounded by the lack of adequately trained physicians and treatment facilities uniformly across the world. On one hand, the medical sciences have made tremendous progress in terms of research and development to treat chronic and emerging diseases; on the other hand, its avail-ability to the larger world population has gaps. As a result, traditional hospitals need to trans-form themselves into smart health management organizations. Pilot projects for smart hospitals and healthcare systems are being implemented at national and regional levels.

On the technology side, the rate of innovation and consequent disruption is exponentially increasing. As per Deloitte's research published in 2019 about the Future of Health, the health-care industry of 2040 will be dramatically different from how we know it today. A little over 20 years ago, the first robot was used to assist in surgery; today robotics is very frequently used in many routinized procedures. In the last 20 years, we have also come a long way from coding the first genome at the cost of millions of dollars to now doing genomics for millions of people at a cost of less than $100. Technological progress around nanotechnology, quantum computing, robotics, biomedical engineering, storage methods and costs, pervasive connectivity, mixed reality, and 3D printing will change the practice of healthcare. AI will play a key underlying role in all of these because we will need new ways to manage and make sense of the massively volu-minous and sometimes transient data which is critical to get the insights that we will need to get research, education, prevention, and care right.

IoT makes the interconnection and interoperability of devices possible, connects physical devices/spaces and medical services, and helps to improve the efficiency and outcomes of medical treatment. Developments in big data, cloud computing, and AI enable an exponential increase in data processing capacity and make numerous decision-making and auxiliary treatment tools possible. IT and mobile Internet technologies, video imaging, and high-resolution telecommunication have further improved the efficiency of communication between people and people as well as between people and things, and this also helps to dramatically increase the operational efficiency of hospitals and healthcare systems – both for research as well as treatment.

Today's healthcare is focused largely on treatment; tomorrow's healthcare will transition more to focus on health. We will see the shift from treatment to predictive and preventive posture enabled by technology and AI.

THE CRITICAL ROLE OF AI IN THE HEALTHCARE OF THE FUTURE

As the focus of healthcare changes from diagnosis and treatment to proactive health management, preventive interventions, and lifecycle engagement, we will also see a shift to more personalized and targeted healthcare, experiences to promote wellness, and a transformation in the role of healthcare facilities like hospitals and micro-clinics.

There are several major issues that the healthcare of the future needs to address. From an analytics standpoint, there are five key problem areas where we need advanced techniques like AI to play a huge role:

1. **Avoiding the approach of averages and creating a personalized context to healthcare.** Today a majority of the hypotheses around health are based on what happens to average populations in age groups, regions/races, and gender demonstrating a certain behavior or symptom. The effectiveness of any healthcare intervention is limited by what the individual's physiological and psychological response to that intervention is, how the individual's unique genetic composition is predisposed to respond, and other extenuating circumstances that might impact it. There is an increasing shift to highly personalize and contextualize the individual to health and care. This requires a complete unique makeup of every individual with context to a large number of health markers that need minute monitoring and analysis to design interventions. We are now talking about converging massive amounts of data from multiple branches of medical sciences and running massively complex analytics that can only be done by deep learning and other AI tools.
2. **Integrating the events, patterns, and experiences across an individual's lifecycle concerning health to create new insights and interventions.** When we extend the scope of healthcare to an individual's entire lifecycle and environment, we have to coalesce the points made above in a continuum to achieve the desired outcomes. Now we have just amplified the integration of systems and complexity of analytics.
3. **Making available all knowledge and resources related to research, diagnosis, and treatment.** Medical sciences have a legacy of several thousands of years across many civilizations around the world. In the last century, a lot of advancement has happened in medical sciences to understand problems and causality and find treatments. In the last several decades, such information has been increasingly digitized and a lot of it is easily available today to the general population. But as the medical sciences have become more complex, more specialization has also come in to address the complexity. Since we are dealing with people's lives and sometimes those of a broader population in case of an epidemic situation,

timely response to symptoms and evolving situations becomes critical. Given the nature of complexity, possible unique precedence of events in other situations, and the presence of knowledge in a different part of the world, we need better tools to integrate knowledge on a real-time basis and disseminate it to the location and situation where needed. Enabling technologies like advanced telecommunication, mixed reality systems, and massive stores of unstructured data organized in a graph model for flexible indexing and sorting are already available. AI techniques help make these enabling technologies effective. There is more work to be done in developing more capabilities around these new digital technologies and analytics to reframe how knowledge management happens in the healthcare industry.

4. **Combining the clinical systems and operational systems to create unified outcomes and experiences.** Historically, the different technology systems in the healthcare industry and especially the hospitals evolved and were managed in silos. There has been increasing realization for some time that to achieve broader outcomes than served by any of these individual systems requires deeper and seamless integration across the various systems. For example, patient care in hospital rooms requires hospital information systems, electronic medical records systems, in-room patient systems like entertainment, nurse-call systems, specialized medical systems, HVAC systems, and building automation systems, with several such systems to be cohesively integrated. There is a bigger need for system integration and the ability to respond in real-time to address the emerging needs of patients. We will need AI techniques for the new insights to emerge from such an integrated information ecosystem.

5. **Improving capacity management.** Capacity management is one of the greatest present-day challenges for the healthcare industry anywhere in the world, including in the most developed economies. Nearly every major hospital administrator will cite this as one of their top-three issues and as a solution to reducing expenses, enhancing efficiency, and increasing the scope of care provided. Medical issues are rising and so is the population and aging population in most parts of the world, but the number of hospitals or healthcare professionals is not increasing proportionately. Available monies for treatment and research on a per-capita basis are also not increasing, but spend is. The big issue in capacity management is being able to predict the tipping point of utilization across the ecosystem, which usually dramatically drives up waiting times and stress in the system once the threshold of 85% is reached. Capacity management can be improved by improved situational awareness and evening out variability across an incoming volume of medical transactions, time, space, and assets across a very complex ecosystem with thousands of independent elements. James Scheulen, Chief Administrator of John Hopkins, considers this as one of his most important agenda items and through a thoughtful approach and appropriate use of technology and analytics has achieved significant results, including 35% reduction in patient waiting, 70% reduction in postsurgery OR holds, 11–80% reduction in bed assignment across various departments, among other exemplary accomplishments. Active capacity management lies at the intersection of quality, safety, outcomes, service, and efficiency. It leads to very high patient satisfaction scores and the effectiveness of treatment. Without AI techniques, understanding the dynamic influence of various elements of the healthcare ecosystem as well as predicting performance and behavior is nearly impossible to undertake active capacity management.

Additionally, many AI techniques are already being deployed in research and diagnostics functions, and their usage will continue to rise with time as there is more availability of data and tools, increasing complexity of the problems to solve, and expanded capacity of AI professionals to solve new problems.

Specific AI techniques like Natural Language Processing are increasingly being used in engagement platforms between healthcare systems and patients to make it more simplified and streamlined, education platforms to make knowledge more accessible and understandable, and in detecting patterns of events. The impact of AI in healthcare in the future will be limited only by the lack of human imagination.

In the next two sections we will dig deeper into two major areas of transformation: personal health cloud and smart hospitals.

 PERSONAL HEALTH CLOUD

The concept of person-oriented health cloud will be one of the most transformative developments over the next several years. Today we can already find many technology companies offering healthcare-oriented capabilities on a cloud platform; this is not new. Salesforce has already adapted its core CRM for patient management and patient experience. We also see some very innovative applications like Unite US (www.uniteus.com), which takes a community approach to coordinated healthcare-related actions, and Health Cloud (www.healthcloudsa.com), a South Africa–based startup that is attempting to create a platform for open information and insight exchange between various participants in the healthcare industry. Healthcare technologies have been a very vibrant space for investments for a very long time given the opportunities that exist. In 2017, more than $40 billion was spent on digital technology startups by venture capital funds, a number which has increased a lot since then. Even large healthcare systems and healthcare companies are making portfolio investments into the growing innovation and disruption network. So clearly we will see more and more cloud and analytical applications, many of which will solve real problems, scale, and help improve healthcare in the future.

However, there is one untapped area that will get more focus. In one of the earlier sections, we discussed how the healthcare industry is largely driven by the law of averages, which potentially suboptimizes the effectiveness of any diagnosis, treatment, and long-term care. Our current health and future well-being are impacted by several different parameters like current vital statistics, sleep patterns, food habits, work habits, workout habits, family history, environmental factors at home-work-transit, historical response to certain treatments and allergies, the health of other family members, mental state and pressures, the evolution of physical conditions over time to show a pattern and detect the motion of those emerging patterns, genetic signatures, and community signatures. All such information exists, but exists in silos, rarely associated and contextualized, and not considered to the level of depth for appropriate diagnostics or remedial purposes. Similarly, there is new information available around causality, treatments, and medicines every day, a large portion of which is not accessible for individual consumption or contextualization

The focus on understanding details about an individual has been recognized for some time now. The idea behind the development of genomics at an individual level is to start the process of understanding the person instead of just looking at patterns. What is missing today is a network of nodes of person-centric information repositories capturing the different types of data described in the above paragraph.

Developing technology infrastructure and enabling the business ecosystem for personal health cloud is complicated, will require significant investments, will take time, and most importantly will take coordinated action between many current industry participants and possibly even the development of several new players. Whenever there is a fundamental shift in the industry structure and incentives of incumbent participants, this level of complexity and resistance is not unprecedented. Whether it is online retail models driven by Amazon or completely different models of consuming music like those ushered in by Apple, the path to transition has never been simple. The primary challenges behind the development of personal health cloud are driven by many factors, such as:

a. **Absence of primary player with access to majority information.** Presently, the insurance providers, healthcare systems, and individuals, collectively have a lot of the information, but not all of the information. To get a comprehensive picture of the individual, more investigation and collection of information will be required. Such high-touch and person-dependent activities for large populations are difficult. Imagine doing census for the first time but with a couple of orders of magnitude complexity. One could always start with collecting as much as possible for as many as possible, but the lack of adequate data will impact the efficacy of the information.

b. **Lack of anchor beneficiary other than the individual.** Persistent investment of money and time for such a complex endeavor requires that there is a single or small group of major beneficiaries with enough economic interest so that they can change the demand and/or supply economics. In the foreseeable future, the primary beneficiary for a personal health cloud is the individual. But in this case, the "individual" is a very fragmented beneficiary group because the benefits kick in only when healthcare services are required, something that at an individual level is unpredictable and (hopefully) infrequent. When we look at a large pool of people together as a collective, the benefits are more favorable, but there is no immediate natural organization of people into a collective in any of the existing industry structures. The one constituent which can change the equation dramatically driving quicker development and adoption of personal health cloud is the State. Governments can legislate, create an incentive, or take any other number of measures to drive action. For the State, there are clear incentives for improving health and care at an aggregate level. The other potential catalyst for such a development could be a large technology company like Microsoft or Google or AWS that may have other incentives of driving consumption and near-monopolistic preference for their technology by being an early and decisive mover.

c. **Developmental complexity.** The development of the technology infrastructure has a lot of inherent complexity as well. We will need a graph database approach for the underlying data management framework. Building massive scale and very flexible graph databases have architectural and programming challenges and require a higher order of technical acumen and capability. Given the diversity of data, metadata management adds another layer of complexity. Ensuring the security and privacy of highly sensitive personal and health data at this scale is not something that has been done before. Deciding who can access what data under what circumstances requires some serious policy-level thinking. Finally, building the tools to properly access and interrogate the data adds another major layer of complexity; we will need new AI-enabled and Controlled Natural Language–powered user-experience tools to leverage the data from personal health cloud systems.

d. **Unclear business models.** We have discussed in this section that building a personal health cloud can get expensive and complex with no immediately clear beneficiary with adequate financial capacity. Even if this idea gets developed, it is unclear how the benefits will get monetized because they do not conform to or support any existing industry structures. Once more succinct business models for data monetization emerge, we will see greater efforts toward development.

We firmly believe that these challenges will get addressed in the near to medium time horizon. The benefits of the idea far outweigh the challenges and disincentives. As has happened many times in the past, people and organizations will come together in a collective to solve common problems and further the common good. In building such personal health cloud repositories, serious issues have to be solved around organizing the data, ensuring security and privacy of the data, enabling access of the data to other systems and people, keeping the data current and relevant, and continuously proactively analyzing the data for new insights. AI techniques around Deep Neural Networks, Recursive Neural Networks, Long-Short Term Memory Models, Controlled Natural Language, and others will need to be employed to achieve these audacious goals of managing the personal health digital vault.

There are many profound implications of such a personal health cloud ecosystem that will lead to new business models and disruptions. The first and most important implication is the democratization of information and power to the individual. Today, the healthcare ecosystem players have an edge because they control information and knowledge; with the personal health cloud ecosystem that will shift. Hospitals and other healthcare institutions will have to exchange and broker information through new information networks and methods requiring potentially significant changes to their operational processes and technology infrastructure.

There will be many tricky situations to resolve as well. For example, the personal health cloud ecosystem will surely personalize healthcare and make it more effective, potentially bringing down the cost for care over time. This will require a complete overhaul of how we think about medical insurance today. While we want the costs to come down and insurance premiums to reflect that, we might be wary of being penalized for factors like genetics or environment, over which we have little control. The role of government will also change significantly in this new environment, bringing new policy, regulatory, and administrative implications. We will be discovering and addressing new topics around ethics and morality as information and insights take new shapes.

 SMART HOSPITALS OF THE FUTURE

The concept of smart hospitals has been talked about for many years now. Research firm Frost and Sullivan defines smart hospitals as those that optimize, redesign, or build new clinical processes, management systems, and potentially even infrastructure enabled by underlying digitized networking infrastructure of interconnected assets to provide a valuable service or insight which was not possible or available earlier to achieve better patient care, experience, and operational efficiency. They distinguish between a digital hospital and a digitally enabled smart hospital. In their definition, a digital hospital has sensors everywhere that are networked, but a smart one derives new insights and value from that network. A smart hospital is not just technologically enriched but is also sensitive in its response to emerging needs and experienced issues.

Taking this definition a bit further, smart hospitals or healthcare facilities of the future will expand beyond one single smart physical facility into a network of nodes of capability delivery to achieve better health outcomes and care from home to hospitals. There is an argument to be made that in the future, the physical hospitals that we know today where all aspects of healthcare converge to care for the patients will be replaced or supplemented by virtual centers of specific capabilities and specializations. The healthcare system of the future will be an amalgamated ecosystem of people, knowledge, and infrastructure that will be connected, be aware, and be adaptive to the health needs of the patients as well as the broader population.

We shall first describe the AI-enabled hospital of the future.

In any such hospital, there are four different types of information systems:

1. **Clinical systems.** These are systems that are required by a healthcare facility for medical diagnosis and treatment. Such systems typically include electronic health or medical records, intensive-care systems, imaging systems, emergency response systems, nurse-call systems, in-room systems for functions such as bed management, surgical systems, testing systems, etc. In normal treatment environments, clinical systems capture more than 30 measurements per day, but in intensive or special-care scenarios, this number could end up being 60 times more. These systems are the foundation of medical practice. They have strong decision-support systems. Often, many of these devices and data from them are required together in unison to perform one diagnostic or treatment chain. The clinical systems' information systems need an exceptionally high-fidelity and quick transmission. There is usually also a need for traceability of information and insights as well as longtime storage of both. A very large population of such devices is already connected and data from them is being collected and processed in real time. As per a report from Allied Market Research published in June 2019, more than 3.7 million devices are already connected and this population is rapidly growing due to increased proliferation of IoT, the advancement of medical technology, and progress in telehealth. Maintenance of medical devices and clinical systems is critical to healthcare success and often leads to ancillary information systems.

2. **Operational systems.** These are the systems that are not required for the core practice of medicine but are critical for the functioning of the hospital or the healthcare system. For example, healthcare operational systems include office automation, hospital information or resource management system, real-time location tracking systems for assets, research management system, the entire backbone of healthcare, prescription management system, compliance management systems, etc. The operational systems have to frequently integrate and interact with the other types of information systems in the healthcare ecosystem.

3. **Facility systems.** Winston Churchill once famously remarked[4] that "we shape our buildings and then our buildings shape us." Like any other building, any modern hospital will

have hundreds if not thousands of sensors and devices. Such sensors and devices along with their management systems keep the hospitals functional and safe. These sensors and systems address the hospital's needs around power management, heating, ventilation, air-conditioning, energy management, plumbing, safety, security, mobility (elevators/escalators) and specialized delivery systems, location tracking and navigation, lighting, cleaning and housekeeping, and other such systems to effectively run the facility. Typically, we will find building management systems coordinating actions and performance across all of these facility systems. Additionally, we will also find facility management systems to assist in the operations and maintenance of the hospital facilities. Most hospitals will have dozens of maintenance staff and a higher number of contract staff, so it is possible to find systems to manage the workforce as well. Hospitals usually require fairly stringent operating conditions for the most part, in terms of environmental conditions and/or security and safety measures. Nearly all systems in hospitals including the facility systems are subject to compliance requirements around their state of health and performance, which can get audited by authorities from time to time. There is almost no tolerance for suboptimal functioning or downtime for any facility system in hospitals, making their configuration and application unique as compared to other types of facilities. More data and at a higher frequency is captured from hospital facility systems.

4. **External knowledge systems.** These are systems that are not necessarily tied to any particular hospital or healthcare system but are required for completing the information ecosystem. Medical knowledge management systems, weather, and other news or event feed systems, health advisory systems, patient information systems (if part of a bigger network), insurance management systems, etc. are examples of external knowledge and engagement systems. Such systems will have information from different sources getting updated at very different nondeterministic frequencies and mostly in very different formats. Creating context around such information is very difficult due to their lack of inherent correlation.

These information systems will be based rarely on a unified and more often on a distributed IT and communication backbone.

Data from these various systems flows into a common repository that acts as the digital vault. In this vault, several things happen – the data first gets sanitized, it then gets sorted and stored securely, interrelationships and context between various aspects of the data get established, the data gets enriched and tagged, and finally the data is prepared for analytics. While it seems a lot is going on here, it all happens in micro- and subseconds. The neural network of the hospital information ecosystem then runs the data through its massively capable analytical engine to create actionable insights. The purpose of these insights is primarily around:

1. Improving patient outcomes
2. Optimizing capacity of assets and resources
3. Increasing operational efficiency

The output is visible in a collection of user experience applications around patient experience, workflow management, and other such functions. (See Figure 3.3.)

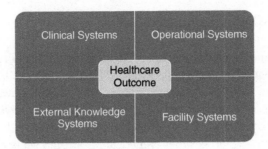

FIGURE 3.3 Healthcare Information Systems

The Bee'ah Group under Khaled's leadership is working on a futuristic hospital project. With the unprecedented pandemic hitting the world, we are revisiting and reshaping our strategy to reflect on what the hospital of the future or " future-proof hospital" will look or be like. Number of profound trends have accelerated which we are taking into account:

1. Concept of integrated connected system (which refers to more scalable and smaller specialty/community centers network that enables more flexible capacity and controlled/safe access mechanism while all being connected to a single digital infrastructure)
2. Leveraging digital technology across the hospital entry, testing, operation, and exit to go contact-less as possible (minimizing human/surface contact)
3. Acceleration of telehealth, virtual care and connected health hubs (which covers cloud-based IT solutions, AI application and analytics to support multidisciplinary approach towards treatment decisions and more efficient system while managing patient flow and scaling care during crises
4. Care comes to your doorstep where possible: selected services to be provided by hospitals through mobile healthcare vehicles that enables quick and direct screening, examination and testing (e.g. mini hospital in a mobile shipping container)

Following are some of the technologies and innovations that UAE have invented/adopted:

1. Laser testing technology – user friendly and enable much faster mass screening with results available in seconds
2. "Super-intelligent" helmets capable "used to diagnose people from a safe distance, enabling them to handle crowds, obtain vital reading and analyze data"
3. Drones – used in national disinfection and sterilization
4. Deployment of robot TAF35 on the streets to support the sterilization operations. The robot can be controlled from a distance of 300 meters and is capable of pumping large quantities of sanitizing and disinfecting materials.
5. ALHOSN app – depends on the use of short-term Bluetooth signals to show whether the person is in close proximity to people who have had contact with patients infected with COVID virus. This is to help contain the spread of COVID. To complement the effort for tracing, an electronic wristband linked to ALHOSN was given to individuals testing positive.

AI APPLICATIONS IN HEALTHCARE

Now let us examine some AI applications that provide more anticipatory capabilities to medical professionals and systems. The scope of applying AI is much broader than this list. With time, availability of data, and more analyst-friendly tools, this list will grow. When thinking about the AI applications, it is critical to remember that AI should be effectively used only when and where there is a need to anticipate a future state or behavior of something with a prescribed or acceptable level of accuracy; for all other analytical or decision support requirements, simpler heuristics-based approaches may be more appropriate and efficient.

Personalized Treatment Programs

Advancements in personal health cloud and genomics will lead to enough specific data about individuals and how they react when exposed to different environmental and medical conditions and how such reactions have evolved. Such data is very useful to predict what the most likely outcome of a new medical intervention might look like and what will be most effective for a specific individual. Sorting through such massive and complex data can only happen through machine learning methods.

Telediagnostics

In medical diagnostics, four factors play a critical role – personal history, clinical examination, evidence-based interpretation, and the doctor's intuition based on knowledge and experience. Personal history has reliability issues because it is highly dependent on feedback from individuals who may not always remember all the events or ignore certain events from reporting because they may not see the relevance, and simply given the length of time and different places where the person might be reporting history a lot of it will get lost. AI will help with the development of personal health clouds and also correlate various aspects of personal history for the specific context being investigated. AI will also help with the capture of history by prompting what additional information to capture based on the analysis of most likely scenarios from history and other references.

High-end diagnostic tools like MRI and other imaging tools or different types of blood and chemistry analysis tools are very effective in identifying problems and narrowing down the potential causes. Such clinical investigations started with a need for highly trained and expert analysts to interpret the data; over time, the same need has been supplemented with remote routinized capabilities, and now is being increasingly taken over by the machine and executed using machine learning techniques. This approach allows the diagnostic process to be faster, be more accurate, cover more cases of diagnosis with the same resources, and be less expensive. This approach is very effective for diagnosing many types of cancer, heart problems, liver-related/kidney-related issues, in addition to normal ailments. Automated ML programs developed using programming language Julia and tools like Contextflow have helped reduced the 20 minutes radiologists used to spend looking for patterns and information down to 2 seconds.

When it comes to more evidence-based techniques, machine learning is particularly helpful to plot the progression of a disease or a series of symptoms to their most likely medical outcome. When coupled with the personalization aspects discussed above, this can be an incredibly powerful tool to determine the right treatment protocol. There are many examples of successful pilots in this space, for example, one conducted by Google Deepmind to pre-detect kidney diseases or the work IBM did to identify possible blindness using retinal study.

We are increasingly using the learning and super-fast processing capabilities of machines to get closer and closer to human intuition.

Drug Discovery

The traditional drug discovery process takes years and billions of dollars of investment. This makes the cost of drugs and hence treatment expensive, with delays in the benefits to masses, and also limits innovation and research to a few very large players in the industry. But AI is changing that. On January 30, 2020, the world's first AI-discovered drug for Obsessive-Compulsive Disorder (OCD) by the code name of DSP-1181 was announced. This was done by British startup Exscientia in collaboration with Japanese pharmaceutical firm Sumitomo Dainippon Pharma. The inventors claim that the algorithm used to discover the drug, a process that took only one year as opposed to several, can be used for discovering other drugs as well. AI is useful not only for the discovery of new drugs but in figuring out the interaction between different drugs when administered simultaneously or as part of the same treatment regime. AI helps sort through and simulate the various permutations-combinations of the implications of drug–drug interaction. Various national organizations like the NHS in the UK are setting up dedicated AI labs for healthcare to promote more research and development. Speeding up the discovery process benefits every stakeholder in the ecosystem

Robotic Surgeries

Surgeries are another area which has so far been considered the exclusive domain of very specialized medical professionals and are also being impacted by the use of AI-assisted robots. Simple, repetitive small tasks like small incisions, putting in stitches, or running probes are activities that can be very effectively learned by robots and used in performing surgeries. The Smart Tissue Autonomous Robot (STAR) developed by John Hopkins four years back is one of the early robots to help with surgeries. STAR consists of tools for suturing as well as fluorescent and 3D imaging, force sensing, and submillimeter positioning. These capabilities, when applied to soft-tissue surgeries, make the process more effective as compared to normal human-driven surgeries for similar soft tissues. This is just the beginning; there continues to be more development in this space each day. Robotic surgery has many advantages – it provides skill augmentation for doctors where there is already a burgeoning gap between supply and demand, reduces the fatigue and stress during surgeries, is more precise in incisions and other such processes thus improving the recovery times, and is expanding the scope of learning from multiple surgeries across the world as learning will not be based on the individual experience of the doctor but collective knowledge of all surgeries across the world.

Emergency Response

Emergency response is probably one of the most frequently occurring and highly stressful activities for medical professionals – be it doctors or nurses or technicians. Effectiveness in emergency response requires a very quick understanding of the situation, triaging the issues, determining causality of problems, and identifying the most optimal next course of action. Given the commonalities at this early stage across a very large number of emergencies, AI algorithms can be deployed effectively with all of the functions described here because we can apply analytics across a very large data pool very quickly. In triage situations, machine learning and neural networks are very effective for situations that have moderate urgency drivers. For patient monitoring, AI techniques are very helpful to identify anomalies and predict future possibilities with less human intervention. Different flavors of neural network techniques are very effective in such modeling activities.

Capacity Planning and Management

Hospital operations are complex ecosystems with a high degree of interdependency, time-sensitiveness, variability, and chances of error. Capacity management problems in healthcare are very similar to the scenarios experienced in major transportation hubs or complex supply chain networks, except that the criticality is of a much higher order. There is always a fixed number of assets and resources in the healthcare environment, but they might be required for many different events suddenly and simultaneously, leading to capacity management issues finally resulting in delays and poor levels of care. AI algorithms can be effectively employed for constraint optimization and the best outcome given the constraints, thus helping with capacity management. Historical analysis of capacity management scenarios and emerging events can be quickly synthesized to arrive at the most optimal scenario. These are immensely helpful when we have to face emergencies due to natural disasters or major law-and-order issues.

Energy Prediction and Diagnostics

Historically, there has been a lot of focus on energy optimization but as a post-facto implementation. But today we have enough sensors, data, and analytical techniques to proactively understand future energy consumption models and be able to take action on such insights. Energy Prediction Model (EPM) using AI is usually based on deep learning, sequence-to-sequence long short-term memory (LSTM) techniques to predict the energy consumption of a whole building, as well as at an equipment or component level, for various external and indoor conditions. This allows peak shaving, load shifting, demand response, and sourcing decision, reducing energy consumption and energy costs on average by 10%. AI-based models have trained adaptively through real-time and historic IoT sensor data. AI Model-based Energy Fault Detection Model is a (deep learning) energy anomaly detection or fault detection and diagnosis (FDD) model that detects anomalous or faulty energy consumption based on the deviation of predicted energy consumption. This capability reduces energy consumption on average by 15%, extending the life of building equipment and reducing maintenance costs. This is a data-driven AI-based model, constructed and tuned autonomously using historic data. An Optimal Control of HVAC System with Deep Neural Network and Reinforcement Learning solution computes optimal operational setpoint for the airside of HVAC systems by taking into consideration thermal mass of the building as thermal storage, predicted energy load, electricity rate structure, zone temperature, humidity, indoor air quality (IAQ), and occupant information. The proposed solution is a data-driven, AI-based model trained in real time through sensor data. The solution reduces energy cost by 20% on average, improving the comfort, wellness, and productivity of building occupants.

Predictive Asset Maintenance

The biggest maintenance concern around assets in the healthcare type of environment is emergency shutdowns. Such shutdowns can have a very significant impact on the operations of clinical systems or facility systems; operators and owners have a very low tolerance for such events. Often multiple redundancies are put in place, which is not only inefficient but also expensive. AI is very effective in predicting such events and recommending remedial measures. In the AI approach, shutdown predictions are posed as an anomaly detection problem. Various state-of-the-art deep learning architectures such as Long Short-Term Memory (LSTM) Auto Encoders and LSTM Variational Auto Encoders are employed for such predictions. Anomaly and faults identified through various existing diagnostics to avert failure and avoid expensive damage of equipment and wasted resources are other major areas of AI implementation. There are broadly two types of optimization problems that need to be solved. The first one is the optimization of short-term decisions (e.g., daily or hourly), which is to optimally assign and route technicians to maintenance tasks and synchronize technicians and resources (equipment, tools, vehicle, etc.) within service level agreements (SLAs) with clients. The second one is the optimization of longer-term decisions (monthly or yearly), which may involve optimally planning resource conservation, retrofits or replacements of equipment, considering operational cost, maintenance cost, replacement cost, failure cost, maintenance budget, and resources. Techniques that can be used here are optimization techniques such as Constraint Programming, Dynamic Programming, Markov Decision Process (MDP), and Mixed Integer Linear Programming (MILP), which interacts with AI-based prediction models.

Model Predictive Maintenance

Most of the maintenance protocols are based on asset condition and health or on some period or maintenance intervention arrived at by studying historical understanding. Model predictive maintenance is a unique concept of selecting maintenance protocol based on optimizing the net present value of the asset calculated using current operating parameters of the asset, projected maintenance costs, and forecasted operational utility costs while simultaneously evaluating the NPV and total cost for other alternative assets, including new ones and/or different types of maintenance protocols, while ensuring that core performance output from the system remains the same or nearly identical. Model predictive maintenance is arrived at by combining AI and heuristic models. This is a more effective technique because one does not have to wait for a long time for enough data and variation to build the models without understanding the underlying physics.

Asset Tracking and Utilization

Real-time asset tracking and utilization knowledge is a big issue in the healthcare space that can be addressed using AI techniques. It has been reported that nurses may end up spending an hour a day looking for equipment and devices like IV pumps, mobile ECG machines, etc. Such wastage is not only a huge productivity drain but also could end up denying the right level of care to the patients. Utilization of high-value specialized assets like lab equipment is another problem that impacts care effectiveness. Knowing availability and usage patterns is very helpful to improve research and clinical outcomes. Several AI techniques help with pattern recognition and recommendations.

Alarm Noise Suppression

Given that there are so many devices both clinical as well as facility-related in any healthcare environment, a large volume of signals gets generated from these devices and systems. In many instances, there is a lot of noise in such signals and it is very difficult to sort through the false-positives or less important problems either manually or through simplistic rules. It is very difficult to understand the systemic contribution to these signals and the noise. For example, in security systems like access control systems, usually 90%+ alarm signals do not merit attention, but the 10% that do can be of critical significance. AI techniques have been very effective in prioritizing the alarm signals with proper context and learning over time.

Compliance Management

Compliance management is a big challenge for any owner/operator/administrator of any healthcare constituent – be it a hospital or a pharmaceutical company. Compliance management usually involves sifting through huge volumes of data and validating that all the requirements are met. AI is very well suited for such activities. In compliance management, more than reporting what responsible people care about is being able to preempt any potential violation. Such measures will require simultaneous pattern analysis of several different and often unrelated variables. This is also a task AI is very well suited for. Since any compliance program usually involves a lot of human intervention, more usage of AI will reduce resulting error possibilities and associated costs.

Cybersecurity and Privacy Assurance

This is an already huge and growing concern in healthcare and several other industries. The number of threat vectors is ever-increasing and the intrusions are becoming increasingly innovative. We will deal with this topic in much greater detail later in the book. What makes this problem critical in the healthcare industry is the sensitivity of data, the amount of data-generation points, and several intrusion points for bad actors. AI-driven anomaly detection and pattern recognition at very high frequency are critical to addressing such issues.

Data Veracity

The quality and accuracy of data are a huge challenge in healthcare and many other disciplines. This problem is exacerbated by the multiplicity of sensors and systems, types and frequency of data, and other variabilities. Cleansing such complex and often unreliable data streams is very cumbersome. Data veracity is the degree to which data is accurate, precise, and trusted. Data veracity problems need to be corrected before introducing the data to ML/AI pipelines (both training and inferencing) so that accurate ML/AL models are developed (trained) and accurate solutions are generated (predicted or inferencing). This problem is frequently encountered while doing failure prediction, anomaly detection, asset health analysis, reliability analysis, predictive maintenance, operational optimization, energy prediction, wellness prediction, security risk analysis, and creating smart recommendations based on AI. Various techniques employed for anomaly detection and recursive pattern recognition are very useful to understand and take action on data veracity problems.

BUSINESS MODELS OF THE FUTURE IN HEALTHCARE

Business models in the healthcare industry have been changing over the last several years. We have seen the consolidation of multiple private practices and smaller outfits into a few large healthcare system players. We have also seen changes in how healthcare insurance works – discounts around active lifestyle management, pooling of resources, more dynamic premium pricing, etc. We have seen the growing participation of remote diagnostics and remote health management. We have also seen the rise of specialization and micro-specialization. Finally, we have also seen increasing globalization of healthcare systems – for example, Cleveland Clinic has a presence not only in US cities outside of Cleveland but also in Abu Dhabi and Toronto. These business model changes are not dramatic; they are more like an extension of existing ones better enabled by technology.

However, in the new digital world we see a few more fundamental changes.

The biggest area of change will be around the pricing and costing of healthcare services. The majority of financial models in the healthcare industry today are based on events and interactions – we get charged for visits, tests, treatments, medicines, and so on. They are not necessarily linked to health outcomes. We will see more outcome-based pricing or financial models in the future. Digital technologies and AI will allow us to better predict and manage health outcomes which are difficult to model today. With greater personalization of healthcare and more precision treatment and medicines, people will want more specific pricing linked to the outcomes they achieve similar to some other industries where we have started seeing such models. The shift will not first start with the patients, but most likely with suppliers to the healthcare industry. The most likely starting point of outcome-based models in the healthcare supplier ecosystem will be with facility services or remote patient services or even diagnostic services. One similar shift that has already happened is around how hospitals do not get compensated much if at all in many countries for treating hospital-acquired infections. Changes in the financial structures and incentives in the healthcare industry will require a whole new level of tracking and transparency that will require more intensive use of technology for compliance. Modifications to the technology infrastructure will also have to be accompanied by substantial change management efforts around people's behaviors and work processes.

The second big area of change in terms of business models will be location-based ones. As information and knowledge get more globally unified and accessible, as remote diagnostic and treatment capabilities become more sophisticated, as the capacity of resources and assets gets more networked, the role of large capital-intensive monolithic facilities will change. While not exact parallels, the roles of bank branches, retail stores, and remote learning also dramatically changed because of digital technologies. The transition will take more time and will never be to the same extent, but there will be a gradual shift driven by tele-health. In such a scenario, the personalization of patient care which is very human-centered and executed in a high-touch model will also have to change. Achieving patient satisfaction and health outcomes will require a more systematic and integrated approach with a seamless flow of information and insights. As physical facilities become less important, more concierge-type approaches will be required in telehealth administration to retain the same level of effectiveness.

The third big disruption in business models will come from the role of the community. Over the years we have moved into a more individual-centric society. With the new generations we are moving back into an interesting intersection of the individual and the community. As the world keeps getting more integrated and our lives keep getting more social, we will see a renewed focus on the community concerning health. When the focus is shifting from reactive treatment to proactive care, there will be a need to influence broader sections of the population beyond the individual.

The fourth big area of disruption will be in terms of long-term care. Present business models are very high-touch. With the increasing population of people who need care on one hand and shrinking care staff on the other hand, to balance the supply and demand AI-powered intelligent agents like chatbots will play a big role in engaging the patients and managing an increasing array of interactions. The use of virtual assistants has already started making a big impact on transforming customer service in other industries.

The fifth big area of disruption will be in the construction and management of hospitals of the future because of the very high proliferation of technology and analytics in the facility systems, more than most other facility types. We will see the emergence of new IoT devices and systems across the entire spectrum of hospital information systems. We will also see new interoperable platforms that break through the existing silos, procurement cycles, and market structures. The technology applications and platform space have already started to become very vibrant with large investments that we have discussed previously in this chapter. We will see very different types of technology specialists and service providers who will integrate the various systems as well as manage their operations. Many of these services will also get tied to outcomes in a managed service environment as opposed to a more traditional resource-cost-based business model.

 SUMMARY

We have always known that healthcare is important for us as individuals and nations as a whole; however, it rarely took center stage in any consideration. The adage *health is wealth* had almost become a cliché before the COVID-19 crisis hit. Now we live in a different world. We have seen how epidemics can create havoc in every aspect of our lives and livelihood. We first wrote this chapter before COVID-19 emerged. Now when we look back on all the topics and transformations we touched upon, everything seems so much more relevant now. We wish these capabilities existed today to help us fight this crisis.

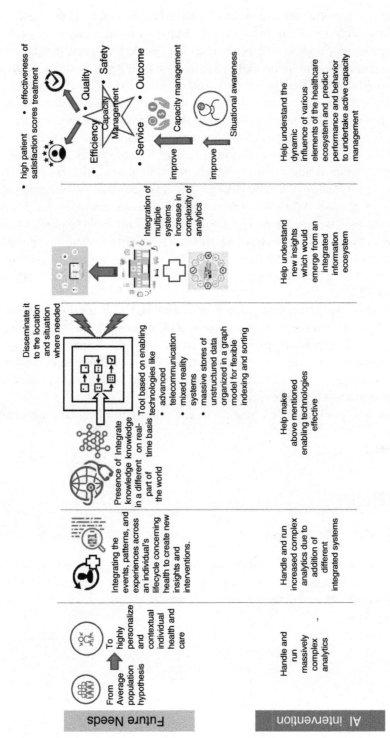

FIGURE 3.4 Impact of AI on Healthcare

For example, if personalized treatment programs had existed and been supported by the personal health cloud, the ability to provide a better treatment regimen to each individual would have been so much better and maybe most lives could have been saved. If telediagnostics were more mature and more pervasive, the load on healthcare facilities might have been less. In some hospitals, robots are being used to carry things to COVID-19 patients to minimize exposure. If the use of robots were more prevalent, we could have reduced the exposure to our frontline medical staff so much more. While AI is already being used for drug discovery, could we have done more? The whole aspect of emergency response now acquires a completely different level of intensity. With more and better use of AI and digital technologies, we could have been more proactive and predictive about infection zones, infection cases, triage process, etc. Nearly every country is now struggling with its medical infrastructure due to this sudden onslaught of crisis. While AI could not have solved the current issue, it surely could have helped us prepare for alternative scenarios better and also could be used to run proactive drills from time to time. Nobody was ready for this and it took the medical community and civic administration days and weeks to figure out how to respond. We could nearly rewrite this entire chapter around COVID-19 and everything would still hold, except that the impact would be even more intensified.

The balance between nature and us has been disturbed. This is causing the environment to change and is also a potential contributing factor to several ecological and epidemiological issues that we see today. In the last several years we have seen SARS, MERS, and now COVOID-19. With each new episode, the impact rises and broadens. We will likely continue to see the emergence of such issues in the future. We need a better-coordinated strategy and tools to tackle these emerging issues. This is where AI can and will help.

Figure 3.4 is a quick recap of how AI might impact the healthcare industry of the future.

Be well; be safe.

REFERENCES

(1) "Healthcare Global Market Opportunities and Strategies to 2022"; ResearchAndMarkets.com; June 2019.
(2) *Macroeconomics and Health: Investing in Health for Economic Development*; Jeffrey D. Sachs; December 2001.
(3) "Digital Health Market Forecast 2019–2025"; *Global Market Insights*; February 2019.
(4) House of Commons Speech; Winston Churchill; October 1944.

CHAPTER 4

Transforming Education with AI

"Education is the premise of progress."

—*Kofi Annan, former UN Secretary General*

 INTRODUCTION

Similar to Healthcare, Education is a very important sector of the economy. While its relative size is smaller, its impact on the future of humanity is equally profound. Globally, the education industry is presently over $6 trillion as per reports from Citi, Goldman Sachs, IBIS Capital, and other market analysis. By 2030, this education industry is expected to be over $10 trillion globally.[1] The growth rate of this market is in mid-single digits and the core of the formal education systems does not change very rapidly in short periods. However, technology-driven learning segments of the industry are growing much faster. HolonIQ's Smart Estimate™ predicts that education technology expenditure fueled by AI and other digital technologies will cross $340 billion by 2025, which is just around the corner. The education industry is highly fragmented with lots of players and many microsegments. Technology is rapidly blurring the lines between these microsegments and morphing the capabilities of the players.

Education has a deep impact on GDP growth. As per data available from The World Bank's World Development Indicators (WDI), every dollar a government spends on education, GDP grows on average by $20 over time. At a macro level, growth in education spend is equally matched by GDP growth. There are many pieces of evidence to suggest that higher literacy rates help drive the fastest GDP growth. We have several examples of how targeted education has reshaped many economies and fueled their high GDP growth. The national agenda of most nations is making education one of the biggest priorities.

For over 1,500 years, the adage *knowledge is power* has been guiding societies and civilizations. In the old days, when access to information was difficult, knowing things or having information was construed as possessing knowledge, and knowledge led to influence and power.

But as the venerable Albert Einstein said, "Information is not knowledge." Today information is bountiful and accessing it has been democratized, making the ability to synthesize information to create new insights as the true sign of knowledge. Winston Churchill said it best: "True genius resides in the capacity for evaluation of uncertain, hazardous, and conflicting information." In this information-rich world, AI and digital technologies are dramatically transforming how we consume and process knowledge.

Knowledge, in general, is becoming more and more accessible every day and it is also becoming easier to search for information. There are many services which even proactively present topical or general information to individuals about current happenings or historical information at a predefined frequency. However, there is a fundamental issue with such access to information – it is usually ranked and presented based on popular ratings, past search histories, paid sponsorships, the perceived interest level of information seeker based on generic demographic analysis, and other factors that are not specifically tied to the individual. Moreover, when we think of learning, every individual has a different way of consuming information and converting it into learning – some prefer random information search from published material, some prefer a more conversational method, while others prefer a more structured approach. Being able to distill information for an individual's specific needs, remove biases from the data, and present it in a method that is most appropriate for the individual is key to making learning more effective. Again, we have the problem of data existing in silos and not being contextualized to the individual for content or delivery.

Simultaneously, we are seeing how the participation of new digital platforms is rapidly increasing over the role of traditional educational institutions like schools and colleges. For example, Google Education Suite has more than 70 million users, up from 50 million in 2015. Similar platforms like Coursera and Pluralsight have close to 50 million users as well. As digital platforms gain more ground, they will become more sophisticated with new capabilities, many of which will be using AI.

The COVID-19 crisis has accelerated the digital transition of learning. Lockdowns in every part of the world abruptly halted the physical-interaction forms of education; institutions had to shift to a remote digital delivery very quickly. Given how quickly educators had to react to the situation, they could only virtualize their interaction with students, not offer a comprehensive digital learning experience. As the world starts slowly to emerge from the COVID-19 pandemic, never before has needs-sustained behavior change and engagement to amplify individual performance and organization outcomes been as critical as it is today. Social distancing, work-from-home, lesser in-person contact, increased reliance on technology, etc. will become the standard norm in our daily lives, professionally and personally.

This is a natural generational transition that was already happening, albeit slowly. The COVID-19 pandemic has just shrunk the timelines and brought it into the immediate timescales. Moreover, this is happening to a world that is still not completely prepared to handle the new norm, emotionally, socially, and from an infrastructural perspective. We have to make significant changes in every aspect of our lives to accept and deal with the new norm. This includes the very social fabric of how we live, interact, and engage with each other. We are faced with a sudden and major cultural change, and faced with change, the natural response of the human brain is a threat response arising from the limbic brain, resistance to change. For the larger population, acceptance of change is an acquired skill that becomes that much more difficult when the limbic brain is active.

AI will change education industry in several ways – transform it from a generic disposition to a more targeted personalized delivery model for higher impact; make education more interactive and immersive with the usage of mixed reality and other digital capabilities; allow for more agile and unfederated learning models; and enable lifecycle management of learning.

IMPROVING PERFORMANCE THROUGH A LEARNING ECOSYSTEM

Learning is a complex neuroscience endeavor deeply involving the brain and its retraining to new stimuli. Learning involves receiving new information, having the motivation and ability to store and process it, and being able to contextualize and apply it to new scenarios. Insights are derived when one can observe an environment or reflect on recent experiences and draw upon past learning to reach a set of potential conclusions for the future. Performance enhancement happens when learning and insights lead to actions.

Learning is a very personalized enterprise. Each person's brain works differently. Each person has different motivators and derives different meanings from the same information presented, including how it is presented. Each person also reacts very differently to experiences. The process for the synthesis of information and the design of responses is also different for each individual. People's reactions to various environmental factors and team dynamics are also different. Hence the way everybody's brain gets rewired to make learning effective is unique. Neuroscience-based learning expert Dr. André Vermeulen explains:

> The scientific studies reveal that a unique combination of brain hemispheres, paired with expressive-receptive, rational-emotional, and sensory and intelligence preferences, make up a person's neurological design. For maximum comprehension and retention, all lobes in both hemispheres of the brain should be involved in information processing.

The more active the learning process is, the more effective it is because different neural networks of the brain get exercised to codify the learning. Effective learning also requires sustained exposure to information and experiences so that the repetitive exercise of different neural networks leads to new pattern formation. Group learning in social settings is found to be more effective in most cases as we tend to adjust more to social context.

Learning theories[2] are constantly evolving since the days of Plato in ancient Greece. Today there are more than 15 popular learning theories, each with their unique nuances. *Cognitivism* is a popular one, explaining many of the different learning techniques. The *transformative learning* theory, first introduced by Jack Mezirow in the late 1970s, focuses on perspective transformation across three dimensions: understanding of the self, changes in the belief system, and changes in lifestyle. Connnectivism postulates that the frame of reference for people changes as they gain new experiences and learning, especially the ones with more life-altering impacts. There is an emerging discipline around *connectivism* that is considered more suitable for the digital age. As per this theory, people extend their learning through formal methods into job experiences, network interactions, and social ecosystems. As per this theory, which mirrors more of how the brain naturally functions, people learn by forming connections across different inputs and stimuli.

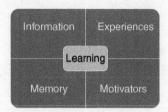

FIGURE 4.1 Learning Ecosystem Framework

Let us use a simple framework to understand the major components of learning. In Figure 4.1, *information* refers to all the sensory inputs we receive, whether auditory or visual, *experiences* are self-explanatory and related to the information directly or obliquely in this case, *motivators* are our unique psychological and physiological markers that take us in a certain direction, and *memory* is the neurosciences elements of learning. This framework will be useful later in the chapter when we talk about how AI can help in the learning process as part of transforming the education industry.

Repeated *application* of *learning* and the right *environment* of application will lead to higher performance. Figure 4.2 depicts this concept.

Most traditional learning techniques were historically designed to cater to common minimum effectiveness for a broad and diverse group and easy delivery mechanisms. Classroom-based delivery models, which are the oldest form of learning methodology, are rooted in broadcasting information and the teacher's interpretation or insights on a mass-scale basis. Textbook-based methods took it one step further, making the same process more repeatable, scalable, and dispersed. As the centuries evolved, new experiential and immersive techniques have

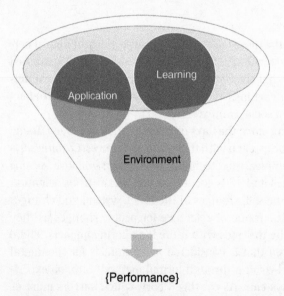

{Performance}

FIGURE 4.2 Learning-to-Performance Framework

been introduced and many of them are more effective for assimilation of information and retention of learning. The latest development is using neurosciences-influenced gaming techniques, which not only are proving to be more effective than anything else but also have proven to be better linked to performance enhancement with a better tie-in between learning and business performance indicators tuned to personal preferences and individual/group performance. More on that later in the chapter.

 ## UNDERSTANDING THE MACROSCOPIC FACTORS DRIVING SMART TECHNIQUES IN THE FUTURE OF THE EDUCATION INDUSTRY

Today we live in an interconnected and interdependent world that is rapidly changing and inherently complex. The issues and opportunities that we are presented with today are unprecedented by any historical standards. We need new skills and capabilities to survive and be successful in this environment, making education critically important. There are several macroscopic factors which are requiring education to be reinvented more smartly. Here are some of the important drivers for this transformation:

Economic Impact

Every nation, every society, is trying to further its economic agenda and improve the lives of its people. In the 20th century, there has been a lot of research seeking the connection between education and its socioeconomic impact. Such research has established a clear linkage between education and economic output. American economist Dr. Edward F. Denison's seminal work[3] on understanding growth in national productivity between 1929 and 1982 in the United States presents some interesting statistics. According to his research, 14% of the growth in output can be attributed to labor education. He also found that return on education ranged between 5 and 10%, which is one of the highest returns on any type of investment in any economy.

In emerging countries, the impact of education on the economy is even higher. As an example, in India, nearly 7.5% of the GDP is contributed by the IT industry and is consistently growing at double-digit rates, most of it driven by global outsourcing. This growth has largely happened over the last 20 years. Today this sector contributes a big portion of the country's exports. Each new IT services job is believed to have a cascading effect of four more jobs in other ancillary sectors supporting the IT industry. In the past 20 years, India's per-capita GDP has increased nearly fivefold from $438 to $2,100 and its GDP ranking in the world moved from 13th to 5th position. The entire GDP growth story is not only due to India building the IT industry, but it had a big role to play. The reason for this economic transformation is attributed to education and a growing young workforce. Yes, labor arbitrage was very helpful in the initial years to attract the business, but today the cost of labor plays a much lesser role while talent availability and capability play a bigger role.

India is not alone; many countries in South East Asia, Eastern Europe, and other places in the world have seen similar transformations. More recently, the UAE is trying to diversify its economy through a focus on emerging digital opportunities and that is being fueled through a strong focus on education and entrepreneurship.

Even in more traditional sectors like agriculture, where the education levels required are also low, the impact of education on economic output is undeniable. A study done on this topic by researchers in Ghana in 2014 found nearly a 2× impact on farm output between no education and secondary education. In a similar study of the Ugandan agricultural industry[4] published by Simon Appleton and Arsene Balihuta in 1996, a 13% improvement in productivity has been attributed to completing primary schooling.

Whichever industry we pick, whichever country we pick, the link between economic growth and increasing levels of education is clear. As we wade through the changing economic landscape, and the impact of other social and technological factors, education will continue to play an increasingly important role in driving growth.

Demography, Rising Aspirations, and Inclusiveness

Today, we live in an interesting juncture in which the world demography is going through an interesting transition. Around the world, we are already over 7.7 billion people and expect to see another 1 billion fellow human beings added in the next 10 years. On one hand, we have a rapidly aging population in the developed world; on the other hand, we have a growing youth population in the developing world. With improvements in healthcare, the average life expectancy is rising nearly everywhere; the focus on addressing child mortality issues in Africa and other underdeveloped regions will further push the population and average age over time. The demographic dividend (i.e. people in the working-age group) is the highest in history, opening up new economic opportunities through an increased workforce. The countries where the youth and the overall population are growing the fastest also have more socioeconomic gaps. While the world is getting more integrated today, more recently we have seen a rise in nationalistic fervor in many parts of the world.

As technology keeps bringing people around the world closer, we are becoming more aware of the opportunities and our aspirations of a better future state for ourselves and the societies that we live in are rising. In an address at the London School of Economics in April 2017, UN Secretary General Dr. Ban Ki Moon talked about the global convergence of aspirations. He explained how increased Internet penetration, digitalization, and social media were dramatically increasing the benchmark used by individuals to measure their aspirations. He talked about examples such as how a poor child in Quibdo, Colombia, can text message with her friend in Bogota and hear all about her school, what she's learning, and the jobs she'll have when she graduates. Similarly, a child in rural Ghana can find out from his cousin what studying at LSE and living in London is like, highlighting that demands for "real" opportunities are rising across the developing world. While aspirations are important to push the developmental agenda of society forward, not being able to meet them is equally dangerous, leading to mass-scale frustrations, conflicts, and fragility of social fabrics. Education is the first step to meeting these aspirations, followed by access to opportunities. Given the amount of ground to be covered and the rapid pace of evolution, it is critical to rethink the education system to be more tuned to people's aspirations and emerging opportunities.

The digital age is also creating some new divides in the different demographic cohorts based on capabilities. Broadly it is accepted that the Millennials are savvier with and more open to technology than the Baby Boomer generation. In the United States, the population of both these cohorts is nearly equal. While people from older generations view their mobile devices as tools to get things done more efficiently, the younger generations view such devices as their primary interface into the world. Socioeconomic background differences also play a key role in people's ability to move forward with digital-age economic opportunities. If we look at the inner cities of most large cities around the world, which are generally less privileged than the suburban population, we see less participation in digital-age economic activities. This distinction is also true for different nations with different developmental profiles. These differences give rise to inequality, leading to tensions that inherently get in the way of progress. Education is the primary tool to bridge such differences and bring about more inclusive growth.

Technological Changes

More than anything else, technology is changing the way we live and work today. The Denison study quoted above also found that technological improvements were responsible for 28% of the growth of the gross national output in the United States between 1929 and 1982. Today, a similar study will show a bigger impact on technology in productive output. Every business, every organization is adopting a digital agenda and redefining its participation in the marketplace.

Automation has become pervasive and we are seeing the increasing role of machines not only in executive routine tasks but also in routine decision making. This is where AI is beginning to play a big role. Many industries and many functions within industries are getting completely redefined. For example, in less than five years, chatbots have reshaped customer service and call center functions. In the coming five years, as natural language processing capabilities further evolve, we will see dramatically reduced participation of humans in this function. Today, software programming capabilities are not limited to the staff in IT or product development organizations; even managers and executives are trying to pick up basic programming skills as they try to learn more about modeling and AI.

In a paper published by the World Economic Forum in March 2019, it is estimated that at least 133 million new roles generated as a result of the new division of labor among humans, machines, and algorithms may emerge globally by 2022. While we have a growing workforce, we are also faced with unprecedented skill shortages in the workplace. Korn Ferry Institute research suggests that by 2030, the global skill shortage will be more than 85 million professionals and skilled workers, impacting new revenue generation opportunities of $8.5 trillion. The skill shortages are fairly global and their impact is being felt universally. There is a timing urgency to this issue as well. The World Economic Forum, in its 2019 discussion on digital skills, estimates that more than half (54%) of all employees will require significant reskilling by 2022, but the problem is likely to be even more acute in some regions. Historically, beyond basic education, the workforce relied on companies to upskill them. Today, that trend is changing; the majority of the workforce is interested in investing their own time and some resources to gain new skills and be better prepared for the future.

Nearly every industry is going through a massive transformation, requiring new skills. What is making this more interesting is the pace of technological change, making current business models and educational practices less effective much quicker than ever before. Every government and every company is rethinking the relevance of current education practices to meet tomorrow's needs.

Globalization

Globalization has been around for a very long time. The last 30 years saw a boom in the globalization of businesses and economies at a very rapid pace. This also changed the socioeconomic fabric of many societies that had assumed leadership positions but were slow to adapt to new realities. The emerging inequalities and tensions have more recently led to sociopolitical pressures and a level of antiglobalization. However, globalization is here to stay and is an irreversible process; only its nature will change.

While the previous phase of globalization was more focused on the movements of goods and services in an integrated global supply chain to take the best advantage of cost and talent at various locations, the new phase will focus more on the exchange of knowledge and skills. The physical face of globalization will change to a more virtual phase. There will be tele-distribution of goods, services, and capabilities to a much larger population in remote areas that were previously unviable. We discussed some of these examples in Chapter 3 on healthcare. Tele-migration is the new trend that we see emerging in workplaces now. People are breaking barriers of national boundaries and physical spaces to participate remotely in the execution of the same work. In his 2019 TED Talks, Richard Baldwin says that "the future of globalization will not be focused on things we make, it will be on things we do."

This changing face of globalization will require a much broader and deeper understanding of the world across various disciplines. This transition will also require a higher level of empathy for and real-time understanding of the local conditions for businesses to be successful. Our knowledge and specialization in functional areas will have to be significantly augmented with other skills and information to be effective in this new global environment. This is driving different approaches to education as well.

 ## THE CRITICAL ROLE OF AI IN THE EDUCATION OF THE FUTURE

As we have discussed so far in this chapter, AI will immensely influence and change the entire education industry. Here are a few areas that we believe will be impacted more.

Personalized Learning

As a concept, personalized learning has existed for more than 60 years, the term first being used by Sam and Beryl Epstein in their 1961 book, *The First Book on Teaching Machines*. However, the definition of the term was also debated among educators and academia. In 2005, Dan Buckley made the definition crisper by tying personalization to the learner. Today there is broad consensus that personalized learning revolves around optimizing the learning approach, content, and pace for the learner based on their needs, interests, and context. As we have seen in our discussion so far on the macroscopic factors influencing education, personalized learning is the need of the hour to make education more effective.

Earlier in the chapter, as part of the learning framework, we discussed the four components – information, experiences, motivators, and memory; each of them are the pillars for designing personalized learning. Such learning environments involve very targeted content whose delivery mechanism changes dynamically based on how the student responds to it. There is a lot of micro-decision-making and reflection that systematically happens in a personalized learning environment. Given the massive requirements of adaptation to appeal to and be effective for a broad population of students, digital technology is the only way to go about it. This trend is already visible in the market.

However, the technology proliferation in learning so far has been focused more on digitizing and customizing the learning process to some degree without realizing the full benefits of personalization. This is where AI steps in. If we have to understand each learner's needs and interests, available information to satisfy those needs and interests, the best method to expose the information and change the method based on effectiveness, the experiences they are gaining every moment, their motivators and how it is changing over time, the memories being formed and how they are being retained, and finally how the rewired brains perform in future, we are talking about a lot of data inputs which are not naturally relatable to each other through any obvious structure. The only way to seek a correlation between these different data streams, observe the changing patterns, understand the drivers for change, and develop insights around the plan for most effective learning outcomes is through AI-driven algorithms and massive data processing engines. We will have to apply a wide array of algorithms from machine learning to recursive neural networks to get a grasp on the enormity and complexity of the subject.

To build a truly personalized learning system, we have to create dynamic context around all of these different information streams, center them around the learner, and use the intended learning outcome as the objective function. To get started, we will need a *personal education cloud* on similar lines of the *personal health cloud* that we discussed in the previous chapter. However, this personalized education or learning cloud will have to be tightly integrated with the rest of the education ecosystem. This is a massive endeavor because the entire industry is very fragmented, always evolving, sometimes parts of it competing with each other, and most importantly, there is no shared incentive between various participants toward the learner's outcome. There are many other challenges to this becoming mainstream:

- The financial flows of the industry are driven by delivery methods and not the outcome, so as the delivery methods change, the revenue models will get impacted and natural change barriers will arise.
- The role and accreditation of the learning institutions get redefined. The bulk of the education industry at all levels, be it K–12 or higher education, is based on preexisting institutions. As the focus shifts from the institution to the individual, the present-day business models will dramatically change. Since the education system is controlled by the institutions and if they are not willing to adapt to the market forces, there will be tension and mutation that we will observe.
- Educators have to get better acquainted with individual learners, whereas previously they could focus more on the learning content. This will require new skills and capabilities in the educators themselves. Their performance management system will have to be retuned to more outcome-oriented objectives. Most educators, especially at lower grades of schools and in early college years, are not paid well or incentivized adequately to drive the kind of change we are discussing here.

- Personalized learning involves a lot of self-reflection and self-assessment. These disciplines are not fully matured in present-day progress management methods. All decisive grading and learning effectiveness rights presently reside with the education system (school or college system) and the educators. Therefore, significant changes will be required to increase the role of the learner in the process.

Other than the learner, there is no immediate beneficiary of the personal education cloud. Consequently, it is unclear who will drive the development and adoption of such an environment. A new player who figures out the technology and the business model will be able to transform the industry in a very profound manner, similar to how Apple changed the music industry.

Done right, personalized learning can make the teacher–student interaction more effective because like most of the delivery and assessment tasks will be addressed by technology, the teacher can focus more on coaching and helping the learner where it is most required. Personalized learning can reduce the stress and agony for teachers as they will see better outcomes from their students; after all, they embarked on this career to build the next generation and not to be bogged down by constraints. There is clear evidence that personalized learning leads to better student achievement. The Bill and Melinda Gates Foundation sponsored an initiative around Next Generation Learning Challenges. In a 2017 report, researchers from RAND corporation found this correlation in the schools that were part of the Challenge, with students improving their scores by 2 percentile points or more in most cases.

Personalized learning does have one big drawback if not addressed adequately. Since a lot of the learning is going to be guided by digital delivery in an automated fashion, that can be easily swayed toward a certain belief system creating deep-rooted biases in the learner. This phenomenon is known as the *echo effect*. We have already seen the echo effect make a big impact in our sociopolitical environments; these days social media influences elections more than nearly anything else.

Personalized learning, however, is just not about developing a personal education cloud; it is more and includes aspects which we will discuss in the next section.

Experiential Learning

Since learning is the eventual rewiring of the brain, experiential learning is one of the best techniques to achieve that goal since repeated doing of something followed by a reflection of the experience is an effective way for the retraining process. The concept has been around since ancient times, Aristotle talks about experiential learning in 350 B.C. in his book *Nichomachean Ethics*. More recently, American education theorist David Kolb developed the modern theories and practices around experiential learning in the 1970s. The effectiveness of experiential learning is unimpeachable. Many studies have found that while after reading one can retain only 10% of the knowledge, which increases to 20% after the use of audio-visual aids during the learning process, experiential learning leads to more than 75% knowledge retention. Considering the efficacy of this technique, we find its implementation pervasive in all levels of learning – from K–12 to corporate learning environments. The use of technology in experiential learning is also quite mainstream as the web and other media become more effective in the distribution of and engagement around learning content.

So now the question is how AI and digital technologies change this game. Let us first investigate the challenges of doing more experiential learning. Our research leads to the following as key challenges:

a. **Limitation of space and physical resources to simulate real-life.** Most schools and colleges are generally constrained on space and capital availability to appropriately build out the facilities required for experiential learning. In every study on this topic, this has been cited as the number-one reason for the present-day gaps in further promoting experiential learning when a learner receives structured education in the early years. This problem poses another problem of learning method dissonance. Laren Resnick, an American educational psychologist, in her research published in 1987 postulated that there is a profound mismatch between how students learn in the classroom and how they will later learn in the community. This is driven by the low proliferation of experiential learning facilities in schools as opposed to the real-life experiences that one is exposed to in the work environment.

b. **The burden on the instructor.** The current largely physical-based with some web-augmentation experiential learning tools and methods require the instructors to do a lot, way more than they might have the bandwidth, resources, or even motivation for. Not only do they have to follow regulations and guidelines in a noncorporate learning environment, but they also frequently design the program, secure the resources, think of creative delivery methods, and finally administer the program. This takes time and is very hard. So even if there is strong positive intent, many instructors are found to resort to more traditional learning methods after some initial trials.

c. **Adaptability to the individual to make the experience more personalized for higher efficacy.** Experiences are unique to each individual. We have talked about the personalization of learning extensively in this chapter. The current experiential learning methods, which are largely physical and often group activities, do not fully take into account the individual learner's needs, current knowledge levels, preferred leaning absorption techniques, motivators, and other such factors.

d. **Social skills of students to participate effectively in group work.** Experiential learning generally is delivered as a group activity. There is research to back up this approach as in real life we have to work as teams to solve problems and make progress on an issue. However, in an increasingly digital and virtual world, the newer generation of learners are lacking many of the social skills to effectively work as a team. We find kids today to be more plugged into their mobile devices than with other humans around. Even in a corporate setting, when a meeting or a class is going on, we see people frequently toying with their devices. The isolation of the individual from the group impedes the learning experience.

e. **Lack of sufficient reflection.** Time is a big constraint in learning environments across the board at all levels. We tend to focus more on delivering experiential learning and leave little time for reflection. But reflection is a very critical component of the process. Also, the process of reflection, which usually ends up as an abrupt unstructured group discussion, can be awkward, making it less effective anyway. Reflection also needs to be captured in real-time for greater value; in prevalent methods that is difficult because reflection time-outs can be interruptive. We need a reflection process that is inconspicuous yet timely and granular.

The advancements of digital technologies and AI help address these issues in three major ways:

1. **Understanding the state and frame of the learner.** As the personal education cloud becomes popular and is enriched with learner information, we will be able to appropriately adapt the learning experience for each individual.
2. **Quickly creating real-life simulated environments inexpensively and with adaptability.** Multimedia convergence of voice-visuals-print and mixed-reality systems like augmented reality, virtual reality, simulation techniques, and others have matured to such an extent today that our reliance on the physical construct of environments is much less than before. Since there is no or very limited physical construct, capital requirements or time taken to build out the simulation is also far less, making experiential learning more affordable and scalable.
3. **Building out a virtual social fabric.** Studies have found that we become more unhinged socially if we do not physically interact with other people; there is a subconscious safety net created by space and time. We are seeing that today in the intense impact of social media on all walks of life. If we develop more virtual platforms for experiential learning, we will be able to create an environment to bring people together on a common plane first before we bring them together physically.

Given the massive amounts of data that we have to deal with to make all of this a reality, the scenarios and simulations that we need to create, and the dynamic adaptability that is required for higher effectiveness, AI techniques will be critical in development and delivery of experiential learning in the future. AI also enables *appreciative inquiry*, a key element of experiential learning and gaming, something which we will get into more in the next section.

Performance-Linked Learning

There is a section of the population and there are periods that everybody goes through in their lives where learning is for the sheer pleasure of knowledge, but for the most part, the objective of learning is participation in gainful economic activities and/or improving performance. Learning is a relatively permanent acquisition of knowledge and consequently changed outlook and/or behavior; performance is the visible measurable output of that relatively short duration of time.

High-performance organizations find learning to be a key enabler to their performance and the two tightly linked together with a driver for better business outcomes. In most organizations, the present learning effectiveness measurement techniques are based on participation and sometimes on canned tests, which are not the best reflection of sustained learning. On rare occasions, companies have used engagement and retention metrics collected in surveys as a proxy for learning effectiveness. In a survey done by Brandon Hall Group, 69% of the companies said that an inability to measure learning's impact is a significant challenge to achieving their learning outcomes, which are usually linked to business results. The idea of linking learning and performance is not new, such as in approaches like Balanced Scorecard promoted by Kaplan and Norton more than 25 years ago, which linked strategy, business goals, human capital objectives, and learning goals all together in a neat framework. However, implementing learning–performance linkage is challenging because of the thousands of variations and nuances that exist in any organization, which is difficult to maintain in a codified manner over time and still be reflective of current-day business realities.

It is widely recognized that the future of work is changing dramatically in the next 5 to 10 years, driven largely by technological changes. This will make workforce reskilling and related impact to performance critical to business success in the future. In a study done by McKinsey of business executives from organizations delivering more than $100 million in revenue, 82% of the respondents view reskilling as a key priority for future business over the next 5-year horizon. However, reskilling is a complex task and difficult to deploy sustainably because of many reasons – employees have to see and internalize a future state and the skills required to realize that future state; they need to feel motivated in pursuing a journey toward that future state; and most importantly learning has to be linked to performance improvements that tell us whether we are making progress in that journey. This is where digital technologies and AI come to the rescue. This starts with gamification.

Games have been used to aid learning for thousands of years. In the last 100 years, a lot of structure has been created around this topic, starting with how Boy Scouts began awarding points for achievements in learning and performance from the early 1900s. It entered the worklife in 1973 when Charles A Coonradt published *The Game of Work*. By the end of that decade, videogames started becoming very popular and led to among other things the birth of the personal computing industry. The word *gamification* was first coined by British programmer Nick Pelling in 2002. The last decade saw a massive explosion in gamification and it has become a tool for reimagining future states. This started with Jane McGonigal's groundbreaking TED Talk, "Gaming Can Make a Better World," in which she prophesies a game-based paradise: "When I look forward to the next decade, I know two things for sure: that we can make any future we can imagine, and we can play any games we want, so I say: Let the world-changing games begin." As Millennials have started to constitute an influential percentage of the workforce in the last five years, gamification has gone viral with applications in every walk of life. Since gamification and game-based learnings are focused on results, incredibly fun, and engaging, their impact is very high and lasts for a long time.

AI and gamification have a very synergistic relationship, one feeding the other. Nearly all games today are developed and delivered on digital platforms and have advanced AI algorithms to execute the game while in play. At the same time, the discipline of AI is being enriched by trying to implement complex games. One of the popular recent examples of the latter is how in 2015 DeepMind's AlphaGo program beat a human professional player in the age-old Chinese game Go with hundreds of billions of possible moves for the first time; two years later an improved version of it defeated the world's number-one player in successive Go matches. To accomplish this, DeepMind data scientists had to do deep research and refinement in Reinforcement Analytics techniques, which is a branch of AI. This research and refinement later helped build out capabilities in other disciplines of healthcare and energy optimization by DeepMind. Today Google is using DeepMind's capabilities for much broader purposes. Incidentally, 20 years ago, IBM's Deep Blue supercomputer defeated world champion Gary Kasparov in chess, another very complex game.

The effectiveness of gamification is further enhanced by Octalysis – a human-centric design framework proposed by Taiwanese-American entrepreneur and gamification expert Yu-Kai Chou

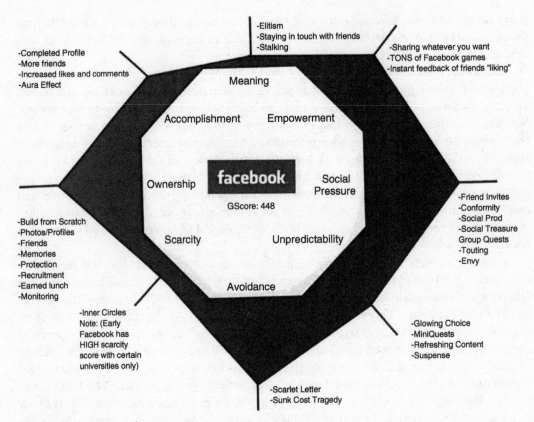

FIGURE 4.3 Octalysis of Facebook Engagement Drivers

Source: Octalysis – the complete Gamification framework, Facebook. © 2020, Yu-kai Chou.

in 2012. The Octalysis framework contains eight core drivers for human motivation which are deeply and directly linked to performance. The eight drivers are meaning, empowerment, social influence, unpredictability, avoidance, scarcity, ownership, and accomplishment. Figure 4.3 is an Octalysis framework representation of what makes Facebook so effective.

Recently, this approach is being integrated into learning and performance management and is delivered through an immersive gamified experience. The Gamification Company (https://www.thegamificationcompany.com) is one of the pioneers in this space with some very impressive solutions and customer success stories. Their SaaS-based gamification platform, Coroebus™, designed and developed on the foundation of NeuroScience of Play and Octalysis principles, gamifies organization KPIs into theme-based game elements. For example, in the Formula 1 theme, "Productivity" can be linked to Driver Points, "On-time Performance" can be linked to Lap points, etc. With multitiered hierarchy, the platform drives a sense of competition and tracks performance at an individual, team, and group level. Theme-based Points, Badges, and Leaderboards ensure sustained engagement supports the platform. Company founder Mr. Rajib Choudhary says, "We have seen our clients across multiple industries from construction to banking to retail being able to improve their learning effectiveness and organizational performance using our approach."

Lifelong Learning

We all accept that change is constant. However, the pace of change has been accelerating with each passing day, and technology is a big driver for the same. In a very interesting infographic published by Jeff Desjardins in *Visual Capitalist* to understand the pace of change, he used a proxy of how long a new technology or a new development takes to reach the first 50 million users. While cars and airplanes, which were invented more than 150 years ago, took 60 years to reach the first 50 million users, computers and mobile phones took just 14 and 12 years respectively to cover the same journey. The Internet, on the other hand, took only 7 years and Facebook 3 years to reach the same level of usage. Pokemon Go, released less than 5 years ago, took only 19 days to reach that level, which means most people in the world had not even heard of the game before it touched 50 million players. Today, we live in a world of hyper-change and have to continuously learn to keep up. The concept of *lifelong learning*, like other most topics discussed in this chapter, has been around for a long time as well but has acquired completely new relevance and a sense of urgency around it more recently.

One of the most important, if not the most important element of lifelong learning is knowing the learner's context and being able to adapt learning content and techniques to the changing context. Learning how to learn is more impactful than the topical subjects one is exposed to temporally. Metacognition is critical to lifelong learning. Dr. Jennifer Livingston of the University of Buffalo made that linkage in her seminal research published in 1997. To make lifelong learning effective, the history and progression of learning need to be carried through life, something that is very difficult today. When we have capabilities like personal learning clouds, this issue will get largely addressed. Personalization of learning is key to its success on a lifetime scale.

Thanks to the proliferation of knowledge on the Internet, we have easy access to a lot of information. However, to be effective in the digital age, having information is only less than half the game. The more important ability is how to process it and what to do with the insights. This requires critical thinking. In nearly every article written about digital literacy, critical thinking/ design thinking are topics that are viewed as very important skills to be successful. To develop or sharpen thinking skills, one has to go through a lot of scenario analysis and simulations. This is the realm of AI and techniques like gamification that are spawned from AI as we have discussed earlier.

A lot of learning still happens through textual content, a trend that will continue well into the coming years. Such information is not usually well-indexed or well-organized. Natural language analysis of unstructured social data in the context of education is another area of application of AI techniques.

The artificial neural network (ANN) algorithms are very attuned to the needs of lifelong learning because they mimic the human brain, have inherent capabilities to address the stochastic process for long-term neuroscience applications, and can also adjust as per local elasticity needs for the current learning needs. The only issue with ANN is that it requires a lot of input signals and takes time for learning. However, that issue is getting resolved with the concept of synaptic plasticity that allows learning to happen very fast. This concept of plasticity in AI was first conceptualized by Donal Hebb in 1949, never having truly found scaled applications due to technological limitations. This problem has been solved in recent times and we see innovative implementations by many companies like Uber. DARPA has also initiated a series of projects across many universities in this area.

Virtual Assistance

Learning is usually a very interactive process between the students and the teachers – be it in schools or colleges or corporates. The teachers end up spending considerable time helping students seek information or validate the information. A lot of these interactions in today's technology spectrum can be classified as routine. Even a lot of the assessment activities do not require human intervention. A lot of these repetitive routinized activities are now being performed by chatbots. As personalized learning gains more ground, in the initial days when the technology infrastructure may not be robust enough, teachers will spend a lot of their time sorting through personal student data. This is another area where virtual assistants will be very useful. Virtual assistants will be immensely beneficial for the administrators because they end up spending a lot of their time answering routine questions from students. In an experiment run at the University of Murcia in Spain, chatbots were able to correctly answer student queries to more than 38,708 questions, answering correctly more than 91% of the time. This approach allowed students to ask anything at any time of the day and positively impacted their motivation. Similarly, if you flip the perspective to a learner, similar arguments and activities are true for the learner and we create the market for learning assistants.

Virtual teaching assistants have started to gain traction. There are several startups like 1MillionBot, Woebot, Botsify, Hubert, and countless others in this space. As data becomes more available and gets more sorted, and as NLP capabilities further evolve, we will see the growth of virtual teaching or learning assistants.

THE CHANGING LANDSCAPE OF LEARNING AT VARIOUS LEVELS

So far in this chapter, we have seen that AI will deeply impact learning and thereby the education industry in a massive way in the coming years. The transformation has already started and will soon reach an inflection point. Now let us see how learning at different levels will get specifically impacted.

K–12

Schools set the foundation for future learning. Every government and society is now turning their attention to making the K–12 programs more geared toward new-age and new-economy skills. This is the stage when maximum impact is also made on young minds. Following are some of the main impact areas of AI:

a. **Teacher productivity.** The current systems put enormous pressure on administrative and compliance-related tasks on the teachers, making them overworked and demotivated. This is leading to high attrition rates in teachers, especially where they are required most. For example, in the inner-city school systems in the United States, teacher attrition is an alarming 16%. New teacher requirements in schools in the developed world are growing anywhere between 5 and 25% while in the developing world with higher population growth rates that need is nearly doubling every year. It is becoming very hard to attract and retain good teachers in the school systems. A recent McKinsey study on Future of Work suggests that automation and AI can save between 20 and 40% of the time teachers spend on routinized tasks that they frequently engage in, like administrative tasks, preparation, grading, and feedback, thus allowing them to spend more time with students on valuable and satisfying tasks like coaching and engagement.

b. **Personalization.** While teachers universally accept that personalization is critical for effective learning, especially in the early years, as per a McKinsey Global Teacher and Student Survey, nearly 70% of teachers cite lack of time as the biggest barrier to personalization. While automation and AI will improve productivity and free up time, teachers will need a deeper understanding of the personalized context of the student where AI will be immensely useful to do preliminary pattern analysis and nonintrusive assessment.

c. **Behavior analytics.** The social consciousness of students is still in the early formative stage during this phase of students' lives. They also are more influenced by their home environment than by the broader social environment during these years. These stimuli have a big influence on the group dynamics and learning effectiveness in school environments. AI is already proven to be very good for behavior and sentiment analytics.

d. **Predicting needs.** Another difficult task for teachers is understanding which students are not able to comprehend what part of the curriculum. There are correlations between different parts of the curriculum as well as in student achievement. This is a complex but solvable analytics problem which AI will address.

e. **Tracking and improving performance.** We are already seeing interesting examples of AI predicting needs, helping designing curriculums, and driving up performance. Squirrel AI Learning in China, which is focused on the K–12 segment, in five years has already touched over 1,700 schools across 200 cities. There are many other similar platforms around the world and new ones are being created nearly every day. Already tens of millions of students are being impacted in their achievements through the use of AI. This trend is not just limited to academic courses like science or language; companies like Bee'ah, which is driving a mission around sustainability in the Middle East and North Africa region, are using AI-driven gamification platforms to better orient students toward a more sustainable lifestyle. The emerging applications of Knowledge Space Theory, which uses mathematical language to define and track knowledge points using a graph concept, are making AI more relevant for learning. Squirrel AI and other education technology companies are using this approach and have found encouraging results. According to Derek Li, founder of Chinese EdTech unicorn Squirrel AI, "In three hours we understand students more than in the three years spent by the best teachers."

The combination of AI with other digital technologies like IoT, 5G, and mixed-reality (MR) systems will make the resultant output a more complete complement to teachers and classrooms. This will enable more virtualization of learning with high effectiveness, ultimately driving more scale and efficacy. The increasing number of sociopolitical events or medical emergencies or nature-driven interruptions often require us to make learning a remote process. We saw this in spades in the recent COVID-19 pandemic. In such events, effective virtual learning ensures that we continue to make the desired progress despite physical constraints.

Higher Education

College and university education is the next frontier of education. The changes we discussed for K–12 school education will equally apply for college education. We see a few additional areas where AI will make an impact:

a. **Admissions.** College authorities are faced with the onerous task of sifting through thousands of applicants every year to select the desired few. This is highly manual and repetitive. Higher education institutions in most parts of the world do want a level of subjectivity in the admission process, and for that reason the admission process is not entirely based on test scores. However, subjective judgment can be very varied based on individual biases and their particular state of mind at the time of assessment. Moreover, the current methods of essays or statements of purpose, interviews, reviewing other leadership attributes, etc. in the limited time that authorities can spend per student do not allow for a holistic evaluation of the student. AI will help solve these various issues. Many universities have already started early efforts in this area. Institutions like Seton Hall University, Quinnipiac University, and others learn about them at microscopic levels through every interaction.

b. **Retention.** Post-admission, retention is one of the major challenges for higher education. AI is being increasingly used to create early warning systems to understand student engagement and predict potential attrition. Education policy experts Manuela Ekowo and Iris Palmer in their paper "The Promise and Peril of Predictive Analytics in Higher Education," cite many examples where this started several years back. Georgia State has been using AI to identify and eliminate achievement gaps in minority students. Temple University is similarly using AI to identify students who might drop out soon and initiate counseling for them, and there are countless such examples already in vogue. A bit intrusive, but by monitoring the financial state of students based on their spending habits and estimated earnings, institutions can use micro-loans and other forms of student aid to drive up retention and develop a deeper relationship with the university.

c. **Administrative support.** This is another area that today requires substantial manual engagement from the university administration staff, time which could be better spent on other tasks that are more effective to further education. We have already talked about how chatbots are being used to address this issue.

d. **Industry immersion programs.** As we have discussed the significance of experiential learning earlier in the chapter, its relevance is even higher when it comes to AI and other digital technologies. There are a lot of challenges and nuances of implementation of these concepts that students do not fully appreciate and that it is hard for teachers to bring into a course without a deep engagement with industries. This is another area where AI is showing early promise – sorting through the myriad problem statements that industry is trying to tackle, matching them with academic resources and student interests, and creating datasets and experimentation platforms.

e. **Active AI challenges.** Taking the immersion programs further, to make learning AI more effective, institutions are coming up with innovative active challenges around AI. One of the best examples that we have seen recently is in Singapore where multiple academic and research institutions have been brought together under one common roof by the National

Research Foundation and the National University of Singapore to solve some big problems for the nation and the world. This allows for the pooling of human ingenuity and resources, including getting the right test-bed of technology and datasets to further the application of AI.

Colleges have one advantage over any other institution of learning – usually, they have highly qualified and experienced academics very conversant with AI and access to inexpensive research help in the form of students. Like any other environment, they also have a lot of use-cases for applying AI. The increasing focus on entrepreneurship and industry engagement will bring a lot of these early AI efforts from colleges and universities to mass-scale practical adoption in the business world. Every business should engage with higher education institutions as extensively as they can to get an early view on how the world will most likely evolve with AI.

Corporate Learning

The global corporate learning industry is more than $300 billion and growing. AI has so far been used extensively in corporate settings in many consumer and content platforms; extending it to learning is a very natural extension. Outside of the K–12 environment, corporate learning is the other area where we will see the early proliferation of AI. The driver for this is the rapidly increasing skill gap and the immediacy of the effectiveness of learning programs. Once again, we believe that the applications we talked about in K–12 and higher education sectors also apply to the corporate learning environment, so we will not repeat that discussion. Here are the additional impact areas that we see:

a. **Specific contextualization.** One of the biggest challenges in the corporate learning environment is the gap between theoretical understanding and applying it to the specific relevance of the business in real situations with real data. Now AI can bridge that gap because the learning can be designed using the specific context of the company instead of something more generic with limited relevance.
b. **Performance linking.** We have discussed this extensively in this chapter earlier. The use of neurosciences, knowledge space theory, and gamification will be the biggest transformation in how companies think about and practice e-learning today. These techniques will also reduce the bias managers employ today in the selection of learning programs for their employees or evaluating their performance.
c. **Knowledge management.** People in the corporate environment usually have foundational skills and capabilities. Where they struggle a lot is seeking out the institutional knowledge that exists within the company to enhance their learning. Knowledge management is an Achilles heel for nearly every organization. The ability of AI to sort through unstructured and unorganized data to present the most relevant information to learners from within the various knowledge databases that exist within companies will be another major area of application. We will soon see chatbots that act as personal concierges that will go out in the wide corporate network and bring us the information and insights.

It is important to remember that not all technology solutions are apt for all scenarios or functions in corporate learning. If there is no clear purpose, adoption will whittle away after the initial excitement. There are examples like Second Life and limited adoption of AR/VR glasses so far in support of this caution. At the same time, there is a need for urgency in taking decisive (if small) steps because the war for talent is only going to intensify.

EXECUTIVE EDUCATION IN AI

One of the biggest gap areas that we see today in greater adoption of AI in corporates is the lack of adequate appreciation of the space at the senior-most executive levels. They hold the purse strings and have the biggest impact on any change. Many universities and professional organizations have started offering capsule courses around AI, but they are largely focused on math, science, and some programming exposure around AI. Consequently, the executives are not able to develop a holistic view of how to approach transforming their business with AI. The right executive-level program will help business leaders and emerging senior management staff be savvier in the opportunities presented by the digital revolution and how to take advantage of it for driving growth in their businesses. Such enablement will subsequently drive more business model and product innovation, deeper customer engagement, and improved financial outcomes.

The following table is an outline of what we think and an effective program should contain.

Topic	Purpose	Key Contents
Introduction to digital technologies	This will help executives understand the key digital technologies, their current state, their evolution, and how they are impacting our lives and different businesses and help them understand the difference between hype and real applications as well as how to interpret technology curves.	Overview of IoT, big data, AI/ML, cloud computing, edge computing, 5G, and other key technologies
Driving growth with digital	This orients executives on how to think about digital transformation and remodeling their business to differentiate and drive growth by taking advantage of new digital capabilities.	Business value-chain mapping; defining new outcomes and new value statements; building technology strategy and understanding data-enabled needs; preparing a digital business case with ROI calculations; building the solution and implementation plan
Design thinking process	This gives executives new tools for complex problem solving and innovating iteratively.	All aspects of the double-D design thinking process
Establishing analytics leadership	With an increasing focus on and availability of data, executives have new opportunities to augment their natural intellect and intuition with analytics. This section will help them understand the significance of analytics in today's business environment, the different analytics techniques, and how to use them for competitive advantage.	Introduction to basic statistics and analytics; understanding the different analytical techniques and where to apply them; developing a framework for applying analytics to business problems; running experiments and modulating business outcomes; building analytics leadership

Topic	Purpose	Key Contents
Demystifying AI	Today there is a lot of hype around AI and ML. Most executives are not familiar with the nuances of the different AI techniques and how to sort through the technical jargon and complexity. This section is to help executives demystify and understand the world of AI, including machine learning, neural networks, natural language processing, etc.	
Understanding the technology landscape	Executives are today inundated with exploding choices around technology and solutions. Nearly every pitch comes with a promise of a complete solution yet mostly addresses only part of the opportunity. This section is to help executives sort through different aspects of technology choices and make informed decisions around technology strategy.	Introduction to core concepts of platforms, data management, workflows, business applications, and user experiences; understanding where and how to create competitive advantage; deciding where to build, what to buy, and when to partner
Dealing with ethics, privacy, and security concerns	This will introduce executives to the emerging concerns, considerations, and regulatory environment around cybersecurity, privacy, and ethics.	Understanding threat vectors, privacy, and cybersecurity concerns; adopting ethical AI practices; regulatory considerations; building a cybersecurity and privacy program
Managing change	This helps executives build a framework and plan for managing change ushered in by the digital revolution.	Understanding changes and their significance in the business flow; building the IMMERSE framework for managing change: Identify, Modulate, Mitigate, Educate, Roleplay, Show, Effect; creating stakeholder groups to drive change; driving effective communication for change management; creating a culture of continuous learning and innovation
Building the organization of future	With the new workforce demographics and the changing nature of work, executives need new tools to motivate and manage people to drive a culture of continuous innovation and disruptive growth. The emerging gig economy is bringing new dimensions to how we think of work and the workforce. Successful organizations are already rethinking how they collaborate across and outside to build competitively advantaged ecosystems. This section is to help them drive cultural transformation with a focus on the digital transformation of businesses.	Understanding the workforce of the future; introduction to gig-economy; recruiting and harnessing talent; managing performance and productivity in a digital world; building innovation ecosystems; measuring innovation effectiveness

Academia and industry have to collaborate more deeply and quickly step up the game to make this a reality.

SUMMARY

Education is the most effective tool for socioeconomic change. Our present geopolitical environment requires a positive socioeconomic change to happen faster and to have a broader and deeper impact, and must make the change more sustainable. To meet the challenges of the day, we need to bring a new level of vibrancy and dynamism into how we think of education. AI will be one of our biggest levers to do so.

As organizations emerge out of the COVID-19 crisis into new ways of working and a very challenging economic environment, they will be required to rapidly refresh their business processes, reskill their workforce, and achieve more output from their employees. This will require new learning, increased engagement, and a renewed sense of accountability. This is where AI and gamification come in as a game-changer. For a fatigued, disengaged conscious brain that is in a state of resistance, using the neuroscience of play takes the subconscious brain into a state of play, builds engagement at a core belief level, and brings about transformation in conscious behaviors and subsequently business outcomes. Companies like The Gamification Company have successfully used gamification principles combined with other behavioral sciences principles such as appreciative inquiry and value creation process to bring about sustained, positive impact on the core human processes that are critical to success.

As the very fabric of our economy changes in this post-COVID-19 era, we will have massive requirements for reskilling our workforce at all levels. While we believe that eventually there will be another period of good economics once we start getting back to normalcy, there will be an undeniable shift in the nature and size of the economic engine in different countries.

The following table captures the summary of how we think AI will transform different levels of education:

Level	Category	Problem Area	AI Role
K–12	Teacher productivity	Administrative and compliance-related tasks; overworked and demotivated workforce; high attrition	Save 20-40% time by handling routine tasks.
	Personalization	70% of the teachers citing lack of time as the biggest barrier to personalization	Get a deeper understanding of the personalized context of each student. Perform nonintrusive assessments.
	Behavioral analytics	Understanding the different stimuli leading to the social consciousness of students	Perform behavior and sentiment analysis.
	Predicting needs	Tracking student comprehension and performance at a deeper level	Predictive diagnostics
	Tracking and improving performance	Understanding comprehensive performance and designing interventions to improve performance	Complement teachers with new insights and recommendations, combine other digital technologies like IoT, 5G and mixed-reality systems.

Level	Category	Problem Area	AI Role
Higher Education	Admissions	Highly manual and repetitive Need for unbiased subjective judgment in the admission process	Analyze and score each micro-interaction.
	Retention	High student attrition	Early warning systems to understand student engagement and predict potential attrition
	Administrative support	Clarifying questions, searching and providing information	Automate using chatbots and virtual assistants.
	Industry immersion programs	Experiential learning	Matching problems and skills, building data labs
	Active AI challenges	To make learning AI more effective	Use the higher education system as a testbed.
Corporate Learning	Specific contextualization	The gap between theoretical understanding and applying it to the specific relevance of the business in real situations with real data	Contextual learning design
	Performance linking	Biases in the selection of learning programs for their employees or evaluating their performance	Objective evaluation and progression using neurosciences, knowledge space theory, and gamification
	Knowledge management	Managing huge repositories of knowledge, classifying and cataloging knowledge artifacts, making search more seamless	Sort through unstructured and unorganized data to present the most relevant information to learners.

The world as we knew it is changing and the way we learn to live and prosper in this new world needs to change. AI will help.

 ## REFERENCES

(1) "Global Education Market in 2030"; Holon IQ Research; June 2018.
(2) *15 Learning Theories in Education*; Paul Stevens-Fulbrook; April 2019.
(3) *Trends in American Economic Growth, 1929-1982*; Edward Fulton Denison; October 1985.
(4) *Education and Agricultural Productivity: Evidence from Uganda*; Simon Appleton and Arsene Balihuta; May 1996.

CHAPTER 5

Transforming Transportation with AI

"If I had asked people what they wanted, they would have said faster horses."
—Attributed to Henry Ford

INTRODUCTION

It has been debated whether Henry Ford uttered the above statement; nevertheless, it set the standard for defining innovation. The history of the transportation industry is rich with innovation examples for thousands of years that have had a very profound impact on humankind. From the first wheel to the steam engine to mass production of vehicles to lean manufacturing to autonomous mobility systems, new technological eras have been ushered in by this industry.

The transportation industry is a massive component of any economy. As per Plunkett Research, globally, the transportation industry is greater than $5 trillion and contributes 6% to the global GDP directly or indirectly. Transportation also has a big impact on the environment and is one of the major sectoral contributors to greenhouse gas emissions. For example, as per Total Logistics, in the EU in the year 2019, 24.3% of emissions were contributed by the transportation industry. It came down a bit from 27% in 2017.[1]

There is a significant growth in digital technologies, smart capabilities, and AI in the transportation industry. Technology is helping the industry become more efficient and more responsive to customer needs, helping prevent fraud and counterfeiting in many key categories like medicines, reducing shrinkage and waste, and enabling a more globalized economy. The proliferation of IoT has been increasing substantially over the years. Augmented Reality (AR) has already found many use-cases in this industry – from simulation and testing during the manufacturing process to managing logistics and distribution in warehouse operations. As per a DHL study, using AR can significantly reduce their costs for picking goods in warehouses, which is nearly half of the operating cost of the warehouse. AR is finding its way into autonomous driving as well. The investment in AR applications in the transportation sector is nearly $15 billion. While the technology and infrastructure for autonomous driving in unconstrained environments like public roads and highways are getting perfected, there is already increasing usage of this technology in more constrained environments like large logistics facilities or manufacturing shop floors. Autonomous vehicles will help tackle the increasing driver shortages for commercial trucking businesses, make travel more efficient and safer, and improve overall economic output. Many studies suggest that the autonomous vehicles industry could be as big as several hundred billion dollars over the next several years. A related field of unmanned aerial vehicles or drones is already growing rapidly, finding new use-cases for transportation and logistics, inspections, geospatial mapping, defense applications, etc. As per a Global Market Insights study, this segment is expected to be $17 billion by 2024. Each of these technology areas and their growth is enabled by AI.

The transportation industry is already at the cusp of a major disruption. We are seeing increasing growth in electric vehicles and are expectantly awaiting the introduction of autonomous vehicles. On top of that, there is a shift, especially in urban areas of developed economies, where the new generation is preferring rideshare options instead of vehicle ownership. From an infrastructure standpoint, we are seeing increasing challenges around congestion, pollution, and productivity loss. The slow shift from an oil-based economy to alternative-energy-based economies is also impacting the transportation industry. Finally, as technology evolves to make communication more interactive, the need for transportation, be it a short distance or long distance, in itself is reducing with people preferring to telecommute more. And this is one industry where AI has already proliferated at a global scale through optimization needs of interactive maps, routing, and other tracking mechanisms.

AI will further transform the transportation industry in many ways – enable new transportation models like autonomous vehicles; change the motivators and barriers for travel; anticipate the needs of travelers and make services on the path more timely and specific with impact on downstream supply chain; redefine how related services like parking and vehicle maintenance or refueling services are understood and addressed today; and have more far-reaching impact on how we live and work.

However, there are a few headwinds to the growth of digital technologies and AI in this industry. Talent deficit in the industry around these new technologies is a definitive barrier that can be overcome through education and talent development interventions. To fully reap the benefits, usage of technology has to permeate the entire value chain of the industry or its different segments. For example, you will get limited benefits by introducing new analytical capabilities to optimize warehouse operations but do nothing with the rest of logistics. Similarly, you cannot optimize people's work-related mobility without converging the various modes of transportation. The value chains are fragmented and sometimes the players do not have a natural incentive to collaborate. This industry usually operates in low-margin environments, making massive investments challenging. So often public bodies and governments have to step in and make substantial investments before the technology can be fully leveraged.

Nevertheless, the opportunities presented by digital transformation and AI are so impactful that the barriers will get addressed through market forces. True to its nature, this industry will not only change itself but drive changes in a lot of other nonrelated industries.

UNDERSTANDING THE MACROSCOPIC FACTORS INFLUENCING THE FUTURE OF THE TRANSPORTATION INDUSTRY

Several socioeconomic-technological factors are influencing the future of the transportation industry, especially how digital technologies and AI will get used in it. Here we will discuss some of the key ones.

Urbanization

This industry is all about moving people and goods from one point to the other. Such movement is heavily dependent on where the population concentrates, which for the last several decades has been urban-centered. According to the United Nation (UN)'s World Urbanization Prospects,[2] in 2018, 55% of the world's population is already residing in urban areas and it is expected to reach 68% by 2050. The development of the transportation industry and urbanization have influenced one another. For example, the development of Segway, or motorized electric roller boards, or electric bikes, all have been driven by the need for fast urban mobility over short distances. There are many forms of urban design and they drive different transportation needs. More and more agglomerated downtown centers are giving way to polycentric designs which allow for greater growth of population and reduce the need for travel.

Workplace Dislocation

Historically, all work used to be done at designated offices and other types of work areas like schools, hospitals, malls, factories, yards, warehouses, etc. Technology is redefining the nature and method of work by enabling more and more remote and/or automated execution of work. We saw in Chapter 3 how telemedicine is reducing the needs for large centralized healthcare facilities; in Chapter 4 we discussed more effective ways of executing learning programs, and so on. The recent crisis around COVID-19 has taken remote working to another level, eliminating a lot of inhibitions and significantly reducing technology, policy, or policy bottlenecks. In many trades, remote working is proving to be more effective. This changing notion of workplace location has an important bearing on transportation as people's needs to travel are changing.

Gig Economy

So far, we discussed that the nature of work is changing and the location of work is changing. The rise of the gig economy is now also changing the relationship employees have with the worker – from a longer-term dedicated relationship to a much more fluid one. This fluidity further transforms the needs of transportation, making it more dynamic. It is estimated that presently about 9 to 10% of the knowledge-based workforce is transitioning to gig-workers, but that number is expected to rise two- or maybe even threefold in the next several years.

Changing Demographic Preferences

A trend of reducing car ownership among younger people has been going on for some time now. In July 2018, BBC's Roger Harbin had reported that in the 1990s, 80% of the people in urban areas like London were driving by the age of 30; now that is true for people under 45. Increasing urbanization, shifting of the residential and economic theatre of action to downtown areas reducing the need to travel, and simultaneous growth of spending patterns among the youth are some of the main reasons for this shift. The economics of transportation, especially if you do not have to travel much, are also not in favor of vehicle ownership. As this trend continues, it will also impact the transportation industry more.

Sustainability

The transportation industry is the fastest-growing sector impacting sustainability. This industry contributes more than 23% of the total greenhouse gas emissions. In developed economies like the United States and western Europe, this contribution is higher. With the increasing climatic issues and erratic natural phenomena, there is a growing concern across the world about containing contributors to climate change. This is driving social and policy pressures on the transportation industry to explore more sustainable alternatives; consequently we are seeing increasing traction on electric vehicles and other sustainable forms of transportation. For example, a recent report by the UK Energy Research Centre suggested that electric vehicles could help reduce UK transport emissions by around 25% by 2050. Electric vehicles are the fastest-growing segment in the big transportation sector, having crossed 5 million units globally in 2018 and growing at an accelerated rate of ˜40% year over year. While there are some pending issues around enough charging stations, they are getting rapidly installed in major cities around the world. The instability of energy markets, fluctuating fuel supplies and prices, concerns about sustainability, and legislative actions like the California initiative to bring 1.5 million zero-emission cars on the roads by 2025 will majorly impact the transportation industry.

Getting Ready for Autonomous Vehicles

Autonomous driving is an important part of the future of transportation. Skeptics argue that the infrastructure to enable autonomous driving will take a long time to get ready because it has never been designed for that purpose and it is impossible to combine manual and autonomous driving. There is some merit to this argument, but the proliferation of autonomous capabilities in different aspects of driving is already becoming popular in terms of advanced driver-assisted systems. With the increasing proliferation of electric vehicles, sensor technologies in predicting micro-driving motions, and software-assisted vehicle operations, there is an increasing readiness for autonomous vehicles. The evolution from partial autonomy to full autonomy will happen gradually yet quickly over the next 10 years through a combination of focus on the type of transportation (goods vs. passenger vs. mass transport), contained geographic areas where the road infrastructure is more amenable, and degree of autonomy. Along with the growth of autonomous vehicles, there is a simultaneous trend of changing vehicle ownership, which we briefly touched upon earlier in this section. The two combined trends will deeply impact other associated industries and disciplines like automobile manufacturing and supply chain, insurance, car dealerships, car servicing, fueling, cabs, etc.

HOW AI WILL CHANGE THE TRANSPORTATION INDUSTRY OF THE FUTURE

Autonomous Driving

Surprisingly, autonomous vehicles (AVs) have a rich history of nearly 100 years. Very early forms of remote-controlled self-driving cars were first demonstrated in 1925 and 1926 in the streets of New York and Milwaukee respectively. American designer Norman Bel Geddes possibly presented the first view of autonomous driving in the 1939 Futurama exhibit in New York. His concept was right, but his prediction was off by more than 60 or 70 years.[3] The technology to support that vision did not exist. The pace was also impeded by the vested interests of the automotive industry that kept on increasing its influence on policy leading to technology and infrastructure development. Over the decades, however, development continued and all major OEMs made some investments and improvements to keep the ideas alive. Mercedes Benz and General Motors possibly had the maximum contribution in the past century, which in this century is being heavily influenced by several new incumbents. The pace of progress and innovation has accelerated dramatically in the past five years since 2015, driven partly by technology stewardship shown by companies like Tesla and support of governments like in Singapore where the first self-driving taxi service nuTonomy was launched in 2016. We have to keep in mind that there are a lot of forces in the multi-trillion-dollar automotive and transportation industry that have an interest in keeping the status quo.

Meanwhile, the adoption of autonomous driving in non-passenger or non-mass transportation modes has been happening more rapidly purely out of necessity. Space exploration and defense have led this front. It is neither possible to have all space vehicles manned nor are there any existing infrastructure issues like other cars on roadways that get in the way of self-driving vehicles in distant space. Similarly, if military space and defense have been the two biggest contributors to the research and development of autonomous vehicles as well as the core enabling technologies like software design, programming, communication, etc., vehicles during conflict situations can be unmanned; it helps save lives and also gives a competitive advantage. Scientific exploration in difficult terrains like deep underwater in the oceans or high atop mountains also uses autonomous driving technologies to conduct their research.

In the mass movement of people and goods on the roads, there have been many technical reasons for the slow progress of autonomous vehicles beyond the reason of incumbency pressures. The most complicated facet of autonomous driving is being able to anticipate the future motion and direction of every other vehicle on the road, not only in the near vicinity but far beyond. This becomes even more complicated when there is a combination of autonomous and driver-pilot vehicles because predicting human behavior and actions at a sub-second level continuously over rapidly changing conditions was considered nearly impossible. The complexity is further accentuated because the human reactions are impacted by social, emotional, medical, and mechanical factors. There is just too much happening too fast; for computers to process all of that is a mammoth task if a traditional rule-based decision-making posture is adopted in vehicle control. This is why AI is enabling autonomous driving and transforming cars to become intelligent thinking machines.

Beyond vehicle control, AI has many other uses in autonomous driving. Usage of natural language programming to be the primary user interface between the vehicle and the passenger is one prime example of such an application. Autonomous vehicles will be driven by your AI-powered digital assistants instead of human drivers. Route optimization, fuel optimization, predictive maintenance, are some other applications of AI in autonomous driving.

The Society of Automotive Engineers has codified six levels of automation to classify the various capabilities of assisted and autonomous driving. It starts at Level 0 where there are some warning signs from sensors attached to the car such as an alarm if you are too close to another car or big object, all the way up to Level 5 where the driving wheel becomes optional and ornamental. To achieve higher degrees of automation, we need three things – a lot of different kinds of sensors on the car to determine its location, state, and environmental conditions; a lot of data coming from the onboard sensors and other inputs like other cars on the road, weather and traffic information, advisories, etc.; and the ability to process the data quickly and effectively, anticipate future actions and events on the road and the route, identify the optimal driving path and conditions for the vehicle, and actuate the control functions. This amount of massive data processing and anticipation is not possible without strong data management capabilities both centrally on the cloud and locally inside the car that can respond to sub-millisecond changes, a software programming paradigm like multi-agent systems, and AI techniques. Figure 5.1 depicts the progression of automation levels with increasing sensors and data analytics.

It has taken a long time for the core enabling technologies to develop. But the progress in the last ten years has been very encouraging. On the sensor side, light detection and ranging sensors (LIDARS) have come a long way in terms of capability, acceptability, and most importantly affordability. On similar lines, other types of visual, auditory, and vibration sensors with the required throughput, performance, miniaturization, and price points also required significant R&D. GPS development to enable precision location-mapping of the automobiles and everything else on the road on a second-by-second basis also took time and effort to develop. While multi-agent systems have been around for decades, the practices and programming surface to enable them for mass-applications is more recent; to get there, we also needed adequate progress on the more modern lightweight messaging channels and graph databases.

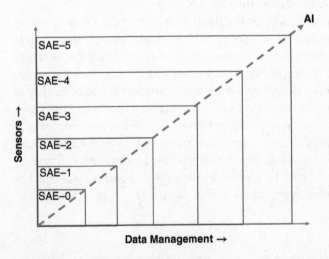

FIGURE 5.1   SAE Automation Levels

While most of the enabling technologies of sensors, data processing, software programming, communication technologies, precision location tracking, vehicle power management, etc. are almost getting there, crossing the last leg in terms of AI will take between 5 and 10 years, possibly the entire decade of the 2020s. The decision making about driving using AI in autonomous vehicles is done through different types of neural networks (ANNs, RNNs, etc.). Today, the accuracy of neural networks starts to taper off after 95% predictability;[4] more data over a lot more time will be required to simulate the outstanding conditions and outlier situations under different driving conditions. Once we cross that chasm, there will be no holding back for autonomous vehicles. We will see their adoption first in limited geo-fenced localities which offer contained environments, then we will see expansion into goods transportation before we see a full-scale application for replacing personal-transportation or mass-transportation.

Another factor that will aid the adoption of autonomous vehicles is the growth of electric vehicles (EVs). Since the engine designs are radically different and weigh less in EVs, it frees up internal resource constraints for AVs. More electrical and electronic circuitry and control systems in vehicles make them more responsive, a critical need for AVs that EVs satisfy. As the technology for solid-state batteries develops further, more power will be available for the increased power needs of AVs. The growth of EVs will be aided by AI as well because algorithms will be able to better predict and optimize the electrical consumption while driving, provide better guidance on charging location and quantum by effectively prosecuting demand and supply against past and emerging trends, and reduce maintenance needs.

It is widely believed that China, which is already a dominant player in the AI space, will also emerge as the catalyst for autonomous vehicles. A McKinsey article from January 2019 on the topic estimates that two-thirds of the travel in China in the next 20 years[5] (i.e. by 2040) will be using AVs. This report estimates the momentum to start in 2023 with early applications of low-speed suburban traffic with SAE-4 level automation and starting to gain real traction from 2027, covering a much wider array of urban and suburban scenarios. Countries like China represent the type and extent of diversity autonomous or, for that matter, any other type of driving will experience anywhere in the world. So once China starts to figure things out for mass-adoption, once Europe starts developing more technology and standards, we will see a global momentum around AV adoption.

In our opinion, AI and autonomous driving will have one of the highest synergistic virtuous cycles of feeding each other's growth and development.

Convergence of Mobility

There is an emerging convergence of mobility among different types of transportation, vehicle ownership, and different levels of automation in the transportation section. In their November 2017 Insights article titled "Forces of Change: The Future of Mobility," Deloitte experts Scott Corwin and Derek M. Pankratz presented a framework on the future interplay among vehicle ownership, asset efficiency, and driving technologies. The diagram in Figure 5.2 represents their framework.

Now this concept is evolving into a more sophisticated converged model and simultaneously the business model is shifting from a product-based one with ownership focus to a service-based one where the usage-based rental is the focus. Bee'ah, the leading environmental management company in the Middle East, partnered with Crescent Enterprises to launch possibly the world's first sustainable converged multimodal transportation network in 2018. Their services range from shared transportation to micro-mobility solutions to freight to collective public transport and up to managing fuel value chain networks.

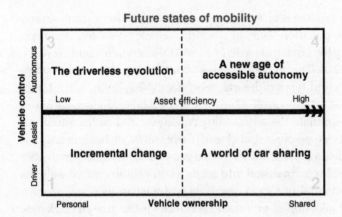

FIGURE 5.2 Deloitte Framework on Future of Mobility

ION/Bee'ah is in the mobility space; whether movement of goods or movement of people to match public aspirations for a safe, clean, reliable, and affordable ways to get from A to B Again. It created an eco-system of mobility solutions tailored to match client's requirements or individual needs to facilitate eco friendly transportations.

Lets take an example of Madar city is using ION's multi-modal transportation system. It's specifically designed to match the complexity of the mobility environment within the city that incorporates human driven and autonomous vehicles and taking into consideration battery levels and booking charging slot. The fleet orchestration platform automates and optimizes the matching, dispatching, and routing to help achieve service level and maximize fleet efficiency. It is simple, you define your service requirement and ION/Bee'ah automates your operations to send the right mission to the right vehicle at the right time, every time.

AI will be the basis of the development of such future network systems. The transition from driving to mobility is quite a profound one. Now instead of trying to optimize point-to-point movement of people and goods, what we are solving for is optimal mobility of people and goods while adapting to other socioeconomic-environmental factors. This nuanced shift is based on a continuous calculation of the optimal path and mode in the context of the changing factors that are highly dynamic. The chosen mode and path have to be matched with the subject's (passenger or goods) constraints and preferences. For example, the health condition of a passenger or storage requirements of goods might be better suited only for certain modes and paths. Planning for demand and supply in such a complex and dynamic environment takes a lot of sophisticated estimation methods. To meet the demand and supply, the estimation algorithms have to be accompanied by control systems that can be modified in real-time with feedback. Once the mode and path are calculated, determining pricing is the next challenge because now the fixed parameters to precisely calculate cost do not hold anymore. Beyond these, we have the challenge of planning for energy networks, availability of the type of required fuel (hydrocarbon-based or electric-based or a hybrid approach), and fueling stations to keep this type of converged transportation network going. AI algorithms are the only way to enable all of this planning, simulation, execution, and feedback loops because no other technique can handle the complexity and dynamism at the speed required.

This shift is also simultaneous with moving away from the hub-and-spoke model in the transportation industry. In 1955, Delta Airlines pioneered the concept of creating a hub-and-spoke system for managing capacity and supply through optimal route design. This model has dominated the thinking and operational design of the transportation industry for the past 50+ years. Beyond transportation, this concept has been applied in many other industries like logistics, software design, data management, communication network design, etc. This approach has served the transportation industry well for a long time while it was dealing with known patterns of movement of goods and people as well as well-defined capacity for transportation. However, this approach has several drawbacks. Design optimality is compromised when unpredictability and variations get introduced to the patterns of movement. Sometimes the cost is inefficient if there is enough traffic between point-to-point movement. Southwest was one of the first to figure this out and created a unique business model that has served them better than most other players in the airlines industry. Single point of failure is a big criticism against this approach; we are all too familiar with major airports getting clogged and ensuing flight delays whenever there is a surge in traffic or an unplanned event like the weather. Many environmentalists are also very vocal against the hub-and-spoke model because it leads to more distances being traveled and consequently more fossil fuel being burned. The network in a hub-and-spoke model lacks adaptability, making it less responsive to new requirements. This approach also does not effectively leverage the multimodal concepts which we believe will be the future.

Vehicle Ownership Models

An interesting emerging trend over the past ten years that is now accelerating and will potentially change the economic models of large portions of the transportation industry is vehicle ownership models. What started as ride-sharing introduced by the likes of Uber and Lyft has expanded to car sharing by the likes of ZipCar and Car2Go. Earlier in the chapter, we briefly touched upon how demographic changes are causing vehicle ownership models to change. But that is not the only reason for this new trend. In their pursuit to balance economic growth, environmental sustainability, infrastructure capacity, and fuel availability, policymakers in many countries are big promoters of shared vehicle ownership models.

Platforms enabling shared vehicle ownership are not limited to startups anymore. Even traditional OEMs like Ford, Cadillac, Hyundai, Lexus, Volvo, Porsche, BMW, and Mercedes have introduced subscription-based usage models which are a variant of the shared ownership models. Such flexible models allow consumers to experience different variants from the same OEM and allow the OEMs to not only understand customer preferences but also improve retention and profitability. It is expected that by 2025, nearly 10% of all new car sales in the United States and Europe[6] will be based on a subscription model.

Once again, AI will have a large role to play in the changing vehicle ownership models. AI will be used to model and predict future trends and inform policymakers, drive production and distribution, decide new network models and routes, shape influence on multimodal transportation development which is largely non-privately owned, and determine the economics of the transportation industry with this new trend. Researchers J. Gerard de Jong, James Fox, Andrew Daly, and Marits Pieters, working with the Institute of Transport Services of the University of

Leeds, published a paper in 2004 titled "A Comparison of Car Ownership Models" in which they highlighted the various AI-models used for prediction and decision support. In the paper, they compared 10 model types based on 16 criteria, ranging from the treatment of supply, through the level of aggregation and data requirements, to the treatment of scrappage. Similar studies have been done by many other academic researchers and policy experts around the world. Real-life statistics have validated the efficacy of such models.

Fuel Economy

The fuel economy is very closely associated with the transportation industry and will also go through a major transformation with the influence of AI. Many of the changes will be driven by the underlying changes in the transportation industry, but some will be more independent.

We have already discussed how autonomous driving, electric vehicles, and shared vehicle ownership models will change transportation, which will directly impact the fuel economy. Adjacent to these developments is another one that will reduce fuel consumption. Vehicles idling or moving at slow speeds also drive greater than optimal fuel consumption. By altering traffic patterns and routes if vehicles are kept in a state motion, this wastage can be addressed. Researchers at Oak Ridge National Laboratory (ORNL) did just that – they combined computer vision inputs from cameras on streets with AI techniques to change the congestion in traffic grids and prioritize movement of different kinds of vehicles based on their fuel efficiency. This is a very unique application of deep learning and neural network algorithms. Similarly, in the shipping industry, computer vision and machine learning are being deployed to optimize routes and travel speed to reduce fuel consumption. European shipping company Stena Line has seen a 2 to 3% reduction in fuel consumption through such implementation of AI in their pilot projects. While AI cannot replace the experience of ship captains and navigators, it surely can assist with very good decision support systems by constantly computing alternatives and finding the best optimal solution. This notion of fuel efficiency extends to nearly all forms of transportation, including airplanes. For example, the French company Safety Line developed and implemented a machine learning tool for Air Austral saving them 6% on fuel consumption by optimizing climb profiles where aircraft spend the maximum fuel.

On the production side, AI is being deployed to help improve asset utilization, drive predictive maintenance, and optimize production schedules to improve returns. The oil and gas industry has heavy capital needs and generally produces lower returns on assets; better efficiency and output will help improve the financials of the producers, a benefit they can extend to consumers and R&D.

Exploration, which is presently very time consuming, heavy-investment intensive, and highly unpredictable, is another area of the industry that will be supported more and more by AI. Deciding where to explore requires analysis and synthesis of multiple disparate and very different data streams like substrata geological information, geophysical information, seismic activity, environmental factors, and other such types of information. Not only does one need to study these information sets, but trace its evolution over hundreds and, if possible, thousands of years. Sometimes the data may not be available and will have to be substituted through simulation. AI can facilitate sorting through and wrangling all of these data- and analytics-related activities effectively and quickly before the serious physical investment starts. Taking a deep-analytics first approach also helps minimize the environmental impact. Early examples of such efforts already exist. For example, in the UK, the Oil and Gas Authority created the country's first National Data

Repository for such purposes. Private oil companies are also equally active in this space – BP is leveraging the capabilities of Houston-based technology startup Belmont Technology, Shell partnered with C3.ai and Microsoft, Baker Hughes partnered with C3.ai, and so on.

AI brings another interesting benefit to the oil and gas industry, which is still the bedrock of the global fuel economy. This industry is not being favored by the new generation of workers. As per an E&Y study, 44% of Millennials, and 62% of those in Gen Z, see oil-and-gas jobs as unappealing.[7] AI can help with automation and process simplification of many tasks as it is doing in other industries, which will ease the talent pressure a bit. When it comes to maintenance and repair tasks, which are usually very knowledge and experience intensive, and where we are seeing major talent drain, AI is a great supplementary tool.

Finally, AI will also help in making the fuel markets more transparent and responsive to demand–supply as well as alternative energy resources. Currently, the energy markets are dominated by a few state players and frequently managed to suit their needs, impacting the rest of the global economy. Several geopolitical issues owe their origination and continuance to oil-related conflicts. AI can help make the world not only more sustainable but possibly more peaceful.

Logistics

Logistics and supply chain are very closely linked with the transportation industry; sometimes they are even considered as one. In the discussion so far, we have already touched upon some of the more direct and obvious applications of AI like route and fuel optimization, network redesign, etc., so we will not get into those again. However, there are other areas of the logistics industry that will be significantly impacted by AI.

Global trade and commerce have made some interesting pivots recently which were driven by geopolitical considerations. The rise of nationalistic fervor and localization of more manufacturing seems to be an agenda in many parts of the world. Trade conflicts have impacted supply chain networks and sometimes entire industries adversely. Future supply chain ecosystems will continue to get more decentralized yet more interconnected; to make them more resilient technologies like AI will be critical. An E&Y study on the subject explains this further:

> Faced with more factories, more markets, and extended supply chain partners with more and different responsibilities, companies need to be on top of total landed cost trade planning, trade land optimization, capital expenditure planning, and even agile tax incentive planning, among others. These greater planning and management capabilities will need to be executed in real-time and must necessarily turn to more advanced technologies to access diverse data points to formulate increasingly complex strategies. Heavy technology evolution may also result in less need and desire for co-location of resources.

We will see logistics operations and supply chain networks significantly reframed with AI capabilities shortly.

Space Exploration

Strictly speaking, space exploration is not part of the transportation industry. On top of that, space exploration has been one of the earliest and most expansive users of AI. A lot of AI development has been driven by space exploration. But it is still important for us to quickly review how AI is going to further transform space exploration because these examples and capabilities will permeate into other industries soon thereafter.

As we reach for the next frontier in space exploration – going to new planets, looking for new stars and galaxies, mapping the history of the evolution of the universe, and sending more unmanned missions into space – we will use more AI capabilities in such pursuits. Spacecraft operation, maintenance, navigation, and control systems already use AI extensively. The same holds for satellites as well. The massive level of image processing done in space exploration uses multiple AI techniques. Without AI, there is no practical way of working through such huge volumes and a variety of data at the expected throughput levels. As per the European Space Agency (ESA), satellites can produce over 150 terabytes of data per day.

Now scientists are expanding AI further for deep space exploration in areas that have unknown gravitational fields, debris, orbits, and environmental conditions. In 2018, NASA sponsored research for autonomous navigation using Ethereum blockchain technology to create a "decentralized, secure, and cognitive networking and computing infrastructure for deep space exploration." Blockchain implementations have faced some flack on Earth; when they get perfected in space we will see new and widespread applications coming back to Earth. In these challenging terrains, communication and networking is another major challenge where AI is being leveraged to optimize networks and dynamically configure them. As we look beyond the known universe, massive-scale image processing will help with discoveries, thus taking image processing and object recognition to completely new heights. With more unmanned exploration in places like Mars happening, the autonomous functioning of scientific systems will have to increase. For example, Mars Rover 2020 autonomous scientific instrument PIXL uses AI extensively. This capability will subsequently transfer to the robotic operation of complex systems on Earth.

As we go beyond Mars, space exploration has to be driven by AI, leading to the completely new development of different types of science, technology, and math to pursue the new goals.

Insurance

Insurance is another related sector that is completely transforming due to the influence of AI. This is not limited only to automotive or transportation-related insurance but across all categories of insurance. Actuarial sciences are the backbone of the insurance industry. Actuarial analytics is not only building models by looking at past data but predicting most likely future outcomes. There are two fundamental complexities in getting high accuracy in actuarial analytics – getting and processing huge volumes of data and adapting or fine-tuning a model with new signals. Historically, actuaries used to create broad cohorts of population based on age, sex, ethnicity, past driving record, medical conditions, road conditions, etc. to predict risks and decide premiums. Getting this right and current has always been a challenge because of the variables and the influence of each individual's behavior/performance on the models. The second big challenge in the way the insurance industry worked traditionally is claims processing. It is very hard for the insurer to know whether a claim is genuine or fraudulent by looking only at claim data and other information about the event or the individuals involved. So, they resort to investigations that make it expensive and time-consuming – ultimately impacting the customer.

AI alleviates both of these challenges. It helps sort through humongous volumes of data to build the right risk models and even personalize it to a great extent for the individual driver or the event or a combination of both. But more importantly, with the advancements in IoT and digital technologies, the models can now take streaming real-time inputs from sensors to understand the current behavior of the individuals and current events to update the risk model. This allows for the potential to adjust premiums to reflect the more accurate probability of risk and pass on benefits to the less risky people or events. This approach, however, opens up another slew of issues around privacy and discrimination which are complex in their ethical and social considerations. AI models also help quickly assess the veracity of claims based on many factors like past behavior of the individual, history and possible extrapolation of the events leading to the claims, and other associated data. Overall, the insurance industry is becoming more personalized but more intrusive. When you overlay this with the changing models of vehicle ownership, now we are in a completely different territory of innovation and new business models.

Product Development and Manufacturing

In our discussions so far, it is clear that the product that we know as an automobile today is significantly changing in design, capability, and functionality in the future, especially because of the growth of autonomous vehicles. The pace of R&D investment in the automotive industry will continue at elevated levels and might even increase a bit in the next few years to focus on net innovation. Most of the R&D pursuits in automotive still pursue very traditional methods of research and simulation. But we have already seen AI playing a role in R&D in more stringent and complicated industries like drug discovery. So it is quite natural to expect AI to change the way R&D processes and throughput currently work today.

Automotive manufacturing is a very complex endeavor with a lot of actions, variations, and players. Lean manufacturing makes this even more complicated because of the precision requirements and time sensitivity. On the manufacturing shop floor, AI has already started to make an impact through Industry 4.0 type initiatives. Robots with better visual recognition and image processing capabilities along with better context awareness are making the production processes faster and improving quality. Better AI-powered decision making will make the supply chain also leaner and more efficient. In many of the supply chain functions, AI-assisted bot technology has enabled Robotic Process Automation, leading to better business results with fewer humans, fewer errors, and fewer process variances. Any downtime in the manufacturing chain is not only very expensive but also very disruptive for all other associated processes. AI is helping solve this problem through better maintenance of the shop floor equipment with predictive diagnostics. A McKinsey study on this subject estimates the benefits to be anywhere between 10 and 20% of the current operating costs, which is huge for an industry under pressure and used to low single-digit profit margins.

Figure 5.3 is a recap of the various influences of AI on the transportation industry.

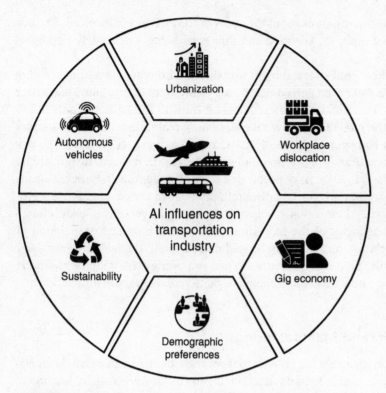

FIGURE 5.3 AI Influences on the Transportation Industry

 IMPACT OF AUTONOMOUS DRIVING BEYOND TRANSPORTATION

At the outset of this chapter, we saw how the transportation industry has led most of the innovation eras in the industrialized world. Later in the chapter, we talked a lot about autonomous driving. In our opinion, this one area of development will have very profound implications for the world in many more ways than we possibly realize today. In this section we will touch upon three such areas of impact.

Software Architecture

Software architecture has evolved since the introduction of software to meet the requirements of the day and operate within the technological constraints. In the mainframe world, architecture was more monolithic, which transitioned to a more service-oriented one in the client-server world. As the web and mobile development continued to become the norm and kept getting more complex and distributed at the same time, the architecture evolved to a more microservices-based architecture. Growth of IoT and cloud computing introduced the paradigm of containerization to this whole mix. With the proliferation of the Internet of Things (IoT), and AI technologies driving them, which requires massive autonomous distributed computing at the edge level, the needs of modern software engineering require agent-based architectures – a concept widely used in both space exploration as well as autonomous driving. We will discuss more multi-agent systems in Chapter 11 of this book.

Pervasive Automation

Automation has existed for centuries, starting with the dawn of the industrial age. We have always considered automation as the best solution for repetitive tasks, starting with the simple ones. Advancements in automation and robotics have expanded the nature of tasks to more complicated ones but with predictable inputs and outputs.

Driving, on the other hand, deals with highly unpredictable inputs and very dynamic environments. If that can be automated, everything except fine arts is subject to automation. Robotic surgeries are probably some of the most complex applications of automation today.

Extensive automation led to the concept of lights-out manufacturing that involves no human intervention in the entire process. As a concept, this was introduced by General Motors several decades back but implemented only in parts of the entire manufacturing plant and process. Toyota interestingly took the opposite position of introducing more manual intervention in the manufacturing process in the last decade to increase flexibility. More recently, there has been substantial development in collaborative robots or cobots that can coexist and work seamlessly with humans and other robots. Cobots are not limited in performing only highly automated industrial processes. Cobots use more sensors and software to adapt.

Pervasive automation will require us to rethink a lot of current-day processes and routines across multiple industries.

Redefinition of Urbanization

Autonomous vehicles might trigger another interesting trend of reverse urbanization. The primary driver for urbanization has been people's desire to be closer to their place of work so that they spend less time commuting, which is largely time wasted as they cannot do any other meaningful work while they are driving. Autonomous driving reverses the problem and makes even commute time productive. Combined with remote working, this might encourage people to be away from urban centers.

If this trend catches on, then everything from retail to education to financial services and every other industry will get impacted, at the least from a locational standpoint, and most likely from an operating model standpoint.

We will have to see how many of these trends evolve.

 SUMMARY

The transportation industry has been going through a massive transformation and that trend will continue for the next several years, These changes are being driven by increasing urbanization, changes in the workplace and work practices, especially after the COVID-19 crisis, the influence of the fast-growing gig economy, changes in how Gen X and Millennials think about vehicle ownership and urban mobility, sustainability considerations, and the rapidly approaching era of autonomous vehicles. The recent crash of oil prices and expectations of continued depression of transportation demand whether it be air or land will further change the dynamics of the transportation industry. In this dynamic environment of influences and changes, AI will play a big role in the transformation of the transportation industry.

Recent advancements in digital technologies and AI will accelerate the development and adoption of autonomous vehicles. This will be one of the most impactful shifts in the automotive industry in over 100 years. Different formats of mobility will converge to give travelers a unified experience. Vehicle ownership and consequently the entire automotive supply chain will change significantly. These shifts will also change the automotive insurance industry profoundly. As the broader changes impact vehicle products and services, the practice of product development and manufacturing will also be completely altered with more automation, robotics, and AI-enabled decision support systems. AI will help logistics networks become more agile and adaptive. AI has been enabling space exploration since the beginning; now we will see an accelerated pace of activity driven by human desire and technological capabilities. Every aspect of the transportation industry will mutate and evolve.

Not only that, but the growth of AI in the transportation industry will also stimulate its use in other industries and create a broader impact on the fundamentals of software development, especially with the rise of multi-agent and autonomous systems. The transportation industry has a history of ushering in big changes in the way we live and work; buoyed by AI, the industry is at the cusp of another major crossover point.

 ## REFERENCES

(1) "Greenhouse Gas Emissions from Transport in Europe"; European Environment Agency; December 2019.
(2) "2018 Revision of World Urbanization Prospects"; United Nations Department of Economic and Social Affairs; May 2018.
(3) "Magic Motorways"; Norman Bel Geddes; 1940.
(4) *Mastering Predictive Analytics with R*; James D Miller, Rui Miguel Forte; August 2017.
(5) "How China Will Help Fuel the Revolution in Autonomous Vehicles"; Luca Pizzuto, Christopher Thomas, Arthur Wang, Ting Wu; January 2019.
(6) "Your Next Car Could Be a Flexible Subscription Model"; Sawant Singh; July 2018.
(7) "Is AI the Fuel Oil and Gas Needs?" Jeff Williams; January 2019.

CHAPTER 6

Transforming Retail with AI

"You cannot run a successful retail business from memory."
—*Attributed to musician John Hartford*

 ## INTRODUCTION

Retail is one of the oldest industries with the biggest impact on the economy of any country. Organized retail has a history of more than 150 years. In the pre-COVID-19 scenario, counting all categories from groceries to clothing to hospitality to electronics to jewelry to automotive retail and so on, this sector is over $25 trillion[1] and represents between a third and a quarter of the global GDP. This sector is one of the biggest employers and is most sensitive to any socioeconomic trends or events. This sector is also poised for some of the biggest transformations in the next 5 to 10 years driven by the recent technological advancements. Billions of dollars are being spent already and benefits worth hundreds of billions are expected to be generated from those investments.

Let us start with a powerful transition case study. Less than 10 years back, Stitch Fix, a startup, was born in San Francisco, which in a few years disrupted this massive industry, even forcing giants like Amazon to study them intently and be influenced by Stitch Fix in some of its operations. From its humble beginnings in 2011, Stitch Fix crossed the $1 billion revenue and 2 million customer-base in a short six years, a feat that took many established players much longer to achieve. This is the first retail company that we can say was built on AI. Stitch Fix took personalization to the extreme and based its business model on a lot size of one. Stitch Fix combines the power of machine learning and human insight into a unique human–machine intelligence system. They collect about 85 data points to understand their customers' demography, style preferences, and state in life to both predict and recommend the most suitable clothes for their customers. Then they ship a few to their customers who are free to keep all of them or keep the one they like best and fits best. Such data combined with other transactional data is then used to further improve the hundreds of algorithms Stitch Fix employs to run its business. This company has built an amazing track record in predicting fashion trends, personalizing customer experiences, and running a cutthroat business very efficiently. This is a company where the Chief Algorithms Officer is one of the topmost leaders in the company.

The story of Stitch Fix is not an isolated one; there are more such in the offing. Most retailers are reporting that they have started using AI in various aspects of their business but as per Constellation Research, more than 92% of the retailers surveyed[2] are spending less than $5 million in applying AI. But this number is increasing as business leaders in the retail industry are learning more about the power of AI to transform their business. Kevin Sterneckert, CMO, Symphony RetailAI, says about the upcoming transition of the Retail industry through AI-influence, "Within five years, every aspect of retail will leverage AI for sensing and reacting to market changes, recommending new approaches, and personalizing decisions. We will see retailers develop hyper-localized assortments and personalized marketing offers that build customer loyalty and create deep engagement between consumers and retailers."

In this chapter, we will investigate the factors that have driven this industry so far, but more importantly, discuss the major disruptions technology will introduce to this industry. These should be a good guidepost for retailers and other associated participants in the industry to strategize about their future role and structure.

UNDERSTANDING HOW AND WHY THE RETAIL INDUSTRY HAS BEEN CHANGING

Trade and commerce have existed for over 10,000 years now, since the inception of human civilization. As mentioned earlier, retail or organized retail as we know it in its current form traces its history to over 150 years. This industry has mirrored various aspects of the society of the day and been an instrument of mass-scale changes in how we live and engage with the economy (Figure 6.1).

Let us now investigate a few of these important influences. The only one we will not touch upon is the technological influences because the rest of the chapter is dedicated to that anyway.

Economic Influences

The direct correlation between a nation's economy and the retail industry is undeniable; it has been established over the years and through multiple economic cycles. For consumer-driven economies, the correlation is much higher compared to others that are more manufacturing or agriculture driven. For example, in the United States, the Retail Exchange-Traded Fund (ETF) has a positive correlation of 0.94 with the nation's GDP, proving the deep influence of the overall economy on the retail sector. In most countries, retail sector growth or momentum is considered a good indicator of future economic growth and current fiscal liquidity in the market. Different aspects of the retail industry like automotive or apparel or groceries all follow different slowdown and recovery cycles; their trajectories are a good measure for the most likely future scenarios. Understanding these trajectories, the global impact, and interlinkages with other industries and economies is a key input to retail business leaders' and policymakers' decision-making processes about investments and interventions.

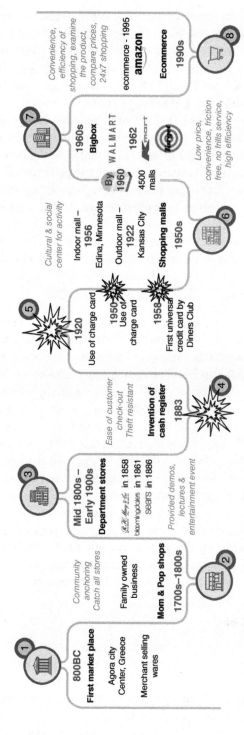

FIGURE 6.1 Evolution of the Retail Industry

Sources: macys.com, Bloomingdales, Transform SR Brands LLC, Walmart, Target Brands, Inc., and Amazon.com, Inc.

Policy Influences

Government policies have a lot of impact on the retail industry, too. In many countries, a big portion of the last mile of the retail industry is constituted of small local businesses. If the government creates policies and incentives to promote such small businesses, they have a positive impact on growth. Even for large players, government policies can be an enabler or a deterrent. For example, in India, which is one of the most potentially rich retail markets, for a very long time, large-format foreign supermarkets were not allowed. However, in the last 10 years the government has been opening up the sector. Large multi-brand stores and increased foreign direct investment were allowed in the country and all major global retailers started establishing a big presence in the country. Now Jeff Bezos considers India as one of his major destinations and is investing over $1 billion to build infrastructure and capacity. With all the policy influences, retail has quickly become one of the largest contributors to the economy, accounting for over 10% of the GDP and generating nearly the same percentage of employment. Policy changes beyond the retail industry can also help or hurt it. Continuing with the India example, two other government policies around demonetization and the introduction of a uniform Goods and Services Tax across the country deeply impacted the retail industry and changed it in significant ways.

Demographic Influences

The next big influence on the retail industry is that of demographic composition and trends in different societies that also have an impact on the economy. Most of the mature economies have an aging population while most of the emerging economies have a very young population. The buying habits can be wildly different based on demographic differences. There are also some patterns between demography, the economy, and people's spending habits. For example, in most developed and developing nations today, the Millennial generation or even Gen Y has a higher proclivity to spend than save for the future, a trend that fuels consumer economy and retail spend. But age distribution in a society and their influence on the economy does not complete the influence picture; there are many more nuances to it. The growth of the population in general and the growth of people in the middle-income economic bracket have a big influence on the retail economy growth. We are seeing more and more multigenerational households in economies that were dominated by nuclear families; this has a meaningful impact on the retail industry as well because it changes the dynamics of household retail spending. For example, in the United States, 40% of Millennials are staying with their parents or other relatives, a percentage that has not been seen to be this high in more than 80 years. Retailers will have to understand and model these various demographic influences on the future of their business.

Sustainability Influences

Environmental sustainability across the retail value chain has got the attention of both retailers and policymakers in a big way only in the last five to six years; however, the intensity of focus is increasing rapidly. Several drivers are making retailers more active to address sustainability concerns. While the retailer may be taking actions at the corporate level, especially concerning their facilities, they have huge exposures in the distant ends of their supply chains that are often in countries in a distant part of the world where environmental safeguards are questionable; but in today's social media–dominated globally integrated world, bad press travels fast and retailers want to save both their brand as well as commitment. Another factor driving this trend is cost considerations. Sustainably using more natural resources can sometimes bring down the cost. In many countries, there are legislative and policy actions. We are seeing a lot of large retailers having leaders and organizations dedicated to driving end-to-end sustainability. Being able to track and manage sustainability across the value chain requires significant data tracking and management.

Epidemic Influences

The recent COVID-19 crisis has impacted every business and every walk of life. It has especially hit the retail industry the hardest and will have a deep and lasting impact. In March 2020, with most countries imposing lockdown measures, the retail industry crashed overnight. Even if there was demand, many companies were not ready to fulfill those needs because they were not ready to operate in a digital world. Till we have a vaccine, cure, and herd immunity figured out for the novel Coronavirus COVID-19, the new normal will include social distancing and lockdowns. Even when countries transition to new normalcy, people buying from physical stores will be dramatically reduced. The economic impact of the crisis will last for a long time, reducing the buying power of the consumers. Buying behaviors for the majority of the population will shift to essential goods.

HOW AI WILL CHANGE THE RETAIL INDUSTRY OF THE FUTURE

Retailers are already spending billions of dollars globally in implementing AI solutions. As per Juniper Research, by 2023, more than $12 billion will be spent by retailers on AI solutions. It is believed that the retail industry might be leading the spend on AI-based analytics and has a very high number of use-cases for AI. There are many functions in the retail industry that will be almost taken over by AI-enabled automation within the next few years. Let us now examine how AI is already changing and is poised to change the different aspects of the retail industry.

Personal Lifestyle Cloud

The success of the retail industry relies on understanding each consumer, connecting with them at the deepest possible level, and servicing their needs in the most efficient and timely manner. This industry has made strides in collecting all kinds of data about customers and transactions. The next frontier of advancement will involve building a 360-degree lifestyle and lifetime view of each customer. The way we believe that the personal cloud concept will transform the healthcare industry, we think the same applies to the retail industry as well. The personal cloud concept in retail will manifest in two areas – deep personalization and lifestyle gamification around the consumer.

The value of personalization has been recognized by the industry already. The rising e-commerce and loyalty programs have led to collecting a lot of information about consumers, especially relating to their preferences derived from purchases, spend patterns, frequency of visit and spend, and so on. However, the approach has been very rudimentary – it only looks at what the consumer has been exploring or buying and draws a linear conclusion of their interest in similar things. For example, if I look for leather shoes, I will be inundated with more ads of leather shoes; if I explore a trip to Italy, I will get pounded by the travel websites. What this approach lacks is the context of why as a consumer I might be interested in something. This knowledge is more useful because it helps with more precise targeting and also finding out what else I might be interested in. Continuing with the same example, if I am looking for leather shoes and I also got a new job, maybe I want to update my entire wardrobe and could be in the market for a new car or a home. Michele Goetz, an AI expert with Forrester, explains how personalization will evolve in the future:

> AI in personalization is much more intent-driven, meaning that marketers need a more robust understanding of customer needs, wants, influences, and relationships. You cannot just log customer behavior that is pulled from search, traffic on-site, or captured from what comes in from the store. Why? AI doesn't care about one-time customer behavior: AI cares about everything. We are looking at what customers prefer and why, and the data must represent that.

Today's analytics do not effectively capture the intent because they rely on a linear correlation between cookies. Tomorrow's analytics will become more sophisticated when we bring more advanced AI-algorithms to traverse through different data streams, seek out associations, interpret intent, and most importantly predict demand and behavior. AI will allow frequent micro-experiments to understand if there are certain nudges from the retailer that can influence consumer behavior. This is the holy grail of success in retail.

Taking personalization a step further, we can synthesize the complete lifestyle of an individual consumer and apply concepts of octalysis to gamify the lifestyle to better understand context and influence behavior. Many credit card companies took the first step toward this with their loyalty programs – crossing over multiple spend categories and rewarding overall spend increase. They also fell short of understanding the *why* behind certain patterns of spend and behaviors. The Gamification Company, about whom we talked in Chapter 4 on education, has taken this a step further by creating a platform that combines all different types of actions an individual undertakes in their daily lives, gamifying them using the octalysis framework, understanding and influencing behavior, and prodding consumers toward certain retailers and services through dynamic reward systems using virtual currency that the consumers earn through their spend and other actions. The early experiments have shown some very promising results in redefining brand loyalties across multiple categories.

Category convergence in retail has been going on for a while and retailers can no longer stay insulated in their primary category. The rapid changes in consumer behavior coupled with category convergence can significantly impact business in retail. Combining the concepts of a digital twin, hyper-personalization, and gamification will arm the retailers with a deep understanding of the consumer and distinctive competitive advantage.

Digital Twin in Retail

The idea of digital twins as a virtual representation of a physical object or an event has been gaining ground in many industries and application areas. Digital twins help in virtual understanding and simulations that are easier and inexpensive. In the retail industry, digital twin enables a new method for modeling and driving the entire business.

To model a retail business, we need an amalgamation of lots of different shopping events. To do so, we have to bring four data streams together – information about the customer, facts about the product, granular transactional details about the experience whether online or in-store, and the outcome of the event. For the point in time of the event, data about the customer and the product(s) is static while the experience data is a streaming time-series data. Even though the customer and product data are static for the moment in time of the event, they could be evolving time-series data. One part of the twin is a design model of the four data streams ending with the desired outcome. The other part of the twin is the data from the real-time event. (See Figure 6.2.)

You can keep making the twins more sophisticated by bringing other data dimensions like a store or channel outlet (could be online as well), seller, and so on. In other industries like autonomous driving or space exploration or medical research, very complex digital twin models have been used for simulation. What we are trying to do here is modulate the outcome by manipulating the levers of experience keeping the customer and the product constant. We can start with some simple use-cases like this and then keep improvising as the systems mature.

We use the digital twin concept to validate the business modeling assumptions based on feedback from real-life inputs. On a small scale, this implementation can help design and improve promotional campaigns. On a more massive scale, one could model an entire business over a longer duration. Digital twins can also be used to make adjustment recommendations in real-time retail experiences based on a very large library of potential outcome patterns. Running experiments in real life is both time consuming and expensive; tweaking them in real time is even more complicated. AI helps simulate those scenarios with the help of these digital twins in a repeatable fashion with little to no investment. Today the science and math around sentiment analysis, social influence analysis, and other psychological or economic catalysts are well developed to make the AI-based predictions close to perfect. While not exactly a retail industry case study, the success of Cambridge Analytica in influencing elections is a testimonial to how far technology has come. We do not need to pursue their sinister activities, but we can use the same concepts and technologies for benefiting consumers and retailers.

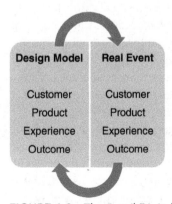

FIGURE 6.2 The Retail Digital Twin Model

Store of the Future

While online channels have got a lot of press in the last few years and the threat of online channels overtaking physical stores has been impending for quite some time, the reality is that most of the retail business still happens through physical stores. The share of online in the total retail business is still less than 10–11%. Even for large fashion houses like Inditex with brands like Zara, Massimo Dutti, Bershka, and others, and strong online channels, the share of business from online is less than 14% and estimated to be in the teens over the next five years. But the stores of the future will be different from how we know them today.

Amazon has been one of the biggest disruptors in the retail industry for more than 20 years now. In December 2016, it took the first step to disrupt the store of the future with its opening of the first Amazon Go store in Seattle that was opened to the general masses in January 2018. This futuristic concept store is the synthesis of AI and some of the most advanced digital technologies like computer vision, sensor fusion, geo-fencing, and others. The store transforms the customer experience completely by making shopping frictionless.

Technology giants like Microsoft have also created similar concept stores because they want to enable retailers with technology and analytics.

The AI-enabled store of the future will distinguish itself primarily in the following three areas:

Automated Shopping and Checkout

A very extensive network of cameras tracks people's movement as well as individual items, their location, and their count. This helps the store system to guide the shopper to the specific location of things they want to buy, and recommend other related products based on their personal history, on other shoppers' behavior, or on current promotions. Sensors on the cart, on the racks, and sometimes on the individual items tabulate the purchased items. Deep learning algorithms not only understand how to guide the customers as they go about the store but also drive the inventory management and other supply chain processes. Location tracking and digital payment systems complete the checkout processes.

Merchandise Management

There are many issues with merchandise management that retailers have to deal with. Managing stock on display and stock in-store is a common challenge across all categories. Understanding the velocity of stock movement is a key related issue that has serious implications for managing logistics. Similarly, the placement of goods and its potential impact on buying behavior is another big issue that retailers struggle with. During the shopping process, customers often pick things from one place and leave them in a different place; replacing things in their right locations is a very manually intensive and cumbersome process across all different types of retailers.

However, some issues are unique to a particular product category. For example, in the fresh produce section, knowing when things are beginning to go bad, something that can be assessed through simple visual inspection like a banana beginning to become discolored, is an important trigger to either start promotion and/or replace the stock on display. In the case of fashion items, the demographic association of purchases is a key indicator that retailers want to track. This is also helpful to start identifying trends.

The visual identification systems of the store of the future inform the inventory management and supply chain systems about stocks, the velocity of stock depletion, an estimated window by when restocking is required, and trigger every aspect of the logistics function. We might finally be able to get sales and operations planning (S&OP) processes right with granular real-time information.

Shopper Analytics

In the store of the future, every micro-action of the shopper is captured and analyzed further to improve the experience as well as increase the income. One of the biggest pieces of data retailers value is how many shoppers enter the store with an intent to purchase but leave without having done so. As an example, in the metro areas of the United States, it is estimated that in the majority of the Walgreens stores, one out of every five and sometimes three shoppers leave without buying because they did not find what they were looking for. The right camera and analytics can pinpoint the specific problems by studying shopper movement. This is a straight revenue-loss issue because often the shopper will explore other stores for the same item. On similar lines, in convenience stores, the biggest source of profit is food and beverages; gas (or petrol/diesel) is only a way to attract customers. A convenience store makes more money selling a refrigerated drink like Slurpee or Icee than it does by selling a tankful of gas. If a store runs out of the food and beverages, it impacts profitability in a major way.

Another key area of analytics is knowing what items to keep in proximity to drive impulse buying. Understanding patterns of what is bought together with what other items and by whom and usually when can help store managers dynamically change their displays and improve the sales. This is another problem that image analytics can provide deep insights into.

Knowing demographic analysis of shoppers, how when they visit, what they buy, how much they spend, what day of the month, and what time of the year contribute to different shopping patterns; what other events might be influencing shopping; whether promotional activity started by one store in the same or different category has any impact on the sales of that store or chain, and so on is very valuable. A lot of this data is available even today in some form or other. But the data is not very reliable because the collection methods are not consistent. If more of the data collection moves to the camera and location-based sensors, and AI techniques are used to correlate and interpret the data, we will get better insights.

The store of the future brings many improvements over the current practices:

a. Personalizes the shopping experience
b. Expedites the checkout process
c. Allows dynamic pricing and pricing experimentations
d. Improves inventory and supply chain efficiency
e. Reduces theft and shrinkage

Ultimately, the store of the future will improve the revenue and profitability of the stores while improving customer loyalty. But not every retailer will be able to implement the concept of the store of the future because such an effort will require substantial investment in technology and reconfiguring the physical space. The ones who will lead and scale this model the fastest will create a disruptive advantage over the competition. Amazon, one of the bellwethers of the retail industry, is planning to lead this space with its plan of more than 2,000 physical Go stores in this decade. First, they shifted shopping away from the stores, now they are bringing it back in a new avatar. Not to be left behind, Walmart is also investing in Walmart Intelligence Retail Lab. On similar lines, Costco is using ML to drive its bakery and fresh food sections to reduce wastage and better meet customer wants. Even smaller players and suppliers to the retail industry are experimenting with similar concepts to get ready for the future.

Retailer of the Future

AI will get more deeply ingrained in a larger variety of functions for most retailers in the future. The pace of AI-adoption is already very high and the trend will continue. AI will be used both in customer-facing applications as well as to streamline internal operations. Since retail is a very scale-driven, intensely competitive, and margin-challenged business, small gains in operational improvements have a multiplier effect on business performance. As per a study published in *Digital World Information*, 26% of the AI implementations will be focused on customers and 74% on operational gains. Multi-category retailers are leading the pack in adopting AI. Large players are already spending about 10% of their IT budgets on AI while the smaller retailers spend about 7% of their IT budget on AI. Here are some of the use-cases that we think retailers of the future will use AI for.

Converged Omnichannel Customer Analytics

Nearly every retailer already has a multi-channel strategy – minimally an online and physical presence. Sometimes, especially when it comes to consumer goods, a store might carry multiple brands. In the online channels it is easier to collect and use the customer data, but collecting the same from physical stores is a very difficult task, more so if it is a nonexclusive store. The collection process is cumbersome and often there is no incentive for the storefront to do so. But as the use of sensors in stores goes up and as we see more and more stores starting to mimic stores of the future, at least in part, such data collection will become easier. However, due to differences in the format, frequency, reliability, and quality of the data, managing such data will be very complicated. This is the biggest challenge to omnichannel customer analytics and getting a full 360-degree view of the customer. When we start overlaying behavioral analytics on top of the identity and transactional analytics, we are in a different realm of analytical complexity. This is where AI will step in to make the synthesis of data and execution of analytics possible.

Predicting Future Trends and Adapting Product Design

Once there is a deep understanding of the customer, their needs and wants, and other trends in the market, AI will be leveraged to more accurately predict future trends and influence the product design process. Such implementations have already started across many categories of retail. McDonald's in the United States has used AI to dynamically adapt the drive-thru menu based on outside weather, time of day, restaurant traffic, and other inventory status. Fast fashion companies like Zara and H&M are using AI to predict trends and optimize their supply chain to take goods from concept to store in two weeks or less. They further use a different set of analytical algorithms to determine that location to send the unused stock based on past performance and trends in that locale or country. Specialized clothing brand North Face is using IBM Watson's cognitive computing capabilities to help customers decide the best fit product for their needs. These are a few of the many early examples. As the technology and analytical tools improve, we will see a complete revolution in what gets designed when.

Optimizing Production Systems and Lot Sizes

To make the entire value chain effective, adaptive product design has to be backed by adaptive manufacturing and fulfillment capabilities. This will be another major use-case for AI among retailers. AI algorithms will be used to study and simulate the sensitivity, capacity, throughput, efficiency, and financial data in the manufacturing process. Given that there is a move toward higher degrees of personalization and possibly smaller lot sizes of goods to support personalization, there is a need to dynamically adjust the manufacturing line and simultaneously optimize scheduling and sequencing. Doing so will require using AI algorithms and AI-backed process automation. The example of Stitch Fix at the beginning of this chapter is an extreme case of personalized production systems. We are beginning to see more emerging initiatives in the same direction.

Pricing and Margin Management

Retail is a very low-net-profit-margin business. The companies in this sector that are profitable operate in a range of 0.5 to 3.5% net margin. The profit margins in this industry have been going down over the last few days, the last few years bringing a sharper decline. Presently, the retail industry is under maximum profit pressures since the 1940s. Many famous brand retailers are going bankrupt, unable to sustain financial health because of escalating competition and depressing volume and prices. In 2019 alone, we saw many names like Barney's New York, Roberto Cavalli, Forever 21, and others go out of business. Therefore, any scope of margin improvement always receives prime attention from any retailer.

Pricing has been considered an important tool for margin improvement. In a McKinsey simulation across the S&P 1500 companies, a 1% improvement in pricing leads to an 8% improvement in net profit.[3] Now, this is across all industries, but the significance is equally true if not more for the retail industry.

In 2017, Deloitte conducted an exhaustive study[4] on the pricing challenge in the retail industry. They concluded that customer engagement and differentiated (or more personalized) offerings are the two biggest drivers for higher pricing. In their study of the FTSE top 350 retailers between 2012 and 2016, they found a 5-year CAGR of 5.2% on revenue and 2% on EBITDA for value and convenience brand, that is, when companies had normal engagement and differentiation. But when companies had a highly differentiated offering and experience, the same growth rates were found to be 18.4% and 14.3% respectively. We can see that the margin is not only going up but the rate of increase is accelerating when companies apply strategies around differentiation and deeper customer engagement. In this chapter, we have already touched upon product-based differentiation and how AI can help achieve that. Later in this chapter, we will discuss more differentiated experiences when we talk about *the shopper of the future.*

For more traditional pricing interventions like dynamic pricing determination based on customer and other factors like inventory, time of day, store performance, etc., testing price elasticity, and other such interventions, AI is more effective than normal heuristics that retailers used traditionally. Kroger has used a combination of smart shelf sensors and customer information with a set of AI-based analytics to offer personalized dynamic pricing through its mobile app.

Customer Service

AI has been so far most widely used in customer service. From the early-stage experiments, we have seen encouraging results like customer satisfaction improvement of 9%, reduced customer complaints by 8%, and 5% lower customer churn. For customer service, AI has been applied in many different ways, such as:

- Intelligent interactive chatbots automate customer service and get deeper insights into customer behaviors, help customers find the right items, help customers learn more about the products and the category, and perform other such functions.
- Natural language voice processing helps better understand human emotions and impact on behavior.
- Long- and short-term memory analytics (LSTM) models to find the right customer agent should the chatbot not be sufficient in customer service.
- Graph-based knowledge management systems have been used to better equip customer service agents.

There are already many pilot projects for such use-cases, and they have been going on for some time now. For example, Pepper, a humanoid robot that runs on AI, has been used by Japan's Softbank to perceive human emotions. In a retail environment in the United States, Pepper led to increased store traffic and sales conversion. Conversica's AI-powered sales assistant tool has been used to improve the sales operations process by identifying and conversing with sales leads generated from online channels. 1-800-Flowers.com has used IBM Watson to create an AI-based gift concierge. There are many more examples across the world like this. As technology improves, we will see more and more use-cases coming up.

Multichannel Inventory Management

With the blurring of different channels through which customers are buying their products, inventory management is getting more and more complicated. Most retailers have a multitude of inventory management systems due to legacy reasons and sometimes additionally use third-party logistics, making the situation even more complicated. Each of these systems brings their different data formats, accuracy levels, frequency of collection, and metadata. Advanced techniques like the AI-based ones become necessary to sort through this web and get the desired insights. Companies like Kohl's, Lowe's, and Walmart that have ship-to-store and store pickup have applied machine-learning practices to expose inventory visibility by tapping into the warehouse and store inventory data.

Fraud Detection and Anti–Money Laundering

Fraud detection, payment security, and anti–money laundering are some other areas where AI has been used not only in retail but in many industries. Issue detection is complex and needs the power of AI because the transactions (even the fraudulent ones) can be so many, small, and seemingly normal that unless you do sophisticated pattern analysis you will most likely miss them. We will get more into this topic in the chapter on AI and finance.

The Shopper of the Future

How we shop has been changing for over 150 years now. In 1861, Pryce Pryce-Jones started the first mail-order business in Wales, United Kingdom, giving consumers the choice of buying from the comfort of their homes. While Tiffany started the same trend in the United States in 1845 with their Blue Book, something that continues even today, Montgomery Ward ushered in a multi-brand mail-order business in 1872. The first decade of the 21st century introduced online shopping and the second decade brought the influence of social media into shopping. Now AI will further change how and from where we shop.

Let us first examine some of the major trends before we go into more specifics about how AI will change shopping.

a. **Social media influence.** Social media has permeated every aspect of our lives. It already has a huge influence on people making shopping choices. Given the amount of time we spend on social media sites, they have become and will continue to be a major source for information and shopping triggers. Social media is also being frequently relied upon by shoppers for reviews and insights into the products. In a recent study, it was revealed that more than 65% of consumers read online reviews before making a purchase decision and 90% of them trust those reviews. So retailers need more sophisticated systems to sniff out an emerging issue about their product or service in any social media or online site, be very responsive to the issue, and be authentic and personal about the response. This will help build trust. Doing this requires advanced sentiment analysis capabilities as well as the ability to synthesize signals and sentiments from multiple unstructured sources.

b. **Shrinking time syndrome.** Two simultaneous trends are impacting how and on what people will want to spend time in the future, especially among Millennials and Gen Z. They are spending more and more time online, nearly 50% more than average adults as per an Ofcom study done in 2017, and more than 70% of them believe that they will have a busier lifestyle in 5–10 years, a period when their spending capacity will be at its peak. This means that retailers can get more loyalty from their customers and consequently more share of their wallets if they figure out how to optimize the customer's time spent with them and leave them with a sense of maximum output and engagement. Not only will people look for value for money but they will also look for value for time. This will have implications on how and where physical stores are located, how they are laid out, how the online channels are organized, at what frequency the retailer tries to engage the customer, and so on. To get this right, retailers will need a lot more data and a lot more details in that data than they might be collecting today, and follow it up with much deeper analytics involving neural networks.

c. **Social consciousness.** Concerns about the environment and ethical supply chain have been increasing. This is happening at an individual level and also in some of the progressive societies where environmental impact is being legislated. In a study conducted by IDG, more than 60% of people under the age of 35 say that environmental and social consciousness is a key factor in their purchase decisions and will continue to be one in the coming years. We have seen rising trends around organic food, natural fibers, banning the usage of plastics for packaging and transport, sustainable supply chains, ethical growing and trade practices, and other such social impact elements. Retailers will have to understand the preferences at an individual level better and design their products and distribution points accordingly.

d. **Redefinition of shopping channels.** Today, there is no clear demarcation between the various shopping channels. It is no longer true that people buy things they want to touch and feel from stores and others from online channels. The purpose of the store is under question. When retailers have pivoted more toward online channels as opposed to their stores, there is no clear indication that their revenue growth has fared better. Customers exhibit very disconnected behaviors concerning what they buy and from where. Since retailers spend a lot of capital and time in the different channels, both physical and virtual, they need to better understand their customers' preferences and also nudge them toward options that create maximum advantage and engagement for them.

e. **Personalization.** Creating a fully personalized shopping experience with the tailored recommendation, pricing, and even product configuration is one of the topmost trends in the retail industry and is very high on nearly every retailer's agenda. Even for more mass-based retailers like Walmart and Amazon, they are putting a lot of premium on personalization. There are many challenges for achieving a high degree of personalization; one of the big ones is mediating the customer's identity and every bit of data about her across the multitude of channels that the retailer exploits to engage with her. With increasing personalization in every other aspect of life, customers have similar expectations in their shopping experience as well, maybe even more so because shopping is a very intimate experience. The other challenge for retailers in achieving personalization is maintaining or increasing profitability. This is an industry built on maximizing returns on mass-scale efforts; when we are trying to shift the DNA of the business to the other extreme, all the fundamentals of the business have to be completely reimagined. This also calls for real-time adaptability that in turn requires high-speed and multivariate analytics to ensure profitability. This is where AI plays a role.

These trends and influences will lead to two major shifts in the shopping experience.

Bot Buying

Bot buying is a relatively new concept that is still in the early stages of development. You might have seen auto-order features on several online retail stores, especially those dealing with groceries. In this model, a predetermined quantity gets shipped to you at a predetermined price for some time. This method is very linearly tied to one item and based on a simple time-based ordering rule. Now imagine putting this model on some serious steroids – an intelligent software program first figures out all the routine things you need based on consumption data derived through some mechanism like stock information from a smart refrigerator or sensors attached to your location, then it finds the best deal for buying those items based on boundary conditions of brand or feature or quality or user-review feedback, and then finally it autonomously orders the goods. For many categories of things we buy, sometime in the future we see that bots will be doing a lot of the buying. These bots will be powered by AI-algorithms to do the three functions we mentioned here. Bot buying will save time and make the shopping process more efficient. This will require retailers to completely reimagine a lot of processes and use technology very creatively because the current ones are all based on either human interactions or simple rules.

Converged Customer Experience

AI will also tackle the problem of extreme and dynamic fragmentation of customer engagement across all dimensions of experience, purchasing, and trust drivers. The AI-based programs will stitch together the micro-moments across all of these experience points, model and extrapolate the next few actions shoppers will most likely take, and make recommendations to adapt those steps to secure a sale or further the customer experience. This approach will help to build deep engagement with the customer.

Warehouse of the Future

The warehousing industry is a very large industry by itself. Globally, warehousing accounts for about $2 trillion in economic activity[5] and has been growing at a moderate mid-single-digit pace. It sits at the intersection of retail, manufacturing, and transportation but is mostly influenced by the retail industry. Warehousing has been going through some transitions. Rising disposable incomes have led to increased consumption by people across most economies (not counting the current COVID-19 situation). More consumption has led to more goods being in demand that drives more need for warehousing. The globalization of demand and supply points has also contributed to the growth of warehousing. However, we are also seeing increasingly abrupt disruptions in economic activity due to political, environmental, or health-related issues. When such disruptions happen, it starts creating different pressures on the warehousing industry. Given the state of the world today and the impending changes that are happening, the warehousing industry is becoming very complex and critical, with an increasing need to be more adaptable, efficient, and inexpensive.

Digital technologies are already making inroads into warehousing and associated logistics functions. Computer vision and robotics have started to find extensive use. These technologies are being used to find storage places, locate inventory, count inventory, drop and pick things, reorganize things, pack and ship material, and create alerts if there is an emergency or other type of threat like theft. Such functions that used to be manually executed are now being automated to bring speed, flexibility, and remove human-induced errors. Labor cost savings are a huge byproduct of this automation. For these automation capabilities to work, massive scale image processing and optimization algorithms are required; that is where AI steps in. Rapid reconfiguration of warehouses is another area where AI techniques are used; the land cost and labor cost both can be optimized through constant reconfiguration as the business evolves.

Amazon has been using robotics, computer vision, drones, and location tracking technologies in its fulfillment centers. In early experiments, they found 5× or higher efficiency when compared to humans. Many postal departments and shipping companies like FedEx are also using similar technologies. The trend will continue. However, there are some challenges with this level of automation that still need to be solved. For example, if a package breaks, the system may not be intuitive enough to handle the situation quickly all by itself. If humans and robots have to work together, optimal task distribution and coordination between them becomes complicated. But as technology progresses and analytics becomes stronger, these issues will find a resolution. Like most other applications of AI and digital technologies, full maturity and complete automation will take a few years. Amazon estimates that before 2030, they will have complete lights-out warehouses, which means there will be no human involvement with the actual operation of the warehouse.

SUMMARY

The retail and consumer products goods (CPG) industry is one of the oldest industries in the world with a deeply synergistic relationship with the health and growth of the economy. As we have seen in this chapter, over the last 150 years, this industry has gone through many transformations and is now at the cusp of another major disruption. The current epidemic crisis is pulling the future forward.

In this chapter, we started our discussion with the economic, policy, demographic, sustainability, and epidemic crisis influences. We then moved on to discuss how AI will change the retail industry of the future, especially in the following areas:

a. Personal lifestyle clouds to get a holistic lifetime view of the individual consumer
b. Digital twins to simulate retail business models
c. Store of the future, which allows for more efficient and personalized experiences for the consumer and better operational efficiency for the store
d. Retailer of the future, which is more tuned to a D2C business model in addition to making their other business models more efficient
e. The shopper of the future, who will be looking for new experiences

The recent COVID-19 crisis is expediting the transitions in this sector. Now retail companies are being required to understand their customers more deeply and individually as the business models continue to shift. Speaking in an exclusive interview with the author, Michael Nilles, Chief Digital and Information Officer of Henkel, the $21 billion German chemicals and CPG giant, says,

> Consumer behavior is fundamentally changing. Personalization and convenience expectations are becoming key and digital channels are the new channel of choice. Corona has accelerated the need for digitization in the CPG industry. Companies successfully mastering to build new digital and data-driven business models like direct-to-consumer (D2C) will be leading the pack. AI is playing a key role in understanding personalization needs around the consumer and customer.

While AI makes a huge impact on customer-facing functions, it has an equally big role to play in the entire company for more efficiency and productivity.

REFERENCES

(1)   "Global Retail Sales 2017–2023"; Liam O'Connell; November 2019.

(2)   "Constellation Research 2018 Artificial Intelligence Study"; Courtney Sato, R. "Ray" Wang; June 2018.

(3)   "The Power of Pricing"; Michael V. Marn, Eric V. Roegner, and Craig C. Zawada; February 2003.

(4)   "The Retail Profitability Challenge"; Deloitte Research; March 2017.

(5)   "Warehouse Market Growth"; *Eye for Transport* editorial; October 2019.

CHAPTER 7

Transforming Financial Services with AI

"We don't have to be smarter than the rest; we have to be more disciplined than the rest."
—*Warren Buffett*

 ## INTRODUCTION

The financial services industry is the bedrock of the world economy. It contributes nearly $20 trillion[1] out of the global GDP of about $90 trillion. Not only is this industry a major contributor, but every dollar of the economy moves through this industry. Banking, insurance, brokerage firms, and other such sectors are the various arms of the financial services industry. The COVID-19 pandemic has badly impacted the global economy and the various sectors like financial services. As the world starts getting back to normalcy after we figure out how to deal with the crisis, we all will be looking at the financial services industry to jumpstart the economy.

This industry historically has been one of the highest spenders on technology; average IT spend as a percentage of revenue is about 7%. This industry also has traditionally been one of the earliest adopters of technology. However, given the stringent regulatory environment that they have to work in, the size of the companies that operate in this industry, and the fast pace of evolution of technology in the last decade, the financial services industry also has a lot of technical debt to deal with, especially a large number of older banks that are still using very antiquated core banking systems.

This is an extremely data-rich industry and success in this industry is heavily dependent on being able to quickly and accurately generate insights out of that data. This industry is also heavily influenced by events and trends outside of the control of this industry (e.g. geopolitical events or health crises). Being right and being early in spotting trends and capitalizing on those trends is key to success in financial services. The world's greatest living moneymaker, Warren

Buffett, has rightly pointed out that growing wealth is all about data and discipline. Hence, this industry also sees big potential with AI. In a study done by Deloitte, 70% of the participating firms believe that AI will transform their business and reported to be engaged with at least some AI initiative. In the same study, the faster-growing companies considered AI to be a big driver for their growth. According to the report, "The top 30% of financial services firms who are front-runners are more adept at integrating AI into the core strategic business of their firms, delivering revenue and cost gains quicker than competitors." There are several examples of companies that have boldly forayed into using AI and digital technologies in their core business and decision-making engine. For example, financial giant BlackRock has built a platform called Aladdin that uses AI and encompasses a range of services for risk management, portfolio management, investment operations, and trade execution to a variety of financial service providers. In 2019, the platform was reportedly managing $17 trillion in assets.

The impact of AI will be seen across the various functions in financial services sectors – from managing customers to managing risks. In this chapter, we will investigate some of the key areas where AI will transform the industry.

 ## HOW AI WILL CHANGE THE FINANCIAL SERVICES INDUSTRY OF THE FUTURE

Like many other industries, AI will have a deep impact on many aspects of the financial services industry. The Cambridge Centre for Alternative Finance (CCAF) at the University of Cambridge Judge Business School and the World Economic Forum (WEF) recently conducted a global survey[2] of 151 companies involved with traditional financial services as well as financial technology companies to understand the impact of AI and digital transformation in the financial services industry. The report of the study was published in January 2020. As per the study, 77% of all respondents anticipate AI to have much-increased significance in their business within two years and 64% anticipate employing AI across multiple functions; however, only 16% reportedly use AI across multiple functions.

Personal Financial Cloud

We first introduced the concept of an individual-centric personal cloud for a specific domain in Chapter 3 on healthcare and used similar concepts in later chapters, too. Once again, we believe that one of the most transformative developments out there in the financial services is the development of a personal financial cloud. Most, if not all of us, have a personal wealth goal to meet our current and future lifestyle needs. In pursuit of that goal, we have earnings, savings, credit cards, other expenses, investments, taxes, obligations, and other instruments of financial transactions. For each of these instruments and transaction types, we usually engage with a different agency and use a different application. Our wealth goals, as well as many of these financial transactions like the value of or return on investments, are impacted by events outside of our control (e.g. stock market performance, geopolitical events, etc.). Usually, such events have historical trends and associated impacts over time. So, if we can plot those and project those forward, we can be better informed about the impact on us and potentially take action accordingly. To make this happen, we need data from all kinds of financial systems and advanced analytics on it centered around the individual. But the ability to predict based on historical trends is not always true.

The recent COVID-19 crisis has been one such event that completely changed the world economy in a very short time with no warning. One could argue that the nature of the crisis and its impact is similar to the Spanish Flu epidemic of 1918. While there are similarities in the epidemic, the global economic structure is very different; now it is a lot more interdependent and integrated. Even in such situations, the impact on an individual level and at an economic level can be better understood by synthesizing data from different sources, applying advanced analytics, and future forecasting possible scenarios based on the interrelationships between the various dimensions of the economy, polity, and society.

Except for very high-net-worth individuals who retain the services of professional wealth managers, most of us do not have a comprehensive view of the present and future of our earnings, obligations, wealth, and the events that shape them, even though all of that data is individually available and can be modeled with some accuracy for future values.

AI will help bring all of this information together, make sense of it, and create new outcomes and business models which will transform how financial institutions engage with individuals. At the core of this transformation lies nudging behaviors and actions at an individual level. American financial commentator, author, and radio host Dave Ramsey once remarked, "Personal finance is only 20% head knowledge. It's 80% behavior!" This is one of the biggest drivers for wealth creation. Today, we are expected to be disciplined and act without proper knowledge and insights about the future; the personal financial cloud will change that by empowering us with knowledge and insights as events happen and as they may evolve.

The challenges for the development of personal financial cloud are very similar to those of personal health cloud described in Chapter 2. To recap here:

a. Absence of primary player with access to majority information
b. Lack of anchor beneficiary other than the individual
c. Developmental complexity
d. Unclear business models

While the personal financial cloud will be very transformative for the industry because it will shift the power from the big companies to the individuals and disrupt every known business model, it will also face a lot of incumbency resistance. One thing is for sure, more people will participate more productively in the financial services industry as a result of the development of the personal financial cloud.

Fraud Detection and Anti–Money Laundering

Most financial services companies consider fraud detection and regulatory compliance as one of the biggest areas for AI to play a role. In the CCAF-WEF study mentioned at the beginning of this section, more than half of the responding companies considered such risk management as the highest usage for AI. Frauds are a big problem for the industry and get very expensive. As per LexisNexis® Risk Solutions' 2019 True Cost of Fraud™ study for the US financial services and lending sectors, for every dollar of fraud loss, financial services companies now incur $3.25 in costs (losses related to the transaction face value for which firms are held liable, plus fees and interest incurred, fines and legal fees, labor and investigation costs, and external recovery expenses), up from $2.92 in 2018. There are similar reports from other agencies and they indicate a similar impact from fraud. With the increase in mobile banking, digital transactions, and cross-border transactions, the rate of fraud has been increasing for the past few years. Fraud not only leads to substantial financial losses for the institution or the merchant but also requires the financial institution, merchant, and consumer to spend unproductive time investigating it and working through it. The insurance industry is also equally impacted if not to a greater extent. As per the US FBI, fraud costs an average household between $400 and $700 in increased premiums. The Coalition Against Insurance Fraud estimates that the annual impact of fraud across all lines of insurance is more than $80 billion in the United States. This problem extends to all parts of the world and the impact is equally devastating in most countries, causing a 10% inefficiency in the industry.

Fraud occurs through multiple vectors – hackers steal credit card and banking information and use that to steal money, more organized criminal enterprise attacks larger financial institutions and siphons money away, terrorists and criminals route their ill-gotten goods through regular financial institutions but after multiple layers of masking, and the list goes on. These crimes are committed sometimes slowly over time and sometimes very suddenly. Whenever something like this happens, usually it breaks a pattern of normal transactions and behaviors. Often there are other associated events as well. For example, if an individual has a certain spend pattern and there is suddenly a high-frequency or location of spend, it could be an indication of fraud. In another example, if there are only inbound deposits to a certain bank account and very specific periodic withdrawals from the account, it may indicate money laundering. Banking transactions at a suspected location outside of the home base by a suspected fraudster or criminal is yet another such example. There are hundreds of movies inspired by real-life events that showcase such innovative techniques. Whether it is banking or insurance or any other type of financial services institution, all of them cite issues with data and lack of timely alerts as their biggest challenge to prevent fraud. In a way, the problem is an oxymoron; this is a data-rich industry but lacks the tools to get insights out of the data.

AI is one of the best tools we have for anomaly detection in any dataset and will be very helpful in detecting such abnormalities indicating potential fraud. AI is very effective in sorting through a high volume of high-frequency transactions and studying them in the context of multiple dimensions and at different layers of granularity. AI programs can do this across multiple unrelated datasets, different networks, a variety of entities, jurisdictions, customers, locations, institutions, and other such variables. Examples of this already exist. FICO's Falcon Platform, which uses AI-driven predictive analytics to provide fraud-detection services to institutions, is one such example.

AI has been applied to detect and prevent fraud in many other innovative ways as well. IT services company Cognizant worked with one of its banking customers to use OCR and deep learning to identify fraudulent signatures on checks. There are hundreds of FinTech companies that are coming up with new solutions and use cases every day.

Customer Service

Since the beginning, customer service has been a very high-touch activity in the financial services industry. It is one of the core drivers for growth and differentiation. The high-touch nature of the function makes it expensive and impedes scalability. Customer service is also highly variable because of the differences in personalities, training, and experience of the agents. Variability drives errors and customer dissatisfaction, which in turn impacts business. Financial services industries have been innovating around their products and services, especially over the last two decades. This has caused additional pressure on the customer service function because of several factors, like training the agents on the new products and services, making them understand the complexity of the business, exposing them to the evolving regulatory environment, and preparing them appropriately for the increasingly global nature of the business. Because of these reasons, customer service as a function is a good candidate for transformation through AI. There are many applications of AI in customer service like chatbots, deep learning of customer and agent behaviors, predictive diagnostic of customer needs, AI-enabled RPA of routine functions, and other such similar functions.

Chatbots are software programs mimicking human interaction. We all have most likely used chatbots in some form already. The concept of chatbots traces back its roots to the 1950s when Alan Turing described what programs should be able to do to demonstrate human-like intelligence. The first chatbots ELIZA and PARRY are more than 50 years old. However, chatbots became more popular and mainstream only in the last five years, starting with Facebook releasing and promoting many of them from 2016 onward.

Chatbots in the financial services sectors are believed to have been first introduced in 2016 by Russia-based Tochka Bank. They launched it on Facebook for a range of financial services, including the possibility of making payments. Barclays Africa quickly followed it up with their chatbot app on Facebook in mid-2016. Since then, nearly all major banks in the world have their own branded chatbots. Bank of America has Erica, American Express has AmEx Chatbot, HDFC Bank from India has EVA, HSBC Bank has Amy, Société Générale has SoBo, Commonwealth Bank of Australia has Ceba, and the list goes on. Each of them offers slightly different functionality, but broadly all of them allow customers to check balances, make payments, activate cards, seek interest rates for different products, pay bills, get reports, etc. The chatbots also allow the institution to seek feedback from customers, suggest new products, and better understand their needs. Today, Bank of America is leading in the usage of chatbots in customer service. As of a year ago, Erica, the Bank of America chatbot, has more than 6 million monthly users, a number which has gone up significantly because of the higher use of remote banking as a result of the COVID-19 crisis. Banks are not the only financial services institutions implementing chatbots. Insurance and other financial services companies are doing the same. Allstate insurance has their chatbot ABie (pronounced as *abbie*), which helps agents quote new insurance policies to customers. In a few years, autonomous vehicles will completely change the landscape of auto insurance and this is driving the insurers to quickly get ready for the new realities.

Chatbots are evolving very rapidly in both their capabilities as well as application use-cases. They have started to handle more complex tasks than the simple routine ones that have been their domain so far. The sophistication of chatbots is being led by three major developments – more advanced algorithms from other domains that can do more complex processing, controlled natural language allowing better conversational intelligence, and merging of multiple AI capabilities beyond NLP and ML to create a more humanoid experience. Tools like DataChat that are based on controlled natural language take NLP interfaces like chatbots to the next level. HDFC Bank in India has done a pilot project called Humanoid Intelligent Robotic Assistant (IRA) as the first interface for customers when they visit branches. Popular messaging platforms like WeChat have implemented chatbot-assisted advanced capabilities to transform e-commerce in China. Better integration between intelligent voice-activated personal agents like Alexa and Google Home with the financial services industry platforms will further drive up the usage of chatbots.

The financial services institutions have a lot of information about their customers. They not only know about the movement of wealth in the customers' lives but also get exposed to a lot of major life events. If they stitch all of that together, they can predict the future needs of their customers and proactively approach them with customized solutions. In the past, this type of service was provided by your friendly neighborhood bank manager – she learns about your upcoming engagement and offers you home and car loans. Now, doing so on a one-to-one basis is not possible. But by synthesizing the data from different sources, including social media, AI programs can predict your needs and either directly create an outreach or prompt the bank staff for an outreach. This is akin to what is already happening in the retail industry, which we have previously discussed. Predictive diagnostics and outreach programs triggered by them can be the biggest driver of cross-selling and upselling. This is true both for an individual as well as institutional customers.

Process automation using AI and RPA is a compelling method to improve operational process efficiencies. For routine tasks, the software can understand the task, figure out the execution path, validate its legitimacy, execute it, and then finally close the loop with the customer, the bank, and the internal systems of the bank. AI will be more effective than humans in identifying anomalies and risks in the execution of the task, thus making it more effective. For example, AI will have a higher chance of identifying fraud as discussed above than humans. Many banks have run pilot projects in this type of application. For example, Bank of New York Mellon ran a pilot initiative a few years back and got some impressive results in their account closing process which traversed multiple systems. They recorded an 88% improvement in the processing time, 100% accuracy in the validation of closure, and 66% improvement in trade entry time. Similar implementation in the fund transfer process also led to significant savings and reduction of errors. Better process execution like these examples puts more money in the financial institution's bottom line, makes the customer happier and inclined to do more business with the institution, and improves the compliance.

Contract Management

Managing contracts is a constant yet complex activity in every aspect of the financial services industry, and that has been true forever. Each contract may have dozens of clauses and hundreds of scenarios when they might get invoked. While most of the financial instruments follow standard contract terms and conditions, there are specific nuances to how they are applied to every individual situation. Contracts can be hundreds of pages long and are often difficult to follow. At the time of sales, if the agent handling the sales process has customized any of the riders in the contract, the situation becomes even more challenging. Every time an individual or a financial institution needs to use the contract to adjudicate any claim or dispute, it becomes a complicated and sometimes contentious task. Adjudication of a contract is fraught with individual interpretations of the parties involved about the terms and arguing about evidence. This is very frequent in health insurance, auto insurance, and property and casualty insurance industry segments.

Even if there is no problem around the contract terms and conditions, managing the thousands of contract documents is an onerous task for the financial services companies. For example, JP Morgan Chase (JPMC), one of the largest financial institutions in the world, spent over 360,000 person-hours in 2017 to analyze just 12,000 commercial contracts. This is nearly a week per contract! Legal documents need to be analyzed and data captured for many reasons like estimating the risk exposure of the company, knowing trigger points for contract enforcement, and so on. While a major part of the 2008 housing bubble burst leading to the previous major global economic meltdown (before the COVID-19 one) is attributed to the greed of traders and executives in financial services companies who built and nurtured the subprime loans market, part of the problem is also attributed to lack of broader transparency around the contents of the tranches of subprime CDO instruments.

AI can help with managing and interpreting the contract documents. Traditionally, Optical Character Recognition (OCR) technology was used to read and digitize documents. OCR relies on specific matching techniques, so it can give very erroneous results when subjected to variations of font, size, dimensions, partial graphs, images, etc. Using AI techniques like ML and NLP allows the OCR to probabilistically and quickly ascertain the most likely interpretation of the document, thereby significantly improving the accuracy and reliability of OCR. Many companies have tried this and seen huge successes. JPMC implemented a chatbot program called Contract Intelligence (COiN) by which they were able to reduce the 360,000 hours spent on document analysis mentioned above to minutes. In another example, Citibank in its Treasure and Trade Solutions division was able to transform its letter-of-credit business line through the use of similar techniques. There are many AI algorithms for pattern recognition like Random Forest and Gradient Boosting that are very useful for such initiatives.

AI is also useful in putting the contract document together. Often people processing financial instruments and contracts for individual customers have to sift through a lot of different documents to get background information about the customer. This happens frequently because customers are given the choice of providing different types of documentation to substantiate some data such as identification or creditworthiness. Since they are issued by different agencies and the formats could vary based on location, managing the variations gets taxing. AI-augmented OCR can help solve this problem.

AI can help not only at an individual contract level but also at an aggregate level. By extracting, classifying, and cataloging the metadata from the contracts, you can identify new patterns about customer segmentation, salesperson efficiency or expertise in risk management, underwriting efficiency, and other operational parameters.

Underwriting

Underwriting has been at the core of risk management for the banking and insurance industries. For centuries, the process of underwriting has not evolved much; however, AI is changing that. Traditionally, the underwriters have to evaluate every situation and every instrument on a case-by-case basis. Therefore, historically, underwriting has been time-consuming and required a very high degree of specialized knowledge. This also leaves underwriting exposed to high degrees of variability because much is left to the interpretation of the underwriter. Underwriting involves a lot of unstructured and textual information analysis by the professionals to get a comprehensive perspective of the risk scenarios before they can apply their models. This makes the underwriting process further complicated and inefficient.

AI techniques, especially methods like machine learning and natural language understanding (NLU, a variant of natural language processing), are changing underwriting. NLU helps with the abstraction of relevant information from a vast database of unstructured data and machine learning helps with pattern recognition for risks. AI models will also help personalize and contextualize risks more accurately for different individual customers and what they are insuring. For example, today the risk and resulting premium for a property and casualty insurance for a home of a certain size and age in a certain area are the same for all homes qualifying with those criteria. However, the actual risk profile varies a lot based on the automation and early warning technologies in the home, its maintenance, usage by the owners or occupants, proximity to other high-risk things like large water bodies or trees, etc. AI will be able to create a unique digital twin of what is being insured and forecast its risk with high probability. AI will automate a lot of the repetitive manual tasks, bringing process efficiencies.

A better underwriting arising out of better estimation of the risk will potentially reduce the insurance premiums. This will benefit the customers and also help expand the industry.

Real-Time Risk Management

Underwriting is only half of the problem. The other half is actively managing the risk through the life of the instrument or the contract. The results of such monitoring can be used to update the risk models and the underwriting process for other contracts. The updated risk models can be used to dynamically update the premium of existing contracts, too. This is already happening to some degree in auto insurance as well as health insurance. Companies like State Farm and Allstate in the United States introduced such models more than five years back. They take telemetry data from the vehicle's onboard diagnostics and other data streams like traffic cameras, law enforcement databases for traffic violations, etc. to change insurance premiums. Similarly, health insurance companies are using data from wearables like Apple Watch and Fitbit to monitor the health and provide discounts or adjust premiums. Now there is a new possibility of synthesizing completely disparate data streams like health and driving data to create a more comprehensive profile. Mixed with other lifestyle data, this could take real-time risk management to higher level.

Sales Management

Like any other industry, the financial services industry has standard products and services that the various companies offer to their individual and institutional customers. However, there is one big difference. Sales in the financial services industry is a very contextual activity and very personal. Even though many people buy the same deposit scheme or the same stock or the same insurance, the circumstances under which they do that and their drivers for the purchase can be very different. Except for insurance, the type of instrument one chooses to transact in most cases is optional and discretionary. Since money is intensely personal, and a lot of an individual's esteem and future is tied to the financial choices they make, they prefer to make them with the people who seem to understand them the best and appreciate the situation the best, hence the earlier comment about sales being contextual. This makes the sales process very hard because people doing selling have very little time and very few tools to quickly gather information about their customers to understand their context and personalize the sales process. This is the fundamental reason why AI will transform the sales process in the financial services industry. Many financial institutions like Morgan Stanley with their Next Best Action platform have begun using AI to augment the knowledge and options available to the wealth advisors. They use algorithms to find the best possible investment opportunities meeting their customers' preferences by scanning the entire market.

Chatbots will be one of the most common tools employed in the sales process. There are pilot implementations already underway at many firms. Chatbots are also being increasingly used for lead generation in many industries, including financial services. When a customer approaches a company, say a bank, for some customer service, the chatbot upon completion of the service can use that opportunity to position some new related offering or get feedback that can be used to determine an appropriate offering.

Customer churn is a huge problem in the entire financial services industry. A 12–15% churn rate is sometimes considered low in this industry, which at times could be as high as 28–30%. Companies spend a fortune and go through unimaginable heroics to reduce customer churn. Poor customer service is often cited as the biggest contributor to churn, but there are other institutional reasons also. With increasing chatbots, the pressure on customer service agents will be reduced, allowing them to provide better quality service. Additionally, AI can help stitch together every individual customer's series of experiences and engagements with the company to predict his or her most likely probability of leaving the company. Research experiments and pilot projects have shown that by using AI algorithms like the *random forest method*, people have been able to predict churn with a greater than 90% accuracy. Now, if the company is armed with such insights, it can take proactive steps to reduce churn before it happens.

Credit risk scoring is a common step during most financial services sales. The traditional methods of credit scoring are very archaic as they are based on static rules. The heuristics approach cannot develop a holistic perspective of an individual's financial present and estimate the future. For example, if somebody does not have a steady salary, does not open new bank accounts or credit cards, or does not buy a new house, their credit score will most likely get diminished, ignoring the fact that the individual might be sitting on a pile of cash in fixed deposits and has invested in some startup companies that are growing very rapidly. AI will help create a more complete picture of a person's financial status by synthesizing data from multiple sources and forecasting future potential.

As a part of the sales process, Know Your Customer (KYC) documentation and activities is also an important step. We discussed the KYC documentation enablement using AI previously. Similar to credit risk scoring, AI can help create a holistic digital twin of every individual customer and prospect.

Loan Management

Loans are at the core of the financial services industry; that is how most of them make money outside of insurance. However, the loan administration process in many countries is very arduous. For example, in the United States, the average home loan processing time is 47 days. Over the years, this number has not changed much. Given that the total mortgage debt in the United States is nearly $10 trillion, any improvement in the loan processing time can help improve the throughput of this industry. Moreover, this is a huge inconvenience for the borrowers in addition to being an unnecessary expenditure.

A large part of the problem lies in the amount of documentation and processing, very similar to the problem faced during underwriting. This is something AI-enabled OCR and NLU/NLP techniques can help. AI can help identify process inefficiencies and bottlenecks to smoothen the process. AI can also help forecast future valuation and risks to bake them into the mortgage underwriting process. The January 2020 issue of *MReport* talks about Capture 2.0, a collection of broad-based AI techniques to transform the loan management process. Several banks and financial institutions are beginning to experiment with such technology.

Workforce Reformation

Finally, AI will transform the workforce capability and composition of the financial services industry. As we have discussed in this section, several manually intensive functions in the industry will be replaced by technology, leading to redundancies. While this will be compensated a bit by the increased demand in the technology companies serving the financial services industry, the overall workforce will come down. As per the CCAF-WEF study, the respondents estimated a net reduction of approximately 336,000 jobs in the financial services businesses slightly offset by an increase of 37,700 jobs in FinTechs. This workforce shift in turn will trigger many other changes – compensation, employee rights, education, and the nature of work itself in such companies.

 SUMMARY

AI will change the financial services industry and that transformation will happen faster than in most other industries, this much is clear. For this transformation to happen, there are a few hurdles that need to be crossed. Here are some of the nontechnical constraints that will shift in the next few years:

- **Regulatory environment.** This industry is very heavily regulated. Clear explainability and transparency in decision making is an underlying requirement of most regulatory drivers. As the technology and application of AI mature, there will be increased capability in the decision support systems to explain how and why AI programs arrived at a certain conclusion.
- **Increased compliance.** Globally, the financial services industry is under compliance pressure brought upon by the adventurism or corruption of a select few. The trend of tightening operating environments will continue in the future. AI will help alleviate some of the compliance problems.
- **Focus on the consumer.** Changing social and political landscape is shifting the power equation more toward the individual consumer and away from the big financial corporations. Big financial institutions now realize that there are several untapped opportunities if they creatively approach the customer. This phenomenon is also aided by increased awareness and proliferation of consumer technology in financial services. This shift will enable the development of personal financial cloud types of technologies.

■ **Further convergence and morphing of financial services.** Once upon a time, a bank used to be a depositor and a lender, a brokerage firm used to do trading, and likewise, every firm focused on its core competencies. For more than a decade now that is no longer true; now giants like JPMC and Bank of America get involved with everything. Even traditional financial instruments are giving way to a lot of new products and services. This type of convergence and morphing is greatly abetted by AI.

■ **Executive education.** Among all the different industry sectors, the leaders of financial services businesses have taken the lead in educating themselves and their staff on the technology and opportunities around AI. This is true from China to the United States and every country in between. A career banker like Jamie Dimon, CEO of JPMC, is as articulate about AI and digital technologies as the CEOs of leading technology companies. Increasing education will drive increased activity and benefits, creating a virtuous cycle.

There are still several issues around ethics, privacy, and security that need to be resolved before the adoption of AI becomes more mainstream in the financial services sector. We will discuss that more in an upcoming chapter. The technology and application of algorithms also have some way to go, but the gaps are getting filled very quickly.

However, as we have discussed in this chapter, several areas within the financial services spectrum will be significantly impacted by AI in the coming years. Figure 7.1 is a recap of those nine areas.

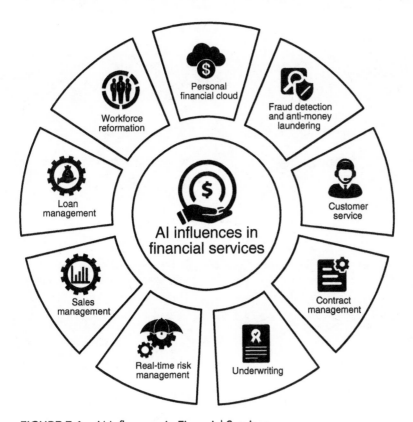

FIGURE 7.1 AI Influences in Financial Services

These are exciting times for both the financial services industry and its beneficiaries. AI will help us reach the next frontier of possibilities for this industry.

 REFERENCES

(1) "What Percentage of the Global Economy Is the Financial Services Sector?"; Sean Ross; February 2020.
(2) "Transforming Paradigms: A Global AI in Financial Services Survey"; Cambridge Centre for Alternative Finance (CCAF) and the World Economic Forum (WEF); January 2020.

CHAPTER 8

Transforming the Built Environment with AI

"A great building must begin with the unmeasurable, must go through measurable means when it is being designed and, in the end, must be unmeasurable."

—Louis Kahn

INTRODUCTION

Visionary American architect Louis Kahn (1901–1974) said the above in 1930 while talking about design. What he said about design is true for every aspect of a built environment. As businesses and institutions go through their digital transformation, there is an increasing realization that their facilities play a pivotal role in this transformation journey. Businesses and institutions are defined by their mission, strategy, operating model, and people. Each business and each institution has a mission that is enabled, augmented, and executed by its workforce, operating in its workspaces, through its workflows. They all come together in a building. Therefore, the digital transformation of buildings becomes a critical component of the digital transformation agenda of any organization. Citizens' experiences and city-scale decision making is also being rapidly impacted by design, data, and digital technologies.

These changes are driving significant economic opportunities. The size of the smart workplace market by 2023 is estimated to be $47 billion as per a recent McKinsey study. The global smart cities market is expected to be over $230 billion in the next five years. According to Navigant, which has a similar take on the market, the intelligent building solutions market will grow at a CAGR of 16% and reach a size of over $100 billion by 2030.

The overall industry size is huge and the possibilities of disruption can become bigger than some of the numbers quoted. Globally, the construction industry is about $10 trillion and contributes 13% of the world's GDP. This is a slow-moving and change-resistant industry. As per a McKinsey study of the sector, productivity in the industry has been going down, and currently, that impact stands at $1.6 trillion. If we just consider the different products and technologies that go into buildings, that market size is more than $500 billion. So we have a lot of opportunities to make a difference with AI and some of the more recent digital technologies.

Buildings today are complex technology ecosystems and a key enabler for businesses and institutions to achieve their goals. The growth of connected endpoints has reached an inflection point of exponential growth in both homes and buildings, a trend that extends seamlessly into enterprises and cities. The last two years have been pivotal in that transition. A new phase of digitization is taking off in the buildings sector as providers adopt new generations of IoT-enabled technologies, mobile-based solutions, and software powered by more advanced analytics.

The current improvements in the Internet of Things (IoT) technologies are redefining how building management is perceived and executed. Different building domains like HVAC, fire, security, and lighting, which historically evolved in silos due to specialized networks, bandwidth constraints, procurement cycles, and functional separations, are now being evaluated for convergence to create better outcomes and experiences for building operators and occupants. Building automation and management are now being reshaped by new digital technologies and the power of data analytics. This combined with a rich and diverse set of intelligent equipment, rapid strides in standard communication protocols, and a demand for future-proof infrastructure has led businesses across industries to consider and/or pursue a digital transformation of their built environment.

The business value created by the use of digital technologies and AI is undeniable. Let us illustrate this with an example of a very large global technology company, let's call it X Co. X Co's commercial mission relies on efficient and expedient product development and customer service to meet the demands of today's digital world. X Co has about 300 facilities collectively representing 20+ million square feet globally, many of which are over 30 years old. Last year they spent $500+ million on operating these facilities. There is an opportunity to save over $30 million in utilities and maintenance spend while saving another nearly $90 million through better space utilization. This is achieved by eliminating the variations in the operating envelopes of the various buildings and using the best cost operation as a benchmark and transferring those best practices to 70% of the facilities. X Co has a gap in their expected versus actual average revenue per employee, which they believe can be bridged through higher productivity. Their modest goal is to improve revenue realization per employee by $1,000 per annum; this represents $1 billion in income improvements across their 100,000 employee base. By synthesizing data from multiple different building systems and sensors, identifying improvement opportunities through analytics, and closing the loop with actionable insights flowed back into the sensors and system, one can achieve the operating cost improvements. By understanding the usage of space, flow of people, and working behaviors of employees, space utilization can be optimized. Employee productivity can be impacted by creating a more engaging and inviting workplace that drives collaboration and allows people more focus on jobs to be done. This can be done through the use of workplace design and personalized technology that allows employees to manage their environment, find various services and utilities in the facility, find and collaborate with colleagues, with individuals tracking personal activities, and be more engaged with the spaces and events in those spaces. In several pilot projects at similar facilities, we have seen 20% uptake on productivity, a significant reduction in attrition, a huge jump in innovation, reduction in space requirements, reduction in energy consumption, and many other benefits. In every business in every facility we can find such opportunities to improve the business outcome and results.

Digital technologies have the potential to bring major efficiency improvements to this labor-intensive sector and help revive business models that are coming under pressure. As the role of digital buildings gets redefined and more intertwined with that of the smart enterprise and smart cities, new possibilities and requirements open up.

UNDERSTANDING WHY THE BUILT ENVIRONMENT IS CHANGING

Even though the building and construction industry has been slow to change and adopt technology, several factors are forcing it to change now. Let us investigate some of them here.

A Better Tie-in with the Mission of the Business

Each business has a very specific mission and faces some unique challenges in pursuit of that mission. The mission of the building has to support the mission of the businesses. More and more business leaders have begun to realize this and are requiring the actions in support of this alignment from their building managers.

In one of our earlier chapters on how AI will transform the retail industry, we talked about the very competitive and high-pressure landscape in which the industry has to operate. McKinsey Global Institute did a study on how new disruptions will impact the economic performance of the sector. We have discussed them in the chapter. According to that study, nearly $30–$80 billion out of $410 billion to $1.2 trillion of economic impact by 2025 will be caused by advancements in building technologies, namely around energy management and condition-based maintenance. This is based on a 20% improvement in the $250 billion annual energy spend by retail outlets and impacting the $490 billion maintenance-repair-replacement spend by 10–40% cost reduction, 3–5% extended asset life, and 50% reduction of downtime. In an adjacent space, layout optimization of stores is viewed as the third-largest contributor to improving operating costs by $79–$158 billion through a 5% improvement in the $6 trillion operating costs of the stores. This is one example of how buildings support the commercial mission of increasing profit envelops of the already tightly squeezed retail industry.

In another example, let us consider hospitals and healthcare facilities that we discussed in one of the earlier chapters as well. The mission of healthcare organizations is to provide quality care to patients that leads to well-being and/or recovery. Critical stakeholders include patients and their families, healthcare professionals, healthcare administrators, insurance companies, and federal and state governments. The addressable components of this mission are improved patient health outcomes, increased physician and nurse productivity, increased customer (i.e., patient and family) satisfaction, and intelligent asset tracking and management. Figure 8.1 is a quick snapshot of how these mission components can be achieved and what some of the hospital facility managers say about these topics.

In another example, the mission of technology and engineering companies is to help customers with new products and solutions to be more effective in their core businesses. By creating

Mission Elements	Potential Systems-Enabled Activities	Commentary
Improved patient health outcomes	• Granular control of temperature settings to adjust hospital room environment to case specific needs • Optimized lighting in exam and operating rooms and medicine stations to minimize human error	• *"Smart systems... should also help patients get better faster. The adjustment of controls is a focus for the hospital in order to sustain and improve outcomes. It's easier to identify what surroundings a patient might need to achieve their outcomes with sensors"* – Senior Consultant, Healthcare Facilities Planning Firm
Increased physician and nurse productivity	• Proactive exam/operating room preparation to deliver ideal work environment immediately upon patient and physician/nurse arrival • Physician/nurse location tracking to page closest available professional in emergency situations	• *"You want the fire station communications, overhead paging, and others all connected. You want the lights to go on when a patient is in distress and for other systems to alert"* – Director of Facilities Management, Hospital
Increased customer (i.e., patient and family) satisfaction	• Patient/family control (or perception thereof) of hospital or exam room temperature, lighting, entertainment • Increased remote communication between patients/families and health care professionals	• *"Patient experience is going to be a big driver. Their comfort, their education, and their entertainment are going to be connected. Those are the reasons why they are there. That is part of the hospital performance and the bottom line"* – Director of Facilities Management, Hospital
Intelligent asset tracking and management	• Ability to more easily locate and optimize placement of tools and equipment for medical procedures	• *"You can use the building systems to streamline patient care by tracking location of the patients themselves and also of the devices doctors need to use"* – Senior Consultant, Healthcare Facilities Planning Firm

FIGURE 8.1 Healthcare Mission and Building Systems

new and better products faster, with better features, better support, and more inexpensively, such companies further their commercial interests. They can do so if their employees are more productive. The workplace-built environment has a big role to play in improving such productivity as we shall see later in this chapter. We gave an example in this context in the introduction to this chapter.

On similar lines, we will find example after example in every industry segment of how the built environment accentuates the mission of the business. This realization is driving new expectations and thereby new changes in the built environment.

Technical Complexity and Serviceability

Today, there is a tremendous amount of technology and complexity involved in managing the built environment. Let us take an example of an average building about 10,000 square meters or about 100,000 square feet. This building is likely to have about 100 meters and sensors. If designed well to optimally use most available technology, this building is likely to have more than 50 subsystems. There will be more than 100 variations of the data captured by these systems because markets differ, usages of buildings differ, technologies used in those subsystems differ, the ways they are designed and installed differ, and so on. Between these various subsystems, in this building, close to half a million sample data points are captured every day; annually this leads to more than 10 gigabytes of data. If you have the data from a few hundred average-sized buildings like the one we discussed just now, in a year it will have generated more than the entire data generated by all the users doing "Likes" in Facebook for the same entire year; this is how enormous the data from buildings is. However, there is a problem with the data. On average at least 5% of the data collected is unreliable; this happens because of network communication issues, sensor accuracy, or other reasons.

The equipment and systems in buildings may have a life of 10–15 years compared to double the time the average building survives without major reconstruction. Diversity of usage and occupancy, the evolution of technology, and changing external factors (such as weather) means that customer expectations are always evolving. With occupants and running business, complete shutdown and repair/replacement is a rare event. There is always a mix of systems, suppliers, and protocols in buildings. A single building may have systems from 30+ suppliers and 10+ protocols. So service and upgrades are rarely isolated and immune to cascading impact. Regulations and building codes change over time. Consistent drive to reduce energy consumption, carbon emission and cost, equipment service, and optimization is an ongoing activity.

People managing buildings have a very challenging job. They have many different stakeholders to satisfy. Occupants want comfort and safety. If something goes wrong, the occupants want the issues to be responded to very quickly. They also do not want to be impacted by any building improvement projects. The service team has to address all the complaints from occupants, ensure all the equipment and systems in the building are working fine, find capable people to maintain the occupants, and do all this within limited budgets. The executive team, on the other hand, is looking at how best to extend the asset life and the value of the property. They are also looking at reducing the operating cost of the building, which includes the energy costs. These sometimes require initiating improvements that the facility service team does not have the bandwidth to deal with and occupants do not have the time to be interrupted with. The suppliers and the contractors on one hand struggle to keep up with spare parts and maintenance activities, and on the other hand try to keep up with finding qualified resources to support the building manager.

There are many models on how building systems and equipment have been maintained historically. These usually revolve around ensuring the equipment and systems keep up their expected performance. All of these models are generally human-intensive. Given the multitude of systems and interdependencies involved, maintenance becomes very complex. The way we maintain building systems today has several limitations. Isolated equipment optimization does not necessarily provide system-wide benefit. Inability to correlate tons of historic data with real-time/near-real-time data has meant that corrective actions might not be entirely accurate. Change in building usage (e.g. warehouse vs. commercial office) has meant that existing systems have to be almost fully redesigned or replaced. Changing government regulations usually drive stopgap corrective actions rather than top-down system-level optimization.

Demographic Changes and Occupant Expectations

Millennials are becoming the dominant segment of the workforce in most countries and they are already a majority in many. This generation has grown up as digital natives. Their workstyles are more flexible. Having been exposed to mobile devices from a very young age and being able to control different aspects of their lives using such devices, this generation expects similar capabilities in their workplace as well. They want to be able to interact with and control their environment, find services in the workplace, collaborate with colleagues, and find their way around. The work environment matters as much to them as the work content. According to Dell, 82% of Millennial employees may change their employment if they are not satisfied with the workplace.

Not tied specifically to any age-group, there is an increasing trend of remote working. This trend was generally higher in developed economies like the United States (25%) or the UK (43%). The recent COVID-19 health crisis has amplified the need and possibility of remote working even more and has made this a global phenomenon. When more and more people are working remotely, it has a very different implication both for workplace design as well as how the buildings are managed. Sensor technology plays a critical role in understanding space utilization and workspace booking. But we will need more advanced analytics, ideally AI-enabled, to understand the patterns of usage of workspaces so that the rest of the building systems can be tuned for optimal performance.

Asset Value and Operating Costs

The spending on the built environment is substantial. For example, in the United States, in 2015, the GDP was $18.225 trillion. Out of that, about $1.4 trillion or 7.7% was spent on nonresidential commercial buildings. Nearly a trillion dollars of that was spent on maintenance, repair, and related capital expenditures. The graphs in Figure 8.2 show a breakdown of these spend items and the shaded spend categories are ones that are addressable through technology.

Companies are always trying to reduce their cost base and therefore building managers have to always operate under a constrained environment. As economies and businesses come

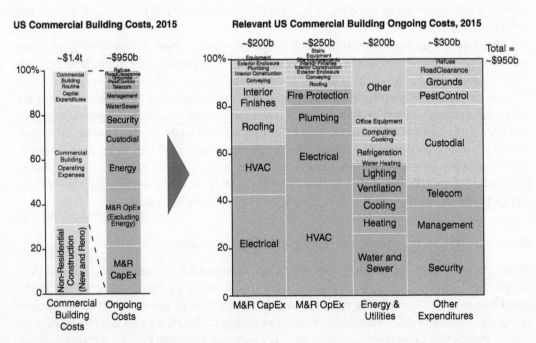

FIGURE 8.2 US Building Spend in 2015

under fiscal pressure, they look at all possible options to reduce spend. In the last decade, we have seen a tumultuous economic environment around the world. Because of the current COVID-19 crisis, we foresee the global economy will be very distressed. So, there will be a natural pressure for businesses to reduce the spending on the built environment. This will accelerate the usage of affordable yet effective technologies in the built environment.

Policy Influences

Depleting energy resources, rising cost of energy, and the threat of climate change has elevated energy concerns into a global imperative. In the context of modern-day national imperatives, effective energy management has become a strategic value, with the changing world economic and ecological variables influencing business in more ways than understood in the past.

According to the International Energy Agency, buildings contribute more than 30% of the world's energy consumption. This is higher than in most other sectors. In more developed countries, this percentage is higher. This problem is going to become more acute with increased urbanization. The urban population grew from 746M in 1950 to 3.9B in 2014 and is expected to surpass 6B by 2045. In 1990, the world had only 10 megacities, cities with a population of more than 10 million inhabitants. In 2014, this number was 28 and by 2030 we expect more than 41 such megacities; these statistics are as per a UN study. Just three countries – India, China, and Nigeria – will account for 37% of the projected growth in the urban population between 2014 and 2050. With depleting energy resources globally, there is a strong focus on reducing energy consumption in almost every sector, including buildings. Buildings also waste a lot, nearly 30% of the energy they consume. This makes the need for energy consumption even more acute.

Around the world, multiple national and regional "energy efficiency" policies have sprung up, and many more are in the process of being formulated. Table 8.1 captures some of the prominent ones.

Many of these policy influences have a straight correlation with the built environment and consequently drive changes in building construction, maintenance, and technologies.

The other major policy influence is from the General Data Protection Regulation (GDPR), a new European Union (EU) law introduced in May 2018. This law governs how personally identifiable information (PII) is managed and covers any system that is collecting PII. It gives individuals more control over their personal information. These data protection standards pertain to any information that can, directly or indirectly, identify a living person (e.g. a name, email address, ID number, geolocation information, or picture). While the law applies to the EU, it extends to any business or any geography that had a presence in the EU or has people from the EU. Therefore most of the global companies are implementing provisions of GDPR. Failure to comply invites heavy fines – up to 4% of a business's annual revenue for the prior year or $20M, whichever is greater.

Buildings today are rich with technology and data. A lot of this data is connected with individuals and qualifies as per the types of data mentioned above. Consequently, many building systems like surveillance systems, or security systems, or even building control systems that interact with occupant-facing systems have to adapt to these new regulations.

TABLE 8.1 Policy Influences for Energy Management

Type of Instrument	Policy Instrument	Definition	Examples
Legislative Instruments	Laws and regulations	Law: legal rules that govern a specific action, process, product, etc.	New Zealand's Minimum Energy Performance Standards (MEPS); India's Energy Conservation Act
		Regulation: outlines how the law should be implemented	
	Standards	Provide technical and design guidance notes (e.g. for equipment)	BEE Star Rating for Electronic Appliances
	Codes of practice	Give practical advice/guidance on how to comply with legislation (e.g. Building Code)	US Green Building Code – LEED (Leadership in Energy and Environment Design)
Economic Instruments	Fiscal	Taxes, fees, charges levied on producers and consumers	Denmark Carbon Dioxide Act
	Subsidies	Grants, soft loans, tax allowances	New York State Energy Research and Development Authority rebate program
	Property and tradable rights	Licenses, rights (e.g. water, emissions)	
	Bonds & deposit funds	Money returned when environmental behavior is met	UK Carbon Reduction Commitment (CRC)
Voluntary Instruments	Voluntary agreements	Commitment from business to protect the environment	Sustainability commitments of business organizations
	Programs & projects	To increase awareness, skills, and knowledge	For example, voluntary information, demonstration projects
	Research & Development	New technologies, processes, products	

DEFINING A DIGITAL BUILDING

To understand the current state of technologies in a building, we need to first appreciate the evolution of data in managing building operations. This concept was shared by Sudhi in his 2014 article, "A Roadmap to the Internet of Buildings," in *Greenbiz*. (See Figure 8.3.)

Horizon 1

Till the late 1960s, most of the control activities in a building were manually managed. There was very little data stored or processed outside of standard logbooks. The building technician was the primary action owner, and decisions were made based on standard practices, experience, and intuition, though not necessarily in that order.

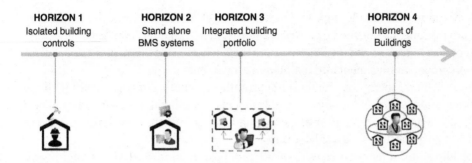

FIGURE 8.3   Evolution of Data and Technologies in Buildings

Horizon 2

Since the 1980s, with the advent of computers, digital controls started to be introduced into building controls. This led to the advent of the building management systems, which meant that while there was greater automation in building operations, a large variety of data was also stored in system archives. The value of data analytics was, however, still not fully realized due to issues with integrating data from multiple systems, access to fast and effective analytical tools, and concerns for data fidelity. Buildings were therefore still managed primarily by a dedicated building manager.

Horizon 3

Changing building landscape, enhanced automation and control techniques, and the need for greater standardization in operations led to portfolio-managed scenarios. This meant that a greater area was now possible to be managed by building management personnel, leading to increased levels of "datafication." Data was now recorded from multiple systems throughout the portfolio – providing simple opportunities for optimization through internal benchmarking. The focus then shifted to identifying patterns in energy consumption in buildings and driving initiatives to manage such consumption. Data started to become the primary catalyst for actions in a building. However, we were still limited by technical constraints around what type of data could be used and how much of it could be leveraged.

Horizon 4

We are now in the era of digital buildings.

The concept of smart buildings has been around for some time now. The era of smart buildings was largely driven through automation. According to the definition by the Intelligent Buildings Institute (IBI) in the United States, an "intelligent building is one that provides a productive and cost-effective environment through optimization of its four basic components – structure, systems, services, and management – and the interrelationships between them." The definition by European Intelligent Building Group (EIBG) further classifies an intelligent building as one that "incorporates the best available concepts, materials, systems, and technologies, integrating these to achieve a building which meets or exceeds the performance requirements of the building stakeholders." Based on these definitions, the use of advanced technologies is a key component and enabler of the improved performance of buildings. However, technology and systems are just one part of the larger building ecosystem. Buildings can be designed and built for high performance and energy efficiency, but such advanced technologies can be all for naught without proper management and maintenance over time.

But building owners, operators, and most importantly occupants are not satisfied with the benefits of automation – they want more. There is a demand for buildings now to be enabled with pervasive digital technologies and leverage data emanating from them to change outcomes and experiences for the various stakeholder groups.

Digital buildings are integrated ecosystems of architecture, design, systems, and operations that deliver tangible value and aspirations of the occupants, operators, and owners. Many new digital technologies are impacting buildings – IoT, cloud computing, graph databases, new communication methodologies like 5G and NB IoT, AI and natural language processing, distributed ledger authentication, mixed-reality immersive experience systems, multi-agent systems, and others that are fast impacting how building sensors and systems work. As a collective, they define the new world of digital technologies with very transformative capabilities.

There are five contributing factors to why the building industry has started focusing on data and digital technologies recently:

1. It was very difficult, slow, and expensive to collect and store all the data for meaningful analytics.
2. Popular technology choices required large volumes of structured, normalized, and error-free data. The diversity of buildings, subsystems in buildings, and usage make such an effort monumental.
3. Building data has too much variation and too many reliability issues, causing data to lose usability and normal analytics to report too many exceptions.
4. Not all building-related information is available in a digital data format. Paper records can be scanned and converted to digital formats, but converting them into data formats has been quite challenging without enabling technologies.
5. In the absence of more robust commercial models, high-volume performance data from buildings and subsystems was used for alarms and event management, relegating the data to play a more operationally supportive role.

We should keep in mind that the concept of IoT is not new to the building industry. Building automation systems have been making sense of sensor data and driving control actions for decades now. But the new IoT capabilities around miniaturization of electronics to enable data communication and cloud connectivity for mechatronic devices are enabling greater leverage of sensor data in system optimization and energy efficiency.

Big data technologies are enabling us to capture data from different sources, in diverse formats, and with varying contexts. From being a catalyst, data is now becoming a driver of actions. Less human effort is required to manage even though the complexity around data has increased massively. We will see interoperability and seamless data interchange among:

a. Various subsystems in a building
b. Buildings and external utilities (such as smart grids or smart cities

c. Networks of buildings
d. The larger ecosystem of smart equipment
e. Increased interface with building stakeholders
 A digital building will mirror the attributes and behaviors of an intelligent living organism.

HOW AI WILL CHANGE THE BUILT ENVIRONMENT OF THE FUTURE

AI is starting to flourish and making a breakthrough in the building industry. It is transforming the energy and building industries with intelligent solutions that can make buildings more intelligent, safe, energy-efficient, and environmentally sustainable, and can improve the comfort, wellness, and productivity of building occupants. In this section, we will talk about the major areas of the built environment where AI will make a substantial impact.

AI-Driven Adaptive Buildings

Buildings are like living, breathing entities that operate in a very dynamic environment. New digital technologies and analytical capabilities, including AI, allow the management of this type of changing environment to make buildings more adaptive and self-learning. The objective is to reduce operating costs, improve asset value, including brand recognition, and most importantly enhance the productivity of people and assets. The AI-powered buildings are self-conscious and self-healing.

Self-Conscious Buildings

Imagine your building recognizes that you are entering it and starts talking to you. When you need assistance, the building understands your needs and helps you work faster, safer, and with greater ease. Imagine a digital assistant that can talk to other digital agents, such as a conference room agent to schedule a meeting room, send meeting invitations to others, and share the agenda with others. Imagine the conference room agent starts the audiovisual systems, starts the conference bridge, and makes the presentation ready before a meeting starts.

Your personal agent could announce your arrival at the main entrance before you arrive. Door access control agents could announce you as being on time or late arrival for a meeting. Meeting room agents could take attendance and estimate the arrival time of attendees who are running late. This all could happen in a completely autonomous fashion with contemporary digital technologies that are available in the marketplace today.

Your digital assistants have capabilities beyond simple chatbots or digital record-keepers; they are goal-oriented intelligent software agents that can develop a plan to solve a problem while optimizing tasks that matter to you. For example, a security digital assistant will make continuous interactions and negotiations with the smart environment to obtain privileges to access enterprise resources. They are the ultimate version of digital twins for smart environments and are the foundation for the highly personalized self-conscious socially oriented environment.

The benefits of the described smart environment span the building and include multi-system integration, smart meeting rooms, advanced access management, smart parking, digital signage, smart space for productivity, driverless electric vehicles, enhanced restaurant experience, advanced safety and security, comprehensive applications for employees, visitors and facilities managers, and a modernized document management system.

Self-Healing Buildings

Imagine air handling units, controllers, sensors, and actuators are automatically discovered and paired, configured, and integrated into the building's automation system. The system strives to achieve the plug-and-play paradigm in a way such that all building subsystems shall automatically be configured and integrated into a building control network (BCN). This means both connectivity establishment and download of configuration parameters are software-driven.

When a device is introduced into the BCN and powered on, it is immediately recognized and registered by the network. The neighboring devices then automatically adjust their technical and control parameters to provide the required coverage and capacity and at the same time avoid interference with other devices on the BCN. The sequence of operations shall be suggested, refined, developed, and commissioned through spoken language–based conversations among the owner, technician, and intelligent software agents (e.g. the sequence of operation recommendation agents).

Every controller contains hundreds of configuration parameters that control various aspects of buildings. Each of these can be altered to change BCN behavior based on observations of both the building management controller itself and measurements at the field devices or networked sensors. One of the first self-organizing building control network features establishes neighbor relations automatically (ANR) while others optimize the sequence of operations to meet a set of optimization goals.

A very illustrative self-optimization use-case is the automatic switch-off of a percentage of cold air supplied during the night hours or unoccupied hours in the summer (fans go into sleep mode when the building is unoccupied). The neighboring control system would then reconfigure the parameters to keep the entire area covered by the air supply. In case of sudden growth in cold-air demand for any reason, the sleeping fans wake up almost instantaneously. These sequences of operations for optimization can be learned and selected through advanced machine learning and intelligent software agents.

The smart connected HVAC devices (or subcomponents) can report their failures through the agreed messaging mechanism. These failure notifications will be seen as the physical world changes to other systems and subsystems. For example, we may have two air-supply fans associated with conference room B. One of the fans reports a motor failure, then another fan may increase fan speed to supply sufficient cold or hot air to meet a goal (e.g. conference room B's temperature should be 24 degrees Celsius). This is called a self-healing mechanism aimed at reducing the impacts from the failure, for example, by adjusting parameters and algorithms in neighboring controllers so that other nodes can support the areas that were supported by the failing node. When a paired temperature sensor has failed, using neighboring sensor values would be a better approach than simply doing nothing or reporting it.

The corrective action is made by a fan controller software, not a centralized building automation system. An intelligent fan control software will consider "What will happen if I do such-and-such?" and "Will that achieve my goals?" These corrective actions can be learned through various learning approaches such as deep reinforcement learning.

The idea of a self-conscious and self-healing building seems a bit farfetched, but in reality this is here and now. Bee'ah is a company that has pulled the future of AI in buildings forward through its new global HQ. This is the first building with intelligent agents for everyone, every place, and all assets. This is also the first building with a semantic knowledge graph and common building data model that enables Azure Digital Twin to replicate Bee'ah's physical world by modeling the relationships among people, places, and devices. This enables unique experiences by correlating data across the digital and physical worlds. The innovative building allows natural user interactions with building subsystems (e.g., texting, voice). Every Bee'ah employee has their own Personal Virtual Digital Assistant. They have a single point of access to all building-related services, leveraging state-of-the-art technologies like facial recognition and robotics. Bee'ah can provide a uniquely integrated ambient experience to all its employees, driving higher productivity and better engagement. Bee'ah HQ's AI-powered self-healing mechanism aims at reducing the impacts from the failure, for example, by adjusting parameters and algorithms in neighboring controllers so that other nodes can support the areas that were supported by the failing node.

Occupant Productivity

According to a 2013 World Green Building Council report, the built environment has a big role to play in employee productivity. According to the report, the following levers impact individual productivity:

- Individual temperature control: +3%
- Improved ventilation: +11%
- Better lighting: +23%
- Access to the natural environment: +18%

In 2016, Facilities Management market leader Jones LaSalle Lang (JLL) introduced the 3-30-300 model to spend in real-estate. According to this model, it is estimated that per square foot of space, companies spend $3 in energy, $30 in utilities, and $300 in employee cost. This was meant to be a rule-of-thumb calculation with regional and building usage variations. Since then, the focus on using smart technologies has shifted from reducing the operating cost to improving employee productivity. Most business owners and building managers have implemented initiatives to improve the built environment to boost productivity. But their efficacy has been limited. In a study conducted by workplace analytics and research firm Leesman, 43% of the 250,000 surveyed employees of various corporations across 67 countries reported that their workplace environment does not help them be more productive.

In the last few years, we have seen several applications come up that address the abovementioned dimensions of productivity, but they all had limited success. More recently, we are seeing AI helping improve productivity solutions. One such area of involvement for AI is enabling frictionless experiences.

Frictionless Experiences

Building occupants have to interface with different kinds of building systems and services a lot through the course of their day. A large portion of these interactions is cumbersome, disconnected, and discordant. Whether it is organizing a meeting or getting food from the cafeteria, we end up wasting time in these routine tasks where there is little need for human ingenuity. Such wastage and friction defocus us from the jobs to be done, thus impacting our productivity. AI can enable frictionless experiences to address this problem. Let us use an example of frictionless meetings to explain this.

The future meeting room is intelligent and has a persona to serve the purpose of the space. Each meeting room will have a unique identity, AI-enabled assistance for automated optimal reservation, distribution, and preparation of meeting notes via a conversation with agents. Face and voice recognition can identify the speaker to create an interactive and immersive meeting experience. Your digital assistants have capabilities beyond simple chatbots or digital record-keepers; they are goal-oriented, intelligent software agents that can develop a plan to solve a problem while optimizing tasks that matter to you.

Imagine a digital assistant that can talk to a conference room agent to schedule a meeting room, send meeting invites, and share the agenda with a PowerPoint presentation on your behalf. Imagine the conference room agent starts the audiovisual systems, starts the conference bridge, and prepares the presentation before a meeting starts.

Agents could announce your arrival at the main entrance five minutes before the meeting time to a door access control agent, which can transmit your potential 10-minutes-late arrival for the meeting to a meeting room agent. If you are delayed in the parking lot, the people in the meeting room are informed about it while the door access agent can anticipate your arrival and obtain necessary authentication information about you and provide validation processes to allow the door access. These scenarios could happen completely autonomously with contemporary digital technologies.

Some of the use-cases for a smart meeting experience are:

- As a facility manager, predetermine what meeting style is most useful for which project team – standing vs. seated.
- As a facility manager, I want to understand meeting room utilization to better plan space.
- As a facility manager, I want to know when I need to repair and replace equipment.
- As a facility manager, I want to know when I need to refill supplies to the meeting room (e.g. batteries).
- As a meeting organizer, I can initiate video/audio recording with a meeting room agent.
- As a meeting organizer, I can request the distribution of recorded meeting notes to the target distribution list.
- As a presenter, I don't need to wire the screen.
- As a meeting participant, I want to know directions on how I can get to the conference room.
- As a meeting participant, I want to feel comfortable and productive in a meeting.

The dozens of tasks that we perform every day in conjunction with the systems in the workplace can similarly be converted into frictionless experiences.

Another big driver for frictionless experiences is eliminating hardware and networking costs. Frictionless access control is a good example of that. In this method, we use cameras from the surveillance system to replace large parts of the traditional access control. The camera recognizes the individual, validates her face with that of employees or registered visitors, cross-checks against the access rights, and then grants access. Not only does this method make the process faster and much less intrusive, but it also increases the level of security compliance because now nobody can move around with somebody else's physical access card. The system automatically identifies areas of congregation in violation of preset policies and alerts the security staff. In implementing frictionless access control, the entire cost for access controller hardware, card readers, and other sensors and the associated networking costs are eliminated. The AI-based cyber-physical alert system will better identify and manage abnormal patterns of employee movement and presence.

Predictive and Remote Maintenance

Historically, operating and managing buildings has been a very labor-intensive process requiring very specialized knowledge. In a recent Verdantix survey of building owners and operators, respondents identified labor efficiency as the number of goals for digital technologies in the buildings. They also expressed a desire for 20% reduction in work content through more intelligent automation; 15% reduction in energy and maintenance management through remote diagnostics, analytics, and predictive technologies; and 30% improvement in space management among other goals around business outcomes, employee experiences, and social impact.

Managing buildings is very expensive, too. For a 15-story-high, 250,000-square-foot building in a major metropolitan city such as Chicago or New York, over its 50-year life, nearly $150 million will be spent in total maintenance and repair. This building would have cost between $3.5 and $5 million during the initial construction phase. Nearly $100 billion is spent annually on building maintenance and repair in the United States.

Managing buildings is founded on the inherent predictability of a building's state once the relevant causal variables are known. In general, one can predict the future state of a building given the current state, controllable actions to steer the state to a desired one, and external disturbances. AI allows us to capture the variables, build the understanding, and derive the desired actions to achieve the objectives. AI adapts to the constantly evolving nature of the building and its ecosystem and is the mainstay of an effective digital transformation. Taking an AI-centric approach to building maintenance is better because as the environment, condition of assets, usage of spaces and assets, and other parameters of a building's operation change, AI can find new boundary conditions for optimal frontier which are never captured in a more heuristic approach.

Predictive maintenance requires an integrated approach that enables collecting sensor data from a lot of devices and equipment to drive comprehensive improvement actions in buildings. The data requirements for such a maintenance regime include operational data from different building systems and devices, data from various IT systems about the products and services performed on them, fault data, environment data, and depending on the system, there could be many other types of data required.

AI-enabled predictive maintenance pays for itself. In the building example quoted above, the estimated maintenance and repair spend will be about $35 million out of the total $150 million. Through simulations, we have seen that 13% of this cost can be saved by using AI to move into a more proactive condition-based maintenance regime. For building equipment and systems, in fact for the entire building as a whole, more issues and thereby more spend

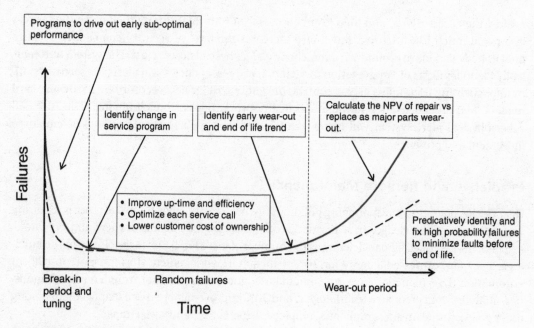

FIGURE 8.4   Impact of Predictive Maintenance

happen in the early days during construction and then again toward the later years. Using AI to drive predictive maintenance also reduces failures, improves asset reliability, and contributes to better operational efficiency. In Figure 8.4 we can see how using AI flattens the curve of failures over time.

The building maintenance industry is also facing a severe talent shortage globally. In the matured economies with older building stock and a lot of technical debt, there is an aging technician population with very few Millennials joining the trade. In some of the more emerging economies with newer and rapidly growing building stock, there is a general lack of maintenance technicians because most of the qualified technical people purpose careers in other disciplines. So technology is the only answer to solve the skill and capacity issues.

AI-enabled mixed-reality (MR) systems like augmented reality and virtual reality are helping address this issue. Connected assets communicate the condition and issues, MR sensors are used to further investigate and analyze the problem, and then advanced algorithms recommend the fix or intervention. This way very experienced technicians do not have to be deployed onsite where less-skilled people can be remotely enabled to perform most if not all of the functions. Many building technology companies have already deployed this on a massive scale. Schindler and Thyssenkrupp have been the leaders in this space.

AI also helps with knowledge management in maintenance. While there are a lot of available knowledge items for maintaining buildings and different systems therein, they are in a different multimedia format and usually unstructured. A big portion of knowledge is contained in the heads of experienced technicians. In such an environment, timely accessing of the required information is a herculean task. We can use AI algorithms to sift through the multimedia multi-format information and find out relevant information. We can also use sensors and other methods to capture the actions and potentially the reasoning of experienced technicians to train the knowledge systems for use by less experienced people. AI-techniques like natural language processing can be employed to easily and more expediently access information from structured sources as well.

In industries such as the aviation industry AI has been used to change the complete business model around asset usage and maintenance. The *power by the hour* model which has been used by companies like GE and Pratt and Whitney is a good example of such applications. Similar implementations in the building industry can completely change the business model, too.

Converged Security

Over the past 10 years there has been a step-change in data source proliferation, causing security analysts to be overwhelmed by levels and layers of connectivity and growth of IP-networked sensors. Besides, the security organization is overloaded with too much external data from weather, public safety CCTV and video, social media, and ever-growing cybersecurity issues. The volume and velocity of these data sources are now demanding a different approach to the managing and processing of security events. The ability to translate data, internally and externally, into a meaningful context for the enterprise fits well into the security analyst function, which today deals with three undesired outcomes:

1. A largely reactive posture to security incidents.
2. Important physical and cybersecurity events are missed (as they appear in the large mass of noise).
3. There is an exponential cost equation for scaling meaningful security systems, causing reduced spending and therefore reduced threat detection for businesses.

We increasingly observe the convergence of physical and cybersecurity, where the above-mentioned internal and external data sources provide an opportunity to synthesize disparate information and events into a probabilistic machine learning model for security managers. The future of security will need to scale quickly across multiple hardware and software interfaces. It will have less and less interaction with people and objects, ultimately defined as a frictionless space. Access control will be guided from a unique digital signature (i.e. smartphone). The video will be led by an artificially intelligent set of sensors that capture the useful images required to assess critical situations. And intrusion detection will become automated and directly connected with the authorities.

We imagine the future of security as a completely automated, algorithm-driven environment where the proactive and reactive actions happen without disruption and in near harmony with the surrounding building environment. The next-generation security operations will enable actionable, intelligent insight with an automated monitoring capability, including a real-time risk dashboard, which correlates security data with all of the organization's assets.

The convergence of physical and digital security to create a more predictive posture will require data synthesis from various disparate sources. This will lead to reduced noise in the system as well as synthetic events that indicate an emerging situation concerning the facility or personnel. Machine learning then helps with risk analysis and response.

Converged security is the next evolution of Physical Security Information Management (PSIM) from an integration play to an intelligent and aware play.

Energy Management, Wellness, and Sustainability

The energy management efforts so far have been largely deficient in achieving their goals. They have been focused on analyzing the current state and finding incremental improvement opportunities. These are largely driven by dashboards, reports, and light analytics. These heuristics-based systems are not capable of taking into account factors that dynamically influence the future:

a. Changing usage patterns of buildings, leading to different, increasing load conditions
b. Efficiency in the design of HVAC systems
c. Occupancy
d. Access to alternative energy sources
e. Weather forecasts
f. Changing utility rates
g. Events

The problem is a multidimensional and multivariate one. The traditional energy management systems are not adaptive and self-learning. AI solves this issue in three different layers – energy prediction modeling, fault detection and diagnostics, and building systems optimization.

AI-Based Energy Prediction Model (EPM) predicts energy consumption of buildings using the deep learning (DL) method of artificial intelligence (AI). The prediction can be made at multiple granularities: whole-building level, tenant level, equipment level, sub-meters level. The prediction resolution can be at sub-daily level (e.g. 15 minutes, 30 minutes, and 1 hour, depending on the energy meter data collection frequency) and daily level. The prediction horizon can be anywhere from 24 hours for a sub-daily resolution to several days for daily resolution. The energy prediction can be for energy consumption in kWh or energy demand (i.e. instantaneous power) in kW. The EPM is a data-driven AI-based model, which is trained autonomously using historic data without manual effort. The model learns what/how building variables impact energy consumption from the historic sensor data on a particular building of interest. The input variables to the EPM model include temporal evolution of historic energy consumption data, indoor zone temperature, operational settings of HVAC, calendar information (time of day, day of the week, day of the year, holidays, etc.), and outdoor condition (air temperature, humidity, wind, solar irradiance, etc.).

The performance of the EPM models is automatically evaluated periodically, and if it is determined necessary, the model is automatically retrained and readjusted (hyper-parameter tuning) using newly collected sensor data to reflect the changes in the building (occupant behavior change, equipment change/degradation, building usage change, etc.). Once an EPM model is trained for a building, it is called at regular intervals to predict the energy consumption of the future for the building. Models similar to the EPM model described here can be applied for other commodities such as natural gas, hot water, chilled water, and heating oil in the future release.

Being able to predict future energy needs is useful because it allows making smart energy demand decisions and smart energy supply decisions. Smarter demand decisions include making a plan to shave upcoming peak demand by shifting demand (load) thus saving demand charge (cost based on peak energy consumption in a pay period). Smarter demand decisions also include planning for reducing load during on-peak periods and thus reducing the time of use (TOU) charges. Smarter supply decisions allow planning to use alternative energy sources (onsite generation, storage, renewable, etc.) and enabling demand response participation.

AI-Based Fault Detection and Diagnosis Model (FDD) detects anomalous or faulty energy consumption based on the deviation of measured energy consumption from predicted energy consumption, and the change of the pattern of the deviation. A significant deviation from the predicted consumption is indicative of an anomalous state and creates a fault alarm. The predicted energy consumption is computed by the Energy Prediction Model (EPM), which is based on the deep learning (DL) method of artificial intelligence (AI).

The FDD can detect faults or anomalies at multiple granularities: whole-building level, tenant level, equipment level, and sub-meters level. The FDD prediction resolution can be at 15-minute, 30-minute, and 1-hour intervals at the same frequency as energy meter data collection. The fault detection is conducted for the past 24 hours, but it can be done for a longer time period of the past. The FDD model detects anomalous or faulty energy consumption for electricity consumption, and other commodities such as natural gas, hot water, chilled water, and heating oil. Fault detection is a useful capability because it can quickly identify conditions that can lead to a significant amount of wasted energy consumption and costs. It can also help in identifying the root causes of faults provided that the users have some knowledge in facility management and predictive maintenance.

AI-based optimization operates by prosecuting the various influencers to energy consumption listed earlier and finding out the most favorable temporal load shifting mechanism as opposed to a constant time-varying consumption model, which is how most building systems are configured. Time-varying consumption increases the cost of electricity producers. Large demand peaks are difficult to supply. This requires a higher capital cost and leads to lower efficiency. The cost is passed to electricity consumers. Therefore, building operators must change behavior or pay higher electricity costs. Hence AI-based techniques are a better alternative than traditional ones.

In the chapter on transportation, we talked about the rise of electric vehicles and autonomous vehicles. This poses another energy management challenge for buildings and campuses – vehicle charging. Instead of being just a consumer of energy, the building now has to become a provider of energy. This introduces another layer of complexity to the already complicated issue of energy management. To address this issue, AI will be used to predict the driving patterns of the employees and regular visitors to identify the most likely charging needs, identify the energy availability and utility rate, and compute the most optimal charging duration and time-slot, keeping in mind best load-balancing and least-cost.

In the next logical extension, AI will also play a big role in enabling and optimizing demand response. The physics of electrical generation and consumption imposes many limitations on how much load can be shed or adjusted. On top of that, one has to keep in view the comfort needs of occupants and other requirements of the building that must not be impacted. AI enables fine-grained control of load shapes that can be highly beneficial to utilities because now they can eliminate expensive and disruptive peaks. Many companies are launching solutions in this space, including several startups. Canadian technology company EnPowered is helping customers in the Ontario region with demand-response using its AI solution. Businesses look to EnPowered's forecasts to eliminate stress, reduce oversight, and avoid unnecessary shutdowns.

In a July 2014 article in *Industrial Automation Asia*, Sudhi identified nine attributes of leading energy management solutions. We need AI to enable several of them, such as looking beyond the visible, thinking globally but acting locally, combining capabilities seamlessly, providing actionable insights with simulated outputs, and being intuitive and self-learning.

Beyond energy management, sustainability has many other dimensions like water and waste management in buildings. AI is used in similar ways to improve conversation efforts around water and other natural resources as well as optimize waste generation and increase diversion away from landfill. Bee'ah, the sustainability and environment management leader in the Middle East and North Africa region, has innovatively applied AI in helping individual customers and large municipalities to improve waste management and diversion from landfill.

Intelligent Homes

So far, we have talked about commercial buildings. But that is not the only place for major impact by AI. AI has entered our personal space and our homes for nearly 10 years with the introduction of Apple Siri and similar voice assistants that use natural language processing and other AI techniques to work. Now AI is present in millions of homes around the world and continues to grow at a fast pace. More generic and more capable voice assistants like Alexa and Google Home that connect to a wide array of devices and functions in our homes are accelerating the pace of growth.

While the majority of the intelligent home or smart home applications revolve around people's ability to control and manage devices, AI is finding increasing usage in other areas like home-based personal healthcare monitoring, energy management, security management, optimizing daily family routines, etc. AI plays an important role in these functions because the AI-enabled programs can mediate between different systems and data, correlate with larger global signal-sets for similar actions to evaluate impact, and perform local optimization in the context of global variations. For example, based on weather, occupancy, and utility rates, in the way we can do energy optimization for commercial buildings using AI, we can do the same for homes as well. By understanding the threat patterns and events in the neighborhood, we can better adapt the security posture automatically in homes. The extensive use of voice and image recognition in homes is also processed through AI-techniques. In research published by Xiao Guo, Zhenjiang Shen, Yajing Zhang, and Teng Wu in August 2019 in "Review of the Application of Artificial Intelligence in Smart Homes," among the various functions of smart homes where AI plays a role the authors attribute a 47% share to voice recognition followed by 36% to image recognition with only 11% attributed to decision making and 6% attributed to prediction making. Now personal robots have started entering our homes as well. Many people are using robotic vacuums as an example. AI-enabled programs are being used to even manage grocery shopping lists by capturing data from refrigerators and pantries. The possibilities are endless and we will continue to see interesting applications in the coming days.

THE FUTURE OF BUILDING SYSTEMS AND TECHNOLOGIES WITH AI

AI is not only fundamentally changing how different functions related to the built environment are managed, but is also profoundly changing the technology and products behind managing these functions. We believe that no part of building technology will be left untouched by AI in the next five-year horizon. In this section, we will discuss a few key areas where the shift has already started.

The Building Operating System

For AI to be effectively applied in buildings, we need a new building operating system. A unified building operating system or a digital vault for buildings is critical to synthesize the different digital capabilities to deliver the outcomes, experiences, and values that people expect from a digital transformation. Such an operating system brings together various capabilities and services to optimize building performance through shared data, insights, and actions by seamlessly interconnecting various systems, devices, utilities in a building, and other enterprise and external information inputs. The digital vault becomes a crucial cog in the wheel because reliable data is the driver for true digital transformation and enterprises need to have data trustworthiness as a differentiator to move forward. This is ensured by having access to the raw data, referential integrity, full context around the data, and knowledge that the data is fully encrypted and protected during transport and usage. With more AI and less human intervention becoming the norm across technology initiatives, enterprises must be confident that systems are set up with true and accurate data synthesis process and related analytics schemas in place. Reconstructing the logic chain of the insights and recommended actions by AI is an ability that transformation initiatives need to have in place.

Digital Twins

Building Information Modeling (BIM) started the first wave of digital information replication by creating a virtual representation of the physical layout of the building with all its sensors and systems. The new-age digital twins in buildings are a real-time synthesis of data from all of the sensors, assets, people, and processes in the building, dynamically depicting their state, health, and associations. Such digital twins enable us to simulate future states and possibilities for AI applications to use. The advancement in building digital twins has been made possible by massive sensorization, pervasive connectivity, and the use of knowledge graphs that make it possible to navigate the large sets of diverse information and contextualize them. For example, a smart building needs to know the floorplans of the buildings from the architect's BIM, the names and IDs of the people who work in the building from HR, and even miscellaneous data like which parking spot is assigned to which person or whether there are special hours for the cafeteria this week. This data has traditionally been held in multiple silos with no connections between the different silos, and certainly no connection to the sensor data of the building, but the knowledge graph changes that. The data virtualization layer can ingest and store this IT data and incorporate it into the knowledge graph for the building. This graph understands the relationships between the different types and sources of data. Digital twins also help manage the different phases of a building lifecycle and the evolution of the building, its systems, and the data across those phases. The Bee'ah HQ mentioned earlier has a similar multimodal digital twin to run the AI-backbone.

Cloud and Edge Architecture

Since the building industry grew in silos, different layers and types of aggregation and communication systems came into being. An HVAC system has its own set of controllers for communicating with field devices, a different set of controllers for performing supervisory functions, and a different software layer to manage the control functions. Similarly, a security system or an elevator system also has a multi-tiered architecture. Such architecture was required due to the fragmentation of OEMs making those systems, limitations in bandwidth and compute capabilities, and the different proprietary communication mechanisms. This multi-tiered architecture is not only inefficient but also expensive. Recent technological advancements are changing all that and now we are moving toward a much simplified two-tiered architecture of the cloud and the edge. All of the sensing, actuation, and control functions in the future will be performed by the intelligent devices while the cloud layer will be used to identify and plan global optimization and control strategies, manage the central configuration and aggregate of all digital twins, and drive other such policy-type interventions. Many incumbent technology players whose current monetization models are tied to the intermediary layers cite several issues like resilience, throughput, speed, reliability, and security to keep justifying the multilayered architecture. But cost economics and capability needs will drive the industry toward a more cloud and edge architecture. Once we make progress in that direction, we will see that AI-algorithms are being autonomously run at the edge with limited reference to the central cloud for best optimal results. This involves the ability to miniaturize the deployment of AI-routines into small packets and integrate them into a network of edge devices. There is progress being made in this regard by companies like Bragi and others. Major technology players like Amazon and Microsoft are also enabling this future architecture.

Intelligent Sensors and Systems

In a cloud-edge architecture for building systems, the capability of edge devices will be very different. Take the example of AirPods if you happen to use them. They are a good example of future intelligent sensors and edge devices combined into one. Both the AirPods work independently but in tandem with inputs from their optical sensors and accelerometers to gauge their placement and usage. These devices learn your behavior over time and adjust their functioning based on your usage of the devices. They have communication and compute capabilities, they can perform self-discovery and self-configuration, and they enable localized optimization. We will see building edge devices start mimicking such capabilities shortly as well. This will be crucial to be able to deploy AI-based optimizations at the edge with little intervention from other layers of the building management system. We also foresee the development of a very capable universal operating system just for building edge devices such as Android did for mobile phones.

In-Building OT Networks

Like many other aspects of technology, the operational technology (OT) networks in buildings also have been slow to evolve. The industry has struggled for a long time to move to wireless and IP networks. But that is all changing now. Developments like 5G, LoRaWAN, and NB-IoT are enabling new possibilities that are critical for a growing amount of high-volume, high-speed, high-fidelity, hi-frequency data exchanges driven by increasing AI-applications. We will see the rigid structures and configuration of networks evolve into more adaptive designs that will use elements of AI to self-organize and self-optimize. The inherent limitations of technologies like 5G in being able to penetrate through the buildings will be compensated by leveraging the high density of edge devices as transport carriers for signals. We will see multiple OT networks converge in a minimally cohesive logical fashion to ensure that the building as a holistic system of systems functions well.

Natural Language Interfaces

Natural language processing (NLP) allows humans and other systems to interact with computer programs using a human language like unstructured syntax and without understanding the underlying programming language or database complexities. The human language can be in the form of speech or text. Eventually, NLP will also extend to gestures, which are another popular form of human expression. NLP is a discipline of AI which is capable of understanding human language and translating it into the machine-readable language. While the roots of NLP go back 60 years, their first consumer application started with the search engines about 20 years ago. In the current business scenario, a humongous amount of data (big data) is being generated from various sources such as emails, audio, documents, web blogs, forums, and social networking sites. NLP techniques have been frequently used in the analysis of big data. As more and more nontechnical users interact with big data systems, they need a more natural interface to interact with such systems. This is where NLP comes in.

There are many challenges in building management systems that NLP can help address very effectively.

To engage with any building management system, the user needs to have a very in-depth understanding of the specific processes and syntaxes of using the system. These systems with archaic software architectures and specific heuristics approaches require the users to follow a specific path to query and action that takes a long time to learn. While executing any path, if the user makes a mistake, they will most likely have to trace back to a common trunk location and restart. This makes both commissioning and operational processes very long, complicated, and frustrating. The growing prevalence of NLP interfaces in the consumer and home automation industries is creating a latent demand for such capabilities in work environments, from which the buildings industry is not immune. The transition from desktop-based user interfaces to mobile ones is a similar transition for reference.

Using NLP, we can make building devices and systems smarter and more interactive.

Building Lifecycle Management

The concept of building lifecycle management (BLM) has been around for several years but very little progress has happened in this regard. The reason for lack of progress can be primarily attributed to split or misaligned incentives between different stakeholders during the building lifecycle. The architect and the contractor will prefer to defer any technology investments that will be most beneficial during the operations stage of the building. Even during the operations stage, there are too many stakeholders – the asset owner, the occupant, the facility manager, OEMs who have supplied to the building, the service providers, the utility providers, and the regulatory authorities. Given the diversity of stakeholders and differences between different buildings and their systems, having a uniform approach and aligned incentive to manage the lifecycle is difficult.

But newer technology-enabled capabilities like advanced BIM, digital twins, building operating systems, and consolidation into simpler cloud-edge network architecture will facilitate the development of BLM. More significantly, large developers and operators will push the industry in this direction. LendLease is one of the largest developers and building operators in the world. Bill Ruh, CEO of LendLease Digital, who previously led the digital transformation of GE and Cisco, says, "We will move from a spreadsheet- and drawing-driven environment to a data, analytics, and AI-driven environment." Similar efforts are being undertaken by many peer companies and large FM companies.

 SUMMARY

Buildings are poised to go through an unprecedented transition. Historically, this industry has been slow to evolve, but now it is poised for a massive transformation.

As we have seen throughout the chapter, AI will influence many aspects of how we engage with and manage buildings. Figure 8.5 shows the state of current technology and how AI will improve it in the future.

Most companies operating in the building industry are going through a transformation. One of the leaders in this space is the elevator giant Schindler. In an exclusive interview with author Sudhi Sinha, Silvio Napoli, chairman of the board of directors of Schindler, tells why he chose to lead and drive the digital transformation initiative:

> To survive the current digital revolution, transforming the business digitally is a strategic imperative for any global industrial company. Do you want to eat lunch or be lunch for your competitors or other incumbents with disruptive data-driven business models and offerings? For us at Schindler, digitalization enables us to enhance the customer experience and safety of our products and services and offers new ways to create value for our customers, users, and employees. Artificial intelligence, fueled by

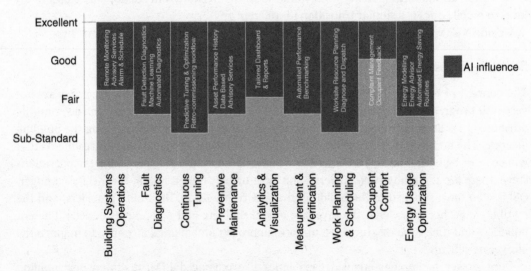

FIGURE 8.5 Impact of AI on Building Management

structured data, will be the engine of our new digital core. Historically, the real estate and construction sector have been rather late in adopting new technologies. Innovation is in Schindler's DNA and we wanted to tap into the potential digitalization offers and serve as a catalyst for the whole industry.

The amount and pace of transformation in this space is quite significant. While Schindler is a great success story by any industry account, in his quintessential humility Mr. Napoli says,

We are digitally transforming our products, our services, and the way we work and it is too early to call [our journey] a success. It is an ongoing process, so is there ever a time to call for victory? Digitalization enables us to innovate, improve customer experience, and apply our engineering excellence in new ways and faster than ever. Combined with a strong entrepreneurial spirit and a clear focus on the longer term, innovation is part of Schindler's DNA and has been a leading force since the company was founded in 1874 in central Switzerland. With that, we were able to grow into one of the world-leading elevator and escalator companies despite a home base in a relatively small country without any big urban areas or high-rise buildings. Agility is essential not to fall behind and our organization is driving change consciously and with a strong sense of urgency.

In this chapter, we have discussed how AI is crucial to make a building truly smart and why it matters. Smart buildings are the foundation for smart communities and many such coming together will create the smart cities of the future (Figure 8.6). More about smart cities in the next chapter.

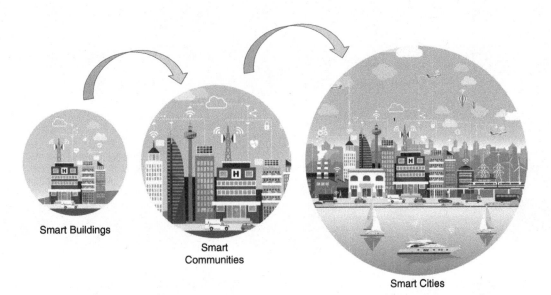

Smart Buildings

Smart Communities

Smart Cities

FIGURE 8.6 From Smart Buildings to Smart Cities

FIGURE 8.7 Office of the Future: Bee'ah's new Global HQ

Source: Zaha Hadid Architects/MIR

CHAPTER 9

Transforming Smart Cities with AI

"Adding lanes to solve traffic problems is like loosening your belt to solve obesity."
—Glen Hemistra

 INTRODUCTION

Urbanization finds its roots more than 5,000 years ago during the Mesopotamian civilization. The industrial revolution increased the pace of urbanization as more economic opportunities formed more rapidly around the cities. However, in the past century, urbanization has been accelerating at an unprecedented rate. We touched upon this briefly in our last chapter. This has also been a reason for the tremendous amount of innovation and economic growth as cities concentrate the talented and motivated into an ecosystem to foster creativity and progress. More than 5 billion people are expected to live in urban centers in the next 10 years. However, the way our cities have grown in the past several decades has followed the same path as futurist Glen Hemistra talks about in the above quote, to keep adding infrastructure and resources to meet the growing needs. City planners and society leaders have realized this fallacy and view smart cities as the panacea to solve the resource crunch issue while allowing for urban expansion to continue. Cities have evolved from human zoos to concrete jungles and now are shaping up to be technology museums.

Traditionally, our cities are built around notions of different infrastructure sectors that usually exist in different silos – roads and buildings, mobility and transportation, connectivity, safety, electricity, water, waste management, parks and communal spaces, and other services. Technology has been increasingly used to make these services more efficient and serve citizens better. A lot of cities have invested in connectivity and basic digitization by creating apps. While such initiatives do help, they do not make the cities smart because neither does the fundamental service delivery of the city change nor does the citizen experience significantly improve.

A smart city is one where digital technologies and data come together to enhance the quality of life of the citizens and help them achieve more. A smart city improves the wellness of its citizens, helps them make their time more productive, makes them feel safer, increases sustainability and better conservation of natural resources, and enhances the experience people have while interacting with the various service delivery functions of the city. A smart city is not technology or infrastructure-centric; instead, it is centered around the human beings who live there. A smart city is an ecosystem of smart capabilities that act in harmony to make it the most desired place to live and work. AI plays a key role in the future development of smart cities. AI will synthesize human intelligence, machine intelligence, and sensor and network orchestration, and empowered platforms will solve several issues that cities currently face and allow for more anticipatory planning and response than the current prevalent models. Simultaneously, there is an emerging need to make services more inclusive and affordable to avoid any discriminatory environment due to the digital, demographic, or economic divide among the citizenry.

While we have seen increased activity around smart cities, we are still in the early stages of that transition. It is being made complicated because retrofitting an existing infrastructure is hard. According to Grand View Research, in 2019, the global smart cities market already crossed $80 billion. As per a recent Bloomberg report, by 2025, the global smart cities market is expected to cross $250 billion. Compared to many other sectors, the spend on AI in smart cities is also expected to increase dramatically in the next few years. According to Omdia, the global smart city AI software market is set to soar to US$4.9 billion in 2025, up from $673.8 million in 2019.

There are emerging examples of smart cities that are beginning to meet our definition. Singapore seems to be at the top of that list as per the IMD Smart City Index published by Swiss business school IMD and the Singapore University of Technology and Design. This survey measures both the city's existing infrastructure and technological provisions and services available to the residents. Residents rated Singapore as high because they believe the technology and infrastructure investments made by the city help improve their lives. Singapore has long been recognized for its many innovations in the smart city space. Now it is accelerating the development and implementation of AI to solve city-scale and societal issues. AI Singapore, a collaborative between many nodal government agencies, academia, and the vibrant startup ecosystem is an effort in that direction. It is focused on issues around healthcare, education, and urban solutions. AI Singapore is taking a very deliberate and targeted approach. For example, its grand challenge in healthcare is, "How can Artificial Intelligence (AI) help primary care teams stop or slow disease progression and complication development in 3H-patients by 20% in 5 years?"

But Singapore is not alone. There are commendable efforts underway in different parts of the world. The ruler of Dubai, Sheikh Makhtoum, launched a slew of 100 initiatives in 2013 to make Dubai one of the smartest cities in the world by 2030. Copenhagen started its smart city efforts by enabling pervasive connectivity; then it quickly pivoted to improving environmental factors like air quality. Developing countries like India are also undertaking smart city initiatives to address their severe infrastructure gaps. In 2015, the Prime Minister of India launched the 100 smart city initiative.

Even the large technology companies are getting involved in the smart cities space. They see this not only as a race to contribute to society but also as a mechanism to further their technology and market presence. Microsoft CityNext is helping cities around the world become more competitive, sustainable, and prosperous. In the Smart City Expo World Congress held in Barcelona in November 2019, Microsoft announced several new features in Azure to make it more attractive for smart city solutions. Google has a similar investment in its arm Sidewalk Labs, which is building a smart city "from the Internet up" in a disused waterfront area of Toronto. The specifications laid out by Sidewalk Labs for this next-generation city describe a completely new infrastructure and a technology/AI-led approach. IBM, Dell, and other technology giants also have been active in this space for several years.

Not to be left behind, industrial companies with products and offerings in the space, be it lighting or be it automation solutions for transportation and power management, companies like Signify (formerly Philips Lighting), Siemens, Schneider, and others, have also made investments and engaged with projects around the world. As we ended the previous chapter, we talked about how smart facilities are a building block for smart cities. These companies figure that they can amplify their business and their contribution by playing in both and extending the learning from one theater to another.

One thing we have seen during the recent COVID-19 crisis, cities with better infrastructure and that are technology-enabled are better positioned to address any emergency. The smart cities' space is already vibrant and irrespective of any economic conditions will continue to grow. In this chapter, we shall investigate the various factors that are driving up the adoption of smart cities and the kind of AI applications that are emerging.

ENABLERS FOR AI IN SMART CITIES

Amsterdam was one of the first cities to invest in making the city "smart" by investing in pervasive connectivity in 1994. After a decade, Cisco and IBM started making significant investments and initiated structured programs to tackle the opportunities arising out of the increasing interest in smart cities. The movement got further momentum in 2011 with the inaugural smart city conference in Barcelona. The last decade has seen explosive growth around smart cities from technology players, in enabling technologies and applications. In the last few years there has been a concerted effort to use AI more extensively to address smart city needs. This is being fueled by simultaneous progress in many enabling technologies; let us now discuss a few of the key ones.

New Communication Technologies Like 5G and LoRaWAN

5G is the next generation of wireless cellular technology which will radically increase the capability of networks to meet the growing needs of passing data between people and between devices. Some of the highlights of 5G technology are:

- **Increased penetration.** Existing networks have limits on the number of devices that can be supported at any one time. 5G will support the ability to deploy large numbers of connected devices and enable them all to be connected, and connected to the Internet. Design goals are to support from 52,547 devices per cell sector of one square kilometer to 1 million devices.
- **Lower latency.** 5G is intended to support a 1mS latency round trip. That means a device, like a car, sends a piece of data to the network and receives a response (such as BRAKE

NOW) in 1mS or less. Not all devices and modes will have very low latency. For IoT-class devices, latency may be tens of seconds, or significantly higher to facilitate low power usage and high battery life.

▥ **Increased throughput.** 5G will support sustained data rates of at least 1Gbps. Currently, IoT devices may be expected to usually have a throughput of tens and very rarely hundreds of kilobits/sec.

▥ **Network slicing.** 5G offers much better network-slicing capabilities over the older generation communication techniques. As the diversity of applications and security requirements have increased, network slicing has become a key criterion for modern networks that have to support a multitude of devices, use-cases, user types, and usage variations.

▥ **Long battery life.** 5G will enable battery-operated devices to keep the modem asleep for very long periods, only waking up very infrequently or when data is to be sent up. For example, a typical device using 5G connectivity transmitting 200 bytes of data every two hours and having two AA batteries will last for 10 years. Some of the specific features added are enhanced discontinuous reception (eDRx), which allows the mobile to sleep for hours at a time without waking up, and power-saving mode (PSM), which can allow the device to sleep for about 10 days without accessing the network.

▥ **Improved coverage.** 5G is also adding features that will allow for reliable communication at extended ranges from the cell. This is accomplished through a combination of advanced coding and smart use of retransmissions to enable signals to be processed further from the cells. Two communication modes that have been added are enhanced machine-type communication (eMTC) and narrowband IoT (NB-IoT). Both of these modes will reduce data rates and increase the uplink functionality, resulting in better in-building penetration or increased cell range.

The biggest difference in 5G will be the cost of telemetry. While the wide-scale implementation of 5G networks is yet to happen, operators like AT&T are publishing rates of $25 per year for a 1GB plan which can be shared by hundreds or thousands of connected devices. There are apprehensions that the modem cost for 5G will be initially higher. The cost curves of new technologies always come down with time and higher penetration.

Many countries have initiatives to roll out 5G and use that infrastructure to step up their smart city initiatives. In 2017, the UK government launched the 5G testbeds and trials program. In 2019, the US Federal Communications Commission picked New York and Salt Lake City as 5G testbeds. China is emerging as the leader in this race. They have an aggressive plan of having 5G coverage across all cities by 2023. They see 5G as the key enable for their leadership in autonomous driving, smart healthcare, smart energy management, and other similar initiatives.

LoRaWAN is another communication technology that is emerging as a popular choice in smart city applications. It shares many benefits of 5G like scalability, low power consumption for IoT devices, low module cost and maintenance, and the ability to transmit data over long distances. It has a few advantages over 5G, the biggest one being not having to invest in expensive infrastructure that takes a long time to build. However, LoRaWAN is not suited for applications that require streaming high-density high-packet-size data nor is it optimal for ultra-low-latency applications. It has its niche in the smart city space. Since there are no or limited licensing requirements for LoRaWAN-type communication protocols, rollouts can happen much faster as well as bundling of other capabilities. In an interesting example, a San Francisco–based startup is rolling out LoRaWAN-based networks in many parts of the United States and has combined it with a blockchain capability to drive new revenue sources and functionality.

There are additional low-power wide-area communication technologies being piloted and promoted in different parts of the world. Sigfox and NB-IoT are two such examples. NB-IoT might work out to be an effective bridge technology over 4G/LTE networks while the infrastructure for 5G is put in place.

The development of all of these technologies is serving one purpose – allowing more endpoints to communicate more data. Hence, all of them will enable the growth of AI in smart cities and other application areas.

The High Density of Video Cameras

Video cameras are one of the most-used sensors in any city.[1] They are used for multiple purposes from surveillance of people to understanding the flow of traffic. We will discuss more how they are and can be used in the future in the next section when we discuss specific applications. China leads the global install base of cameras in the world with over 300 million installed in its numerous cities. In 2018, China had one camera installed for every 4.1 residents. In the United States, that ratio is 4.6. Around the world, by the end of 2021, more than a billion cameras are expected to be installed. The growth of this install base has been massive in the last five years. In 2015, China and the United States had a camera for every 6.8 and 6.9 people respectively, the respective growth percentages being nearly 70% and 50%. The total number of surveillance cameras in the world is already more than 700 million. These are not the only countries; this same phenomenon can be observed in almost every country. During the recent COVID-19 crisis, many countries have used such surveillance devices to monitor the movement of people during lockdowns, for contact tracing, for understanding the sanitation status of localities, and for implementation of containment programs. This will further drive up the installation rate and usage of video surveillance.

This substantial growth of video cameras has led to huge volumes of data being created. Now that authorities have more and more images and information about people, they want to get more and deeper insights. AI has always been the preferred method for such analytics. Such analytics are not only happening at the central level, but a lot of the routine analytics are now being packaged and distributed at the edge, with more unstructured and innovative analytics being performed at the central level. With autonomous vehicles, drones, and other related developments, the number of video sensors will just further explode. The colossal growth of video sensors will continue to fuel the growth of AI in smart cities and other applications.

Increasing Sensorization of Utility Endpoints

Similar to surveillance, various utility services and systems have also seen a massive growth of IoT devices that generate a lot of data enabling a host of different use-cases. For example, smart meters, used primarily in energy management applications, have been growing rapidly. As of 2018, the United States had 86.8 million[2] and the UK has 12.8 million smart meters.[3] Across the world, by the end of 2018, nearly 700 million smart meters existed.[4] This number is rising and we expect that in the next five years, there will be more than a billion smart meters in the world.

Similarly, we are seeing increasing growth of connected lighting, connected thermostats, connected buildings, connected homes, and so on. Even waste bins are also seeing increasing connectivity. The total market of smart connected waste bins is expected to be over $5 billion by 2025. Everything is getting connected and becoming smart.

Each connected product is a sensor that generates and communicates data for analytics. A lot of that data is captured today by individual manufacturers or service providers, but as the use-cases and applications develop, the raw or derived data will become more and more available. This will create a virtuous cycle of feeding into more AI-based analytics, with the benefits of more analytics driving more sensorization and connectivity.

Acceptance of Cloud Computing Platforms

Cloud computing has gained massive acceptance over the past several years. In 2019, the worldwide cloud computing market is estimated to have been $230–$240 billion. Numbers are not available for how much of that spend happened in smart cities. But governments around the world have become more open to using the cloud as their primary platform, especially for smart city applications that require a lot of storage, processing, and analytics. The support of government also comes with restrictions around data sovereignty, cybersecurity, and privacy requirements – requirements that push the technology forward and encourage broader usage.

Now, all the cloud market leaders have come out with their blueprints and services for smart city applications. They are also investing billions of dollars in setting up data centers around the world, building product capabilities, and marketing. There are also partnership ecosystems to bring more players into the fold of using their technology and creating new applications. All of these actions will further drive up the use of cloud in smart cities. With cloud infrastructure, more data will get stored and give rise to the need for more complex analytics, thus pushing forward the agenda for AI in smart cities.

APPLICATIONS OF AI IN SMART CITIES

Smart cities are a rich playground for AI. They usually have a lot of sensors and a lot of data coming from those sensors required for developing reliable models. While there are thousands of use-cases and hundreds of applications possible, we will focus our discussion on a few that impact people's lives and well-being more.

Smart Security and Incident Management

Most of the major cities in the world today have an extensive network of video cameras that capture the movement of people and goods. Some cities use these cameras for many reasons – traffic flow management, traffic violations, identifying congestions, tracking major incidents in real-time, and most often security. From London to Boston to Mumbai to Singapore to Shanghai, in all of these places and more, local law enforcement agencies monitor movement and events for all major hotspots or major areas of interest. The alternative is loss of life and chaos. The Mumbai terror attacks of 2008 are a good example of that. It took the law enforcement agencies a long time to figure out the location and antecedents of the terrorists, even though they were in public areas, because either there were no cameras or many of the ones that were there were not working. These issues have since been addressed. But this is not an isolated example.

As the network of these sensors and the number of images captured continue to rise dramatically, human monitoring ceases to be merely an option. AI is being used already and will be used even more to process these images, find patterns, identify issues, and alert the authorities. Beyond image processing, AI brings other benefits as well. Often the span and depth of the issue cannot be identified by image analysis of a locality. By the time humans can start correlating issues across multiple locations, it will be too late. Also, sometimes, to properly understand the magnitude of the issue, one has to consider data from other disparate systems like social media or newsfeeds. These are two use-cases where AI will be used to synthesize the information, contextualize it, enrich it with the inputs from multiple disparate systems, and then provide the insights to relevant authorities. For example, if there is a large congregation of people happening at a certain place and hate messages are floating around in social media for or against the crowd, it will most likely lead to a law-and-order problem. AI will also dynamically score the severity and impact of the issue for appropriate escalation. Authorities frequently struggle with understanding the pace of escalation. It is very difficult to do that based on experience or simplistic rules because many factors could lead to the escalation of its pace. Given the complexity and fluidity, AI will also guide the response mechanism and adapt it to the evolving landscape of the issue. The COVID-19 crisis is a good case in point for this. This pandemic has been unlike anything we have seen in the past, so there was no appropriate historical reference point. Countries that had a better response to this crisis among other things used AI modeling techniques quickly to understand the vector and velocity of the spread of the disease. They used these models to institute containment measures like lockdowns and diverted their medical and financial resources timely to locations where the models showed rapid increases.

We continue to hear about more and more security issues and incidents every day, but what we do not hear about are the ones that were averted. When insights from AI are combined with human intelligence collected from boots on the ground, it leads to rich and timely predictions that can help save lives, protect the economy, and make people feel safe.

Smart Healthcare

The health of the citizen is key to future societal development and economic prosperity. In a smart city, healthcare initiatives are community-based and ecosystem-focused to promote healthy lifestyles and build a network of major hospitals, specialty-care, and micro-care units throughout the city so that the various needs of the citizens are addressed at the right time by the right professional at the right location. For example, in Singapore there is an initiative called HealthCity Novena toward the development of total integrated care which has been quoted by the World Economic Forum as one of the best practices.

The lifestyle and environmental factors are crucial to promoting health, yet are often ignored. This ignoring does not happen deliberately; it happens because civic and healthcare leaders, in the absence of more specific insights into the long-term impact as per the current trajectory, deprioritize addressing lifestyle and environmental contributors to health problems. Let us take an example to explain this. In a city, there is a gradual rise in problems like diabetes and respiratory infections. Such data can be collected by combining data from various hospitals and clinics about patient visits, pharmacy sales data, insurance claims, and absenteeism data from the workplace. The data items may not be easy to collate or combine because they reside in disparate systems and are present in different formats, but the data is there. Simultaneously, there is data to show that fewer people are walking and instead are using public transportation. Such a conclusion can be put together by combing the data from public transportation systems, the number of cars on the road, and usage of public roads and parks for walking captured through video feeds. Additionally, the air quality data from the city is also seen to be escalating more toward unhealthy levels for some time now. If the medical data about increasing disease occurrence, people's physical exercise data, and air quality data are all combined to understand the problem and extrapolate its impact, the city authorities can undertake several interventions to promote healthier lifestyles, like incentivizing walking through education, more parks, and better walkways. Similarly, by incentivizing car-pooling the environmental impact can be reduced. This type of approach and analysis is better done with the help of AI as opposed to more traditional technology approaches.

The recent COVID-19 crisis has further amplified how healthcare has to be addressed as a community topic rather than just individual-patient or hospital centric. In the last decade, we have seen a rise in the number of epidemics and each new one seems to be more dangerous and impactful than the previous one. These epidemics impact cities more than rural areas for several reasons – high population density that makes spreading of the disease faster and easier, a higher percentage of the population having comorbidities because of the stressful and sometimes unhealthy city lifestyle, shortage of medical resources compared to the population, and for being major transit nodal points for other areas. So as part of smart city initiatives, addressing healthcare issues like this takes center stage now. Here are a few ways in which AI plays a role:

a. Timely identification of high-risk zones
b. Correlating multiple health issues that amplify the impact of a single issue
c. Modeling response efficacy
d. Contact tracing
e. Proactive health monitoring
f. Capacity optimization of healthcare networks

Finally, we are waking up to the significance of healthcare issues for the economy and national security. So, healthcare will get more focus than it already has as part of making cities smarter and more habitable. Combing the AI-impact on general healthcare as discussed in Chapter 3 and the specific smart city interventions will make the world a better and healthier place to live.

Smart Energy Management

In Chapter 8, while discussing the built environment, we have extensively discussed how AI will help with energy management more effectively. The fundamental premise of energy management does not change; energy conservation at a city-scale has to be stitched together from the initiatives at the building level. However, that is not enough. At the larger city-scale, some more macro-level issues have to be addressed. In this section we will discuss such broader issues and how AI will help solve them.

Grid Management

A significant portion of the energy is lost every year due to inefficient grid management, distribution, and transmission. Researchers Sarah Jordaan and Kavita Surana studied the transmission and distribution infrastructures across 142 countries. The found transmission and distribution losses contribute to more carbon emissions than industries like chemicals and parts of transportation. This problem is well recognized by the power sector. Better infrastructure and wiring can compensate for some of the losses. Improved load management and better organizing the distribution network also reduce losses quite a bit. This can be done through improved grid management by using AI and digital technologies. Some of the potential interventions for better managing the grid are:

- **Self-healing grids.** Often grids do not quickly identify issues and outages. Outages and faults put more pressure on the grid, leading to other failures, service disruption, and economic impact for both the customers and the utility. Electrical feedback systems or other IoT sensors can intimate a problem and AI can quickly trace down the root cause, remedial intervention, and initiate a protocol for self-healing of the grid starting with first isolating the network. This will improve the resilience of the grid and make it more adaptable to deal with issues.
- **Responsive learning systems.** Thermostats like Nest in homes popularized the concept of learning occupant behavior to optimize energy consumption. The same is transportable at the grid level by deploying AI-enabled learning systems with responsive capabilities.
- **Massive-scale demand-response.** Demand response has been a popular tool to reduce consumption in many places. The effectiveness of demand-response can be increased by anticipating demand-response scenarios and simulating their impact continuously using AI. Implemented on a massive scale, the benefits accrued will be substantial.

Gamification

Gamification is increasingly becoming a popular tool to change individual behaviors to achieve a common outcome at a community level. We have talked about gamification in the context of education in Chapter 4. Effective gamification solutions use AI as a backbone for scenario-planning and simulations. One emerging application of gamification is in getting individual consumers and buildings to collectively participate in conservation efforts. One of the many solutions from The Gamification Company is targeted on this problem. Opower, now owned by Oracle corporation, uses similar gamification techniques in its customer engagement platform leveraged by several utility companies to drive behavior changes at the individual consumer level.

Community Generation

In many smart cities, the local authorities have promoted individual homeowners and building operators to put in alternative energy generation sources like solar, battery-based solutions, and geothermal solutions. This is converting those homeowners and building operators to prosumers – both producers and consumers. Many places where such initiatives have scaled have ended up in chaotic situations. For example, California has been generating too much solar power causing stress on the grid. AI programs will help identify how much should be generated for optimal results for the individual producer as well as the collective grid. With automated signals and control from the grid, the community generation of electricity can not only solve the energy availability issue but also drive the right economic output for everybody.

Smart Waste Management

With increased urbanization and modern lifestyles, the amount of waste getting generated, especially in cities, is growing at a concerning pace. This is the next major cog in the sustainability wheel. Managing waste is a challenge because most of it gets diverted back to land, impacting the natural balance adversely. Inappropriate handling of waste has been linked to many ecological issues. Globally, waste management is already a big business, estimated to grow to $530 billion by 2025.[5] Waste management, unfortunately, is very fragmented and runs in an archaic manner in most parts of the world. Very few industry leaders like Bee'ah use technology to make waste management more efficient and pursue ambitious goals like zero diversion to landfill.

Bee'ah has been the pioneer in using AI and other digital technologies in various aspects of its business. Here are some of the key areas of waste management where AI applied at a city-scale will bring much-needed improvements:

- **JIT collection and route optimization.** The collection of waste normally follows preset routines. However, this is an acknowledged inefficient process. In many smart cities, waste bins these days are fitted with sensors that can indicate the amount of waste collected. Having that information centrally will enable waste management companies to find the right collection points just in time. AI will help optimize the route for the collection. This will maximize the utilization of the collection trucks, the least impact on the environment, and the highest customer satisfaction and cleanliness.
- **Demand planning and capacity optimization.** Waste management companies have a pretty good idea about the amount of waste generated routinely. They can get a much better idea about out-of-routine waste generation by converging the routine collection data with other event feed data indicating more people and activities such as trade shows, a higher number of tourists, extreme weather conditions limiting human activity, etc. To do so effectively and get the right insights, AI is required in the same way as it is required to predict security threats. Effective demand planning and capacity optimization can make the waste management process more efficient.
- **Waste segregation for recycling.** The different types of waste that are generated these days have also increased. Often, they do not fall in the neat categories of glass, metal, plastic, biodegradable, etc. that have been traditionally used. Till about 10 years back, in nearly all places, segregating waste was a manual process, making it time-consuming and expensive. The same is true for most places even now. But now we have a lot of new sensor technology like video-based sensors, Eddy current sensor-based separators, near infrared sensors, etc. to separate types of waste and process them for recycling or further handling. Many of these sensor technologies are using AI for most probabilistic identification of the types of waste.
- **Gamification.** Sustainable waste management practices at an individual level require similar behavioral changes as does energy management. AI-based gamification platforms

will drive such behavior change in the future. Bee'ah School of Environment Management, which is committed to raising awareness around sustainability and waste management in the communities Bee'ah services, is exploiting such techniques and has found them to be more effective than traditional coaching programs.

While still at a nascent stage, the use of technology is increasing in this space. The spending on waste technologies is expected to rise to $227 million by 2025, growing at a rate of 12%, which is double the industry growth rate of 6%. A good portion of this investment and efforts will be directed toward AI-based solutions.

Smart Transportation

Transportation is usually one of the first focus areas for any new smart city initiative. This is also the topic where some of the earliest AI applications have been implemented to identify traffic patterns to improve flow and inform policy and planning leaders.

- **Traffic control.** Managing traffic flow in cities is complicated yet very important. With the rising number of cars and not enough roads or space and capital to make new ones, the problem keeps getting aggravated. While cities incentivize usage of shared transportation, the problem of expedient and predictable traffic flow remains. Smart cities use video and other sensors to detect the presence, speed, and volume of cars on the road. At traffic signals, there are automated controllers and rules to modulate that flow. This process has existed for many decades. However, it makes the traffic control process much more effective by analyzing and predicting patterns based on historical information, current state, and other event feed that might require more people to travel. Image processing using AI can go far beyond flow analytics and optimization into more behavioral or sectoral insights that are otherwise very challenging.
- **Multimodal transportation planning.** To reduce the pressure on the roadways, promote public transportation or other shared transportation mechanisms, and at the same time give people the most optimal way of going from point A to point B in the desired time under current conditions, city planners are using AI to predict the most optimal combination of options. You can further improve this by future forecasting such scenarios, which will help individuals plan their time better.
- **Smart parking.** Most parking structures in most modern cities have sensors and counters to inform travelers about parking availability. However, such information is usually available by individual parking areas or structures. By pooling all such information at a city-scale and based on patterns (historical as well as current) of vehicle movement, parking preferences, parking durations, the intended destination parking, weather, and other such factors, a more comprehensive system is enabled by AI. With the output from such a system, drivers can be more precisely guided to reduce their parking stress, and optimize their time and costs.
- **Dynamic pricing and taxes.** The most potent tool city administrators have at their disposal to encourage a particular mode or time of travel is through financial incentives of toll pricing and taxation. Instead of having fixed rules around those, AI algorithms can dynamically determine prices or taxes on gas or other utilities involved in transportation based on the objective of a specific time-window.

Many cities are implementing advanced transportation management solutions and have begun to use AI. However, this is challenging because there is a lot of infrastructure investment required in sensors and data management before AI can be applied. Cities like Singapore are leading the way in this direction.

Smart Community Engagement

Another hallmark of smart cities that is beginning to gain importance more recently is the level to which the communities are involved in various aspects of the city. Community engagement helps in many ways – it brings a lot of fresh ideas to the table, informs and encourages the residents to leverage the city resources and smart capabilities, improves policy adherence through voluntary participation, fosters collaboration, promotes harmony between various sections of the society, and makes the city more vibrant. But extensive community engagement in cities is very difficult because there are a lot of different people to cover and a lot of different topics to tackle. Mobile devices become a good delivery mechanism but static applications delivered through them are ineffective because they are impersonal and non-contextual. AI helps address both of these issues. Natural language processing, neural network analysis, and similar AI techniques are very useful in understanding the person to engage, how to engage, actually engaging, and how to interpret the feedback for future exercises.

AI also helps with the design, administration, and prioritization of policy interventions initiated by city authorities. As per a Deloitte report on smart cities, predictive analytics enables city administration to use data to understand which social program interventions have a higher rate of success depending on a specific target situation, and which mix of services could be most helpful.

The example of Cambridge Analytica, while reprehensible at many levels, is a good one of how AI technologies can be used to understand people's motivations and preferences and nudge them to achieve the intended outcome. This is not the place for discussion around ethics; we will do that in an upcoming chapter.

To summarize, Figure 9.1 represents the various key areas of AI influences on smart cities.

 BEST PRACTICES FOR AI INITIATIVES IN SMART CITIES

Executing smart city projects is very complicated. They are capital intensive with long payback times, take a long time, have to work with a variety of complex technologies, and require alignment between multiple stakeholders who are not naturally unified in a cohesive organization. If the project involves making an existing city smart, it gets even more complicated because of existing legacy infrastructure issues, and the disruption it causes for the current citizens. Now when we talk about overlaying AI initiatives on top of that, the challenge is further increased because now we are potentially talking about a lot more sensors, data, and behavior changes. Citizens in such scenarios are naturally suspicious because of privacy and empowerment concerns. In other chapters we have not gone into specific implementation best practices, but we will do so here, because of the specific nuances of these projects and also the positive impact it can create for large sections of the population.

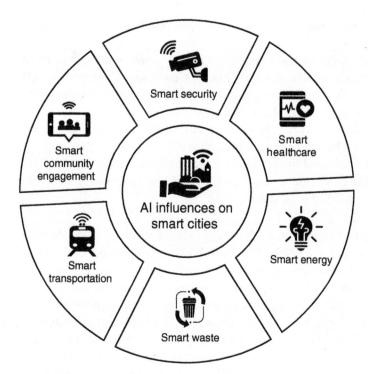

FIGURE 9.1 AI Influences on Smart Cities

Leveraging the PPP Model

Structured Public-Private Partnership (PPP) models have been around for more than 200 years, used extensively during the early infrastructure projects in the United States. Throughout history, their popularity has ebbed and flowed depending on public opinion, government policy, and most importantly liquidity in the market. For example, PPP models became very popular in the 1980s and that trend continued through the rest of the century. In the first two decades of this century, the total number of PPP projects across the world has fallen. However, there have been regional variations to this trend. The effectiveness of PPP models has been long debated with strong arguments and statistics on both sides of the question. The success of PPP projects depends on several factors, including the principal players in the initiative, stability of government policies, quality of the private partner, and so on.

In our opinion, for AI initiatives in the context of smart cities, PPP is the way to go. There are several reasons, such as:

a. **Active engagement of masses.** Any AI solution needs massive amounts of data with high variety. The data also needs to depict changes driven by different conditions. Usually, such solutions will involve interventions that will impact people's behaviors or lifestyles. Higher participation from the masses will improve the effectiveness of getting the data and implementing the recommended changes. So, a business model where not just the government but even the people are actively engaged and feel ownership of the initiative will take it much further.

b. **Large scope and scale.** Whenever the government is involved, usually it attempts solving a big enough problem at a large enough scale. These are the kind of scenarios where AI performs extremely well. It will be very challenging for a single or small group of private players to get enough scope and coverage to make the AI solution effective.

c. **Innovation enablement.** Governments around the world, with few exceptions, are not known for driving innovation. They are built and operated to always minimize risk. Without taking any risk, you cannot innovate. But in solving these complex smart city problems, we need innovation. Private players who have more appetite for risk and experimentation can inject the right amount of innovation in problem-solving.

There are many success stories to substantiate this theory. One of the most successful case studies is Bee'ah. Bee'ah was initiated as a PPP by the Sharjah Municipality in the UAE. This is one of the rare examples of PPP in waste management. Around the world waste management infrastructure is built and operated either by municipal governments or large private players. This is a very traditional sector and it has hardly evolved because there is limited incentive for the operators. The visionary leadership of Sharjah and Bee'ah were able to bridge the misaligned incentives and forge a partnership toward a common greater good. The results in just over a decade of operation are very impressive. Bee'ah has been a pioneer in using technology in various aspects of its business, including setting up a digital business. It is one of the few if not the only waste management company to use AI in improving operations. It has already achieved one of the highest diversions from landfills, more than 76%, and is marching ahead to zero diversion to landfill by 2021. Bee'ah took a burden on public exchequer and converted it into a profit-generating enterprise, which in turn is benefiting the public. With limited resources and starting from a small base, Bee'ah also has been successful in global expansion. It recently won the project to develop the entire waste management infrastructure for the new capital city of Cairo, where more than 7 million people will reside; in comparison, in Sharjah, where Bee'ah started from, the population is less than 1.4 million. Bee'ah has been a beacon of innovation, the perfect blending of visionary leadership, public support base, and private ingenuity.

There are other similar examples. AI Singapore, even though initiated by multiple government agencies and academic institutions, is engaging extensive public participation as part of its grand challenges. Sidewalk Labs in Toronto, mentioned earlier in this chapter, is operating in the PPP model with Google/Alphabet in providing a lot of AI capabilities. Hitachi has expanded its partnership with the city of Copenhagen to create a data platform and analytics engine City Data Exchange toward the goal of making Copenhagen the first carbon-neutral city by 2025. City Data Exchange houses both public and private data so that multiple companies can innovate new solutions using that data.

Building a City Cloud

Solving a lot of smart city problems with AI requires synthesizing data from multiple sources. For example, to make traffic flow smoother and faster, data is required about the vehicles (usually a combination of data from the OEM and the motor vehicles department), their starting point and destination (personal data of the driver), the usual route it takes in case of a habitual driver (a combination of personal data and video-captured data from the road), current traffic (video feed data), toll data (from road operator), fuel tax data (from fuel stations), and so on. This is a classic big data problem – variety, velocity, veracity, volume, variability. We just talked about one problem. Now if we expand our horizon to solving multiple other problems, the complexity of the problem increases manifold, as does the volume of data and processing. So, we need a robust cloud platform to manage that.

The city cloud will be a great technical solution as well as give comfort to city leaders and residents that they have control of their data sovereignty. Data sovereignty is an increasing concern in every part of the world and a key criterion in most solution selection processes. Building a city cloud will also allow the city to evolve its technology and data infrastructure with time. Today, the cloud computing business is still maturing but getting commoditized rapidly. Taking the city cloud approach will also excite the major technology players like Microsoft Azure, Google Cloud, AWS, Alibaba Cloud, etc. as this will become an opportunity for them to bring their bundled offerings as well further their technology with new use-cases. This approach also leads to building a lot of local capabilities in some of these new technologies that will become handy for other economic and technical pursuits.

Creating a Master Plan, but Getting There Iteratively

Every good data scientist will tell you that taking a big-bang approach to developing AI or solving a problem with AI is impractical and unrealistic. You always start with a model and a set of initial hypotheses. As you keep adding more data and fine-tuning the algorithm, you keep improving the reliability of the predictions. On similar lines, your approach to AI for smart city projects should also be iterative within the frameworks of a master plan. The master plan should include a comprehensive view of all the macro issues that you want to tackle using AI; then you should keep building individual solutions and tying them together. As an example, in the traffic flow problem (even though traffic flow in itself does not qualify as a master problem) you could start with flow analytics based on video sensors from the street, and then keep adding predictions and optimization recommendations by considering the other data streams.

Using a Design-Thinking Approach to Design Services and Enhance Experiences

As part of your master-planning exercise, you should create end-to-end customer journeys. Then you should leverage the user-centered iterative design-thinking process to build out the solution. The solution will include both services that the city offers to its residents and experiences that the residents are subjected to while using those services. Often there is a significant gap between intent and implementation, leading to divergence in the service objective and service experience. The human input aspect of design-thinking helps bridge such gaps.

REFERENCES

(1) "Surveillance Market Analysis"; Thomas Ricker; December 2019.
(2) "How Many Smart Meters Are Installed in the United States, and Who Has Them?"; US Energy Information Administration; 2019.
(3) "Smart Metering Implementation Programme Progress Report for 2018"; UK Department of Business, Energy, and Industrial Strategy; December 2018.
(4) "Smart Meters: A Game Changer, but Hurdles Remain"; Valerie Silverthorne; April 2019.
(5) "Waste Management Market Outlook – 2025"; Allied Market Research; September 2019.

CHAPTER 10

Transforming Government and Citizen Services with AI

"He shall despise none, but hear the opinion of all."

—Chanakya

 ## INTRODUCTION

Chanakya was a teacher in ancient India. He authored the famous *Arthashastra* more than 2,000 years ago and is considered as one of the foremost thinkers in governance, economics, military strategy, and diplomacy. Across all ages, objective data and information have been critical for effective governance, as the quote highlights.

This is our final chapter focused on industry sectors. Governance and citizen services are not a classic industry, but like other industries, government, too, is focused on maximizing the welfare and economic progress of its constituents – the people. AI is transforming how governments around the world function very similar to the transformation it is driving in every industry segment. Governance is a big deal, not only because it touches every aspect of our lives today and for the future, but also because collectively all the governments around the world spend over $25 trillion, making it one of the biggest economic activity drivers. AI has been used by governments in many ways for a long time. Defense research has been one of the biggest places of development and application of AI. But the use of AI can be found in more routine activities like automatic address recognition and mail sorting. The US Postal Service, which was one of the earliest and most extensive adopters of this method, is today sorting more than 25 billion pieces of mail annually using AI techniques like machine vision and image processing.

Governments around the world are already spending a lot of money on AI, yet they are being asked to step it up. Center for New American Security (CNAS), a prominent and influential think-tank in Washington, DC, recently released a report in December 2019 titled *The American*

AI Century: A Blueprint for Action. In this report, the think-thank urges the US government to increase its spending on AI to $25 billion by 2025 to keep its technological edge.

Governments have always played a critical role in the research, development, and deployment of new technologies. In the last several decades, the technological superiority of a nation has been one of the biggest factors for a nation's economic prosperity and social progress – look at the United States, China, the UAE, the Scandinavian countries, Singapore, and so many other similar examples. In 1976, the US government used to spend 1.2% of its GDP in R&D; in 2018, the same has come down to 0.7%. Up until the end of the past century, the pivotal position of the United States as the technology and economic leader in the world went unchallenged, but this is no longer true. So, organizations like CNAS are worried. The US federal government is slated to spend only $4 billion in AI R&D in the defense sector and another $1 billion outside of defense in 2020. There are of course additional investments being done by the States, universities, and other public institutions. On the other hand, countries like China are making big bets on AI. They are reportedly outspending everybody else in the world on their AI research and implementation. The latest numbers from China are not clear, but if we look at the analysis done by the Center for Security and Emerging Technologies, in 2018, China is estimated to have spent a total of $8.4 billion in AI R&D while the United States has spent $5.9 billion.

Countries like the UAE are taking a more holistic approach. In October 2017, the UAE government announced the *UAE Strategy for Artificial Intelligence.* The strategy is the first of its kind and focused on development and application in nine sectors: transport, health, space, renewable energy, water, technology, education, environment, and traffic. As a follow-up to that announcement and to make things more concrete, in April 2019, the UAE government announced the *National Artificial Intelligence Strategy 2031.* They have created specific targets like a 50% reduction in spending by the government in its transactional costs by eliminating paper and reducing travel, reducing road accidents and operational costs of the department, and so on. They have appointed a minister in charge of the AI initiatives at the federal government and have dedicated leaders in most of the individual Emirates. The government is building the educational infrastructure around AI, aggressively promoting entrepreneurship in AI, helping build research centers, developing partnerships with other world governments and corporates, and becoming one of the biggest adopters of AI in its operations.

Nearly every developed and developing country in the world is developing an AI agenda. France initiated one in 2017, and Germany has one now as do most other European countries. The UK government is planning to increase its investment in the near-term and catch up as one of the leaders; they believe AI will be able to help them with a lot of problems like healthcare, employment, etc. All of these countries have earmarked billions of dollars for investment in AI. The Government of India also announced its AI Policy in June 2018 with the slogan #AIforAll and a focus on five key sectors: healthcare, agriculture, education, urban-/smart-city infrastructure, and transportation and mobility.

There has been activity at an intergovernmental level also. In October 2015, during the 70th Session of the United Nations General Assembly, there was a discussion on AI, making it the first time for AI to feature in the world body agenda. In 2017, under UN's sponsorship, the Centre for AI and Robotics opened in The Hague, The Netherlands. The UN is leveraging AI to go beyond normal applications and help with global peace and justice. In July 2018, INTERPOL organized the first global meeting on AI and robotics for law enforcement. AI is now a working group or a key focus area for nearly all international bodies.

There are several areas where AI can transform governance and citizen services. We have covered many of them in our previous chapters while discussing specific industries. So, we will not repeat them here. Instead, following is the list for your recap:

- **Healthcare** – emergency response, epidemic management, tele-diagnostics, drug discovery, capacity planning and management, compliance
- **Education** – K–12, higher education, lifelong learning, virtual assistance
- **Transportation** – autonomous driving, transportation infrastructure optimization, fuel economy, logistics, multimodal transportation
- **Financial services** – fraud detection and anti–money laundering
- **Smart cities** – smart security, smart energy, smart waste management, smart transportation, smart community engagement

Governments today have no choice but to focus on AI. Governance has become more complicated and demanding than ever. Citizens today are not only more educated but also well connected as well as aware of their rights. The influence across industries and nations, because we are so interlinked, makes the job of government leaders particularly challenging because there are so many considerations and so much data. AI presents to be a panacea for many of these challenges as it is doing it for many industries.

HOW AI WILL CHANGE THE GOVERNMENT AND CITIZEN SERVICES OF THE FUTURE

In this chapter our focus will be on areas that have not been previously discussed in the book.

Sentiment Analysis

One of the most crucial yet difficult to execute tasks for any government is understanding the mood of people, especially when there are major events or policy changes. Not only that, to understand at a granular level is even more challenging. For example, during the recent COVID-19 crisis, many governments around the world instituted a strict lockdown regimen to reduce the spread of infection. However, in many parts of the world, the citizens were not very supportive and therefore also not very compliant, defeating the purpose of the lockdown in the first place. If we go nearly 10 years back in history during the Arab Spring, governments in Libya, Egypt, Yemen, and other impacted places misjudged the level of resentment of the youth in those countries about present-day socioeconomic conditions. In a lot of countries, we have seen sections of the population being upset with the ruling disposition of the day with something or other; on a few occasions, such feelings have resulted in unfortunate situations. The traditional methods the governments have used to gauge people's reaction, such as sample surveys, listening to their political infrastructure, and getting inputs from government sources on-ground, are all deficient because first they do not cover a broad enough population and second they are not good at judging the extent of problems people might have.

AI can be very helpful here. Sentiment analysis is a method of using natural language processing on mostly unstructured and sometimes structured data to derive subjective insights like how people feel. For example, sentiment analysis can be used on Facebook posts to figure out what people are saying about an issue and what are the underlying tones and to classify the feedback based on factors like demographics. Sentiment analysis has evolved over the last 20 years since the beginning of this century as more and more information has become easily available on the Internet. This technique has been successfully employed to gauge feedback from the voice of customer surveys and online forums. The retail industry, media industry, and other similar ones where public opinions matter a lot frequently use sentiment analysis today. We have seen the use of sentiment analysis significantly rise in politics, especially before elections. In their seminal research paper from July 2010 titled "Identifying Breakpoints in Public Opinion," researchers Cuneyt Gurcan Akcora, Murat Ali Bayir, Murat Demirbas, and Hakan Ferhatosmanoglu were able to statistically identify the major pivot points in public opinion.

Using Twitter data to predict elections has been done for more than a decade. Now, there are more sophisticated datasets from multiple sources along with richer historical information and several new analytical techniques that allow better sentiment analysis. We have seen the application of some of that in elections around the world in the last five years. But sentiment analysis is not only used for understanding people's opinions about something. The output of it is also being used to nudge people slowly to take certain positions. This is like using gamification in bite-size chunks to modulate public opinion and behavior. AI helps get constant feedback and modify the interventions. This territory is very dangerous because of ethical issues, but the tools can be very handy to deal with scenarios like the COVID-19 crisis where there is near unanimity on the course of action of public behavior. Sentiment analysis is also being used by the intelligence community to understand more about the trends in friendly and adversarial countries. In some countries, it is also being used for counterintelligence.

Every day governments are employing new use-cases of sentiment analysis to be more effective.

Designing Socioeconomic Interventions

Another big challenge for governments is to design the right intervention programs to uplift segments of the society or parts of the country, implement them, and understand their effectiveness. Often, even with the best intentions, governments that have a large geographic and diverse demographic coverage go wrong with their welfare programs. However, this classic data analytics problem is best served by AI.

In designing the programs, governments struggle with a few decisions – which groups to target, which interventions to put in, which levers to play with, and understanding the associated impacts. These questions are complicated because they are not independent of each other and only influenced by the topic in question. Sometimes there are many dimensions to the same problem that need to be tackled together. For example, in one country, one of the goals of a social-economic-medical intervention was to reduce child mortality significantly. First, the authorities had to figure out in which parts of the country the problem was most severe, and what had been the trend, and then understand the various influencing factors like healthcare, vaccination programs, mother's health, sanitation, living conditions, education, genetic factors, regional diseases, demographic distribution, and other such types of data. These data points are not fundamentally related to each other but can influence each other heavily. For example, education and vaccination programs can be related; sanitation and education can be related; a mother's health can be related to living conditions, sanitation, and education; and the list goes on. Figuring out this complex web of influences and understanding the weightage of each influence is critical because the goal will be best served by attacking what matters most. In one real-life example, the government started with sanitation and education. This type of analysis requires extensive data collection, cleansing, correlating, and processing as well as extensive advanced statistical analysis usually used in AI programs.

The next most critical action after designing the right intervention is to monitor the effectiveness of the program and modulate the various levers to improve its efficacy. Measuring effectiveness is hard because sometimes there are no singular metrics that show conclusive results. Often, some of these measures take a long time to reach a state of meaningful difference. For example, education and sanitation are long drawn processes that will not immediately lead to reduced child mortality in a short time. But if the parents are continuously trained on the value of healthcare, the different dimensions of being healthy, how to care for the mother during and after pregnancy, and the role sanitation plays in ensuring a more hospitable and healthy environment for the child, over time they will be better equipped to take better care of the child. So, in the meantime we will have to work with a lot of proxy metrics to validate our assumptions and measure effectiveness. This type of approach is frequently taken in AI-driven analytics. Reducing child mortality is a more complex version of the problem of improving an industrial asset's reliability. Yes, the comparison is not fair because one is a human life and the other is something replaceable that money can buy, but if you look at it from an analytical perspective, one is a simpler version of the other.

In countries where the population uses social media extensively, sentiment analysis techniques can be applied to assess the reception and effectiveness of the programs as well.

Citizen Services

One of the primary functions of any government is to provide a range of services to the citizens. But often, citizens are not satisfied with the level of service they get from the government.

The biggest problem citizens face is to get information and clarifications from the government bodies – they do not always know whom to ask. If one can reach the right department with their queries, usually there are no SLAs and if there is an intent for one, it is very hard to track. During certain seasons like the tax season, the extent of the problem becomes much more severe. During emergencies, too, the problem can become severe. On the other side of the problem, government offices are rarely staffed adequately to handle all citizen queries. On top of that, usually a response requires sifting through people and knowledge across multiple departments and that introduces further delays.

AI-based virtual assistants are a good way to address this problem, just as we have seen being done in many other industries like retail and financial services. Many governments around the world have been doing a pilot implementation for such assistants. The Australian Taxation Office (ATO) was one of the first agencies to implement a virtual assistant – "Alex" – on their website in August 2015. Alex responds to queries about personal tax, and importantly, understands conversational language and learns from questions to improve answers. Alex is reported to have achieved a first call resolution rate of 80%, which is significantly more than the industry standard of 60%. Now similar assistants are being launched for many other departments. In the UK, Her Majesty's Revenue and Customs Agency has automated many call center tasks with the help of AI and digital technologies to reduce handling times by 40% and processing costs by 80%.

Government work generally involves a lot of paperwork. Surprisingly, the amount of paper processing has not changed that much in a century. A lot of it might have transitioned from handwritten to digitally captured, but there is paperwork nevertheless. As per Deloitte's research, US government employees spend 500 million hours every year in documentation types of activities. Public officials can serve the citizenry better if there are more hours at their disposal. Automation and using AI techniques like NLP can dramatically reduce the manually intense documentation work that consumes 20–30% of staff time.

Governments usually have many programs and benefits that they would like citizens to take advantage of. For example, there might be free vaccination programs, reduced tax rates if there are children in the family, benefits around job loss or retirement, etc. Often people do not know about them and the governments also do not know when people become eligible for them. One event could trigger multiple benefits. For example, retirement could trigger health-related benefits as well as pension-related benefits. These different benefits are usually handled by different departments, making coordination complicated. This is another problem that governments face where AI can help. Estonia, a small country in eastern Europe but digitally very advanced, has instituted such a program. Marten Kaevats, advisor to the Estonian Government Office on Digital Innovation, believes that AI will help governments become invisible. Estonia's comprehensive digital infrastructure has helped the country reduce its expenditure by 2% of GDP and helped improve citizen satisfaction.

Another area for the use of AI and digital services is the sharing of information about citizens across different government departments. Citizens have too often input the same information items again and again while taking the responsibility for storing them for a long time for posterity. Many countries have implemented unique identifiers for citizens that are commonly used to invoke the various services, but the seamless sharing of information is rare. For example, in many jurisdictions, medical expenses are exempt from income tax, but when filing for taxes, people have to report it separately instead of the various systems capturing such information automatically. The challenge with implementing a system like this is creating a digital twin of the citizen that comprehensively represents every life event however major or minor and creating context around different data streams – both problems on which AI can be applied effectively.

Several government agencies are tasked with inspections and issuing advisories based on those inspections. The method of doing inspections in a time-bound pre-sequenced routinized manner is very expensive and mostly inefficient. Using condition-based inspections, the agencies can direct their limited resources to more targeted areas and do a more thorough investigation. An experiment on similar lines has been done by the Southern Nevada Health District for managing food inspections in the city of Las Vegas. They developed an app for geotagging and natural language processing to identify Twitter users reporting food poisoning and flag the restaurants they visited, generating a list of eateries for investigation. This was how they made inspections active and early instead of reactive or time-bound. It is estimated that by employing this method, food poisoning incidents can be reduced by more than 9,000 incidents every year, and it can avoid more than 500 hospitalization incidents. This type of reduced burden on stretched healthcare or other resources can benefit the cases that are in most need of that service.

Transforming citizen services with the help of digital technologies and AI is very beneficial but extremely challenging at the same time. This calls for changing the technology planning horizon, process, procurement methods, and most importantly the mindset of bureaucrats in taking a more transparent, collaborative, and service-oriented approach to their jobs. The Australian government has done some excellent work in this direction. The Australian Government Digital Transformation Agency has published 13 criteria for digital service standards. They also assess and score the various digital services offered against these published criteria.

It is usually hard for governments to attract the right talent to drive these types of initiatives, but by tapping into people's desire to make an impact in a bigger landscape, this issue can be addressed.

Financial Markets Regulation

Fair and transparent functioning of financial markets is critical to the survival and success of any economy. Government institutions have to monitor and regulate the functioning of financial markets. As long as financial markets have existed, criminals have always tried to manipulate them to make a quick buck for themselves. There are many examples in history where such financial market manipulation has deeply impacted national and sometimes global economies for a long time. The 2008 housing crisis is one of the worst examples. It is a human-engineered crisis that brought the world economy to its knees and from which some countries are still suffering. Ponzi schemes and scams continue to hit financial markets despite regulatory checks and balances.

- Detecting financial market manipulation or criminal behavior can be complicated for many reasons, like when perpetrators use multiple instruments simultaneously that hide the extent of their activity even if they are under watch.
- Many violations happen over a long period through hundreds or thousands of transactions that are difficult to track and stitch together.
- The laws regulating financial transactions can be confusing and interpreting them to see infractions or near-infractions can get very complicated.
- Irregular trading and transactions are not always easy to track.
- Validating the financial statements and claims made by wrongdoers is challenging. For example, one might report a large amount of asset holdings but the assets might already be overleveraged, and these data points are maintained by different institutions in different systems, making it difficult to piece them together and create context around them. This is how most bank frauds happen even today.

Usually, most violations or near violations should create an alarm or an anomaly. AI can help in understanding the patterns of any irregular behavior and in forecasting the magnitude of the problem to understand whether this is a true anomaly or a symptom of bigger malice. Regulators could use the vast data that is already available to them and apply machine learning tools to help predict where they should apply their regulatory efforts. Such tools could be used to identify areas on which to focus regulation and to know whom to investigate and inspect. AI can also be used for identifying collusion and anti-competition attempts by studying patterns of transactions and actions of multiple players simultaneously.

Some governments have started pilot projects in leveraging AI to monitor financial markets and fish out regulatory infractions. Australia Securities & Investments Commission (ASIC) has made AI an integral part of their 2019–2023 Corporate Plan and have been using AI for detecting disclosure issues in financial advice statements, monitoring irregular trading, and using NLP to detect misleading Internet advertisements.

Taxation

Taxes are the main income for governments. Tax fraud is a common problem in most countries that prevents governments from receiving the rightful income that they can further deploy for public welfare, defense, and other critical functions. Tax compliance is very resource-intensive. It is also very difficult because if people do not report correctly or if they route their income through illegal channels or spend their ill-gotten monies in shopping for expensive things or hide assets in other countries, it becomes very difficult for the authorities to find those out and put a cohesive story together. The data for all of this is distributed, disconnected, and varied.

India has one of the most innovative examples of tax fraud detection using AI. The Income Tax department in India is using pictures posted on social media sites like Facebook and Instagram of luxury items like expensive cars, bags, jewelry, etc. to estimate spend by selected individuals and validate that against their income statements filed for taxation. If one has pictures of multiple family members buying expensive Louis Vuitton bags or Cartier watches but shows very little income, he is not reporting some income. Such inconsistencies will be flagged by the platform and that will trigger an investigation. The government of India is spending over $100 million in this initiative titled Project Insight. The government plans to use other sources of data like property data, credit card transaction data, stock market transactions, bank records, and other financial data as well to triangulate the veracity of an individual's income reporting and do that over time. The government expects to improve compliance significantly and use the additional recoveries to fund the numerous welfare programs. Many other countries like the UK, Canada, Belgium, Australia, Singapore, and others have implemented similar programs. The OECD has studied 21 countries that have implemented similar programs and reported cheaper compliance and increased revenues. However, such projects have to be handled carefully because it can infringe on privacy and other rights of individuals.

Document Generation

Governments have to generate a lot of documents, sometimes in response to queries from citizens, sometimes in completing their processes. Government documents take a legal turn, so they tend to be voluminous as well as data-rich. Producing such documents takes a lot of time, is prone to errors, and can get expensive for storage and processing – all actions taking resources away from citizen services that require a personal touch. One of the AI techniques – natural language generation (NLG) – can be quite helpful to address document generation problems. There have been many successful pilots in the legal profession so far. This technique has already been used by many media companies to automatically generate stories for their publications based on event feed and some minimal inputs. Government departments have also started pilots around using this AI methodology. For example, the Japanese Ministry of Economy, Trade, and Industry is using this technique for answering parliamentary questions.

For multilingual countries, especially ones that have lots of official languages or where languages vary a lot by region, government organizations have to spend a lot of money and resources in translating official documents in multiple languages. This is another use-case where NLG can be quite useful.

CREATING A NATIONAL AI AGENDA

To make the use of AI effective and pervasive, governments have to take the lead in developing a national agenda around AI. Many countries like Singapore, Australia, the UAE, a few European countries, and others have done that successfully. This process should start by identifying a nodal agency to coordinate across the various government departments. The nodal agency should be led by a very high-level leader who has a proven track record for large-scale transformations as well as some understanding of AI.

In our research of the various governments that have created a successful national agenda and a few that were not successful, we have found several best practices that are broadly applicable:

1. **Have a specific plan.**
   Whenever there is a specific plan with defined milestones and metrics, it is easy to marshal resources and rally people. The plan should lay out how and by when the functioning of the government will shift with the kind of planned AI interventions. The plan should be visionary, inspirational, impactful, yet have enough intermediate success to celebrate and calibrate. The UAE has developed one of the best plans which you can take a look at.
2. **Define standards.**
   Having a plan is a great start, but it should be quickly followed up with defined standards. This will help set the tone and bring transparency to the process. Earlier in this chapter, we talked about the Australian government's standards in this regard, which is one of the best ones to take a look at for reference.
3. **Improve the educational infrastructure.**
   Any amount of AI initiatives taken by the government or private sector will not be sufficient if the workforce for the future is not ready. This includes upskilling and reskilling. This also includes starting in the earliest years of education and following through the entire higher education stage and beyond. We have discussed AI and education extensively in Chapter 4 and will draw the reader's attention to that for a quick refresher. The Discovery Partners Institute (DPI) initiative taken by the University of Illinois and the State of Illinois in the United States has developed one of the most ambitious plans for creating such an infrastructure to benefit the state economy by billions of dollars of additional economic activity in a new-age economy driven by AI and digital technologies. DPI has other goals like energizing the R&D investments in the State and creating a vibrant entrepreneurial ecosystem. To meet its tall objectives, DPI hired Bill Jackson, an ex-president of Johnson Controls and an accomplished business leader, to lead the DPI.

4. **Create an ecosystem.**

Successful national agendas around all major technology shifts, and especially around AI, have to be driven by an ecosystem approach comprising academia, public institutions, and corporates. This is where different segments of the society and different contributors to the economy are brought together under one common mission and charter to pool their thinking and resources for greater returns. The purpose of the ecosystem should be to:

■ Identify and execute specific areas that can further fundamental research, solve socio-economic issues, and create new commercial business models, thus activating all three stakeholder groups.
■ Drive coordinated efforts across industries and segments of society.
■ Advise the government on policy formation and regulatory matters.

AI Singapore is an extremely good example of how such an ecosystem is getting built. AI Singapore is an effort led by the National University of Singapore and the National Technological University of Singapore with participation from several other universities, the Ministry of Education and other government bodies, and several corporates, including startups. They have focused on the themes of healthcare, education, and urban solutions – topics that are very important for the island nation. Their focus is manifested in very specific actions like the AI in Healthcare Grand Challenge launched in 2018 with a singular focus on the question, "How can Artificial Intelligence (AI) help primary care teams stop or slow disease progression and complication development in 3H-patients by 20% in five years?" 3H for the reader's reference is Hyperlipidemia (high cholesterol), Hypertension (high blood pressure), and Hyperglycemia (diabetes). This is a five-year, two-stage program with a total budget of S\$35m (USD 25m). It is being executed in a multidisciplinary fashion by private-public teams and consortia. Three teams have been selected for stage 1 of this program. Similarly, other programs are being launched in other focus areas.

5. **Form cross-border partnerships.**

The scope and scale of AI are vast. No one country, maybe except the big ones like China and the United States, has all the capabilities and resources to be successful in all of its AI-related efforts. So the government nodal agency can also help further the journey by forming partnerships with the governments, academia, and corporates of other countries. There are some great models for this already. The Singapore Economic Development Board has worked with many foreign institutions to establish dozens of such partnerships and got them to set up shop in Singapore. The Ministry of AI in the UAE is also undertaking similar steps and has signed up many partnerships like the one with India at an intergovernmental level.

6. **Promote entrepreneurship.**

Every new technology shift in the world is successful because of the tension created by the push and pull of the large technology companies on one hand and the startup community on the other hand. Entrepreneurs are good at quickly innovating, inventing new business models and applications, and disrupting the existing status quo. Entrepreneurial initiatives also drive job creation and capacity building. Many companies serious about AI and other digital technologies are making it a national priority to promote entrepreneurship. One of the best scale examples of this is the Atal Innovation Mission started by the Government of India.

A national agenda around AI will be successful when the efforts of the government, the industries, and academia are augmented with the awareness and willingness of the broader population. AI has the power the transform the futures of countries as it does for companies. To take full advantage of the possibilities, the nation has to make it a mission.

 ## SUMMARY

It is clear that in the coming years, every part of the society and economy is getting impacted by AI in a major way. The functioning of civic societies and governments will also be transformed by AI and digital technologies. As discussed in this chapter and the previous ones, we believe that in the public sector, AI will make the maximum impact on public safety, public health, and public welfare – the three areas that will get the most attention anyway in the post-COVID-19 world.

AI is beneficial for public servants as much as it is for the public. A June 2019 report by the European Commission has claimed that AI in the public service can "empower" public servants to make better policies and deliver more efficient services. The report argues that AI requires sustainability to protect the societal and natural environment, growth to secure employment and progress, and inclusion to ensure benefits for everyone.

A recent Capgemini study on the subject of AI in the public sector has estimated spending savings to the tune of \$2.5–\$6 trillion by 2025. With the hardships unleashed by the COVID-19-induced economic slowdown that has put a severe strain on the resources of governments around the world, any savings that can be achieved in providing essential services is very helpful. Additionally, AI can increase the GDP growth by 2-4%, which in today's environment is massive.

The role of the public sector concerning AI is much broader, though. It has to be the standard-bearer for defining the quality of service and ethics around data analytics. The day AI starts to discriminate between people to create new disadvantages for certain segments of the society is the day that will herald the third and very long winter for AI. The public sector has another critical role to play in the future of AI – ethics and privacy. Governments have not only to define the regulatory environment around ethics and privacy but also to lead in implementing them. With the massive scale implementations that are usually associated with any government initiative, the technology and practices around ethics and privacy will also develop further.

Finally, governments have an incredibly important role to play in managing the job displacements that happen due to the increased adoption of AI. Many people fear impending job losses due to the increasing use of robots and AI. There is an expectation of massive redundancies in nearly every sector. A recent Eurobarometer study shows that 74% of the respondents believe there will be job losses due to AI and robotics. However, there is no historical evidence of actual job loss at an aggregate level due to major technology-led transitions. What happens is that one type of job will get displaced by another type. This will require massive reskilling efforts and support for people during times of displacement. Governments need to think about policy interventions in this space as well as become a testbed for managing such displacements through their internal AI implementations.

AI is still new to most people. So governments will have to hold a hand, educate, and promote the right thinking and practices as AI continues to become mainstream.

CHAPTER 11

Building the Right Technology Landscape

"Let's go invent tomorrow instead of worrying about what happened yesterday."

—*Steve Jobs*

 INTRODUCTION

Those immortal words by the indomitable Steve Jobs could not be truer when it comes to building the right technology infrastructure for enabling AI.

On its own, AI is a very specific discipline of statistics to perform unconstrained analytics over large datasets to mimic cognitive capabilities. However, we know by now that exploiting AI for broader implications requires a different kind of institutional approach to technology foundation. We have to start right from where data is generated and acquired, how it flows through the various workflows and work-streams in an organization, how it is processed and managed, and how it is used. We have to think of AI initiatives in terms of integration into the business work processes of an organization extending all the way up to how users engage with the new insights, outcomes, and experiences. Many technology companies will promote their capabilities as the panacea for all problems, but that hypothesis hardly comes true because those solutions may not address the entire ecosystem issue. Doing something bespoke for every situation to address the breadth and depth of possibilities will become time consuming and expensive. In this chapter, we will help business and technology leaders think through the key aspects of the technology ecosystem and how to build the right technology foundation in a scalable and cost affordable manner.

We shall cover the following topics in this chapter:

- Data platform
- Analytics engine

- Multi-agent systems
- Adaptive user experiences
- Universal software gateways
- Technology partner ecosystems

 THE DATA PLATFORM FOR AI

The success of AI projects depends on primarily two things: having the right data and using the right technique. Database management architecture and systems is the most critical component of the technical infrastructure for AI projects.

Database management systems have been around for more than 60 years. With the development of COBOL as the first programming language for popular use, the need for standardized database management techniques was felt, leading to the development of hierarchical system IMS and networked system CODASYL. Since then, database management has gone through a major transformation every decade. The 1970s saw the development of a relational database management system, the 1980s saw the democratization of database management brought to the desktop level, the 1990s saw the introduction of object-oriented techniques, and at the turn of the century new techniques to manage unstructured data started to emerge.

The past decade has been about the development of big data management systems and IoT platforms that could process a lot more volume and variety of data at much velocity. The development of NoSQL and Hadoop File Systems was pivotal in this phase. NoSQL databases enabled the handling of unstructured and non-relational data while Hadoop enabled parallel processing and storage. The new distributed capabilities significantly amplified the ability to apply AI on large and heterogeneous datasets. Within the last 10 years, the development of multi-model *graph databases* has been a game-changer for AI.

AI applications are unique as compared to other analytical applications or IoT applications. One is not a natural evolution of the other, a common mistake many people make. We believe that the underlying data platforms for general analytical applications, IoT applications, and AI applications are distinctive features. Some of the common capabilities required across all the different types of platforms also have specific nuances based on their unique application areas. The following are the critical features and functionalities of the data platform for AI applications.

Diverse Data Handling

AI applications usually involve working with the very expansive and diverse nature of input data. The data is structured, semi-structured, or unstructured. It could be streaming, static, and slow-moving data. Often it involves multimedia data. The data could be in the form of simple values, sensor signals, text, images, illustrations, audio, video, and other formats. The data platform should be able to ingest, store, and process different types and variations of data simultaneously. The data platform should be capable of processing data from different sources, and make it available in one spot. The data platform should be able to ingest data with standard cloud protocols like MQTT, IoTHub, AMQP, and REST, or with specialized connectors developed for old and proprietary protocols. The platform while ingesting and managing data should use industry-leading security practices such as 2048-bit X.509 certificates for SSL for all connections. In most cases, the data platform will have to connect with physical gateway solutions and/or standard APIs to collect the data. Recently we are seeing the emergence of software-defined gateways. The software-defined gateways are more suited for AI applications because they offer more flexibility and control.

Data Contextualization

Data contextualization, sometimes referred to as data virtualization, is the process of unifying heterogeneous device and data management through semantic data relationship modeling. The context is established between disparate types of data from different sources with no apparent relationship among them. Often graph databases are used for this purpose. Data contextualization enriches data with meaningful and configurable relationships. It manages two crucial characteristics of the data: the shape (or schema, entity, model) of the data and the semantics of the data. Contextualization is offered as a native service from the platform and enables developers to integrate their systems into the platform to define data sources and model data transformation without developing or considering how to store, where to store, or how to optimize the search and retrieval. Therefore, virtually no database programming or database administration (DBA) will be required in the process.

Data contextualization is achieved through the construct of smart entities – a unique type of classification or aspect of the data. For example, the weather is an entity, a car is an entity, a person is an entity, age is another entity, and so on. For contextualization, data management service includes multimodal data storage abstraction service, unified metadata management, smart entity management, knowledge graph service for describing the domain of the industry where the AI is being applied, and streaming data management service. As part of data virtualization, aggregation and disaggregation functions should be available with little processing and almost no storage.

Graph Databases

Graph databases are very flexible databases that rely on the principle that all data can be represented as nodes and relationships. Unlike relational and other traditional databases, graph databases do not follow a rigid structure or schema. Data retrievals in graph databases leverage the relationships to traverse through nodes (rather than "join") for very fast data retrieval. If the data being managed is highly connected with many-to-many relationships, a graph database can provide 10× to 1,000× faster data retrieval speeds compared to managing the same data in traditional RDBMS. Not all "graph databases" are created equal. Nonnative graph databases are the database systems that provide node-relationship-like look, feel, and usability without any changes to the way data is stored or queries are handled at a low level. A graph database is assumed to be "native" with the database engine centered on "index-free" adjacency.

The biggest benefits of graph databases over traditional databases are:

■ Ability to retrieve highly connected data fast irrespective of the size of the graph
■ A flexible schema design and management that allows for iterative and incremental application development

- Fast design and development cycles due to modeling database by an idiomatic representation of nodes and relationships
- Support for high concurrency and ability to deliver high availability of database via horizontal scaling leveraging distributed database architecture
- Ability to embed a database within the application

There are, however, some challenges to using graph databases over traditional databases, such as:

- A limited number of native graph database offerings in the market
- Lack of availability of talent (human resources) for implementation and support
- No third-party monitoring tools
- Limited support for legacy application connectivity

Version Control of Analytics

Version-controlling software programs have been around forever to help understand the evolution of the program, test performance, trace issues, and perform such other analysis. In the AI space, data scientists use a chunk of data to create new insights with a certain logic chain. As new data comes in and/or the logic chain (i.e. the algorithm) is tweaked, a new insight is generated. Even if the insights are directionally similar, the way to reach them could be fundamentally different, and knowing that context is critical for transparency, traceability, and fine-tuning. Therefore, a good AI data platform should be able to version not only control programs and data, but also the analytics algorithms, the insights data, and the context in reaching the insight. This is also critical to build trust in the AI. It is important to keep in mind that such version control should be smart and not create too much system overhead in terms of storage or processing.

Interact with NLP Engines

Natural Language Processing (NLP) allows humans and other systems to interact with computer programs using a human language–like unstructured syntax and without understanding the underlying programming language or database complexities. The human language can be in the form of speech or text. Eventually, NLP will also extend to gestures, which are another popular form of human expression. NLP is a discipline of AI which is capable of understanding human language and translating it into the machine-readable language. While the roots of NLP go back over 60 years, their first consumer application started with the search engines about 20 years ago. In the current business scenario, a humongous amount of data (big data) is being generated from various sources such as emails, audio, documents, web blogs, forums, and social networking sites. NLP techniques have been frequently used in the analysis of big data. As more and more nontechnical users interact with big data systems, they need a more natural interface to interact with such systems; this is where NLP comes in. Statistical NLP techniques use probabilistic models to correlate large volumes of unstructured data from multiple sources to create insights. For example, in several leading financial trading platforms we can find such NLP applications that hunt news events related to companies from everywhere to derive insights about their actions, reactions, and possible implications on stock prices.

In the recent past, we have seen NLP applications migrating from basic query and search functions to initiating simple actions. We can see such applications in home automation closer to our industry where the users can command Alexa or Google Home or Cortana to do something.

There are several challenges to the implementation of NLP techniques in any environment. For NLP algorithms to work, they need a semantically enriched dictionary to understand words and interpret intent. Differences in understanding and interpretation come from industry context, language, culture, idioms, and finally individuals, making this somewhat complex due to the variabilities. In designing NLP systems, several tasks need to be kept in consideration like morphological or structural segmentation, grammatical interpretation, parsing, named entity recognition, optical character recognition, and breaking down the intents of words. As NLP applications mature over time, the learning elements of NLP algorithms can self-associate words, idioms, and intents; but even to get started one needs a rich enough dataset to be useful. NLP also requires extensive and fast computing capabilities considering the huge datasets involved.

As more and more AI interactions transition to NLP-based techniques, the AI data platform must be able to seamlessly connect with standard NLP engines.

One recent and promising development in this space is the application of *controlled natural language*. In this method of NLP, there is a thin layer constraining the flexibility of human language that analysts and other users can employ in interacting with the data. There is a library of words, both verbs and nouns, that are defined, and "recipes" of analytics are created with minimal training. Think of the language used by cops or airline traffic controllers with their specific phrases like "10-4" and "copy" as part of a controlled natural language library. Wisconsin startup DataChat, founded by the very impressive serial entrepreneur and professor of UW–Madison, Dr. Jignesh Patel, has built a remarkable tool for allowing users to leverage controlled natural language capabilities on any type of database, greatly simplifying AI and other analytics. Jignesh and his team are able to combine artificial intelligence (AI) with business intelligence (BI) to create *conversational intelligence* (CI), a huge leap in furthering AI.

Cloud-Native Architecture

Ideal AI data platforms are cloud-native – they have been designed with a cloud-first approach and in a cloud-agnostic fashion. While it is possible to convert any on-premises-based data management system into a cloud-based one or connect to a cloud environment, in doing so there is a lot of inherent system overhead that gets transferred during the migration or interface process. A cloud-native architecture will maximize the leverage of cloud IaaS and PaaS services out of the box. The services in a cloud-native architecture are abstracted to a high enough level that they can be easily switched across to those from different vendors and even run across multiple vendor environments if there is a need. Cloud-native architectures usually support a multi-tenant deployment model, ensuring that there is infrastructure simplification and cost optimization. Furthermore, a cloud-native architecture will support containerization, virtualization, microservices, and multi-agent systems for maximum flexibility and adaptability.

Multi-Threaded Identity Management

AI systems have to deal with a lot of different types of identities of users, devices, and systems feeding data. The data in itself has an identity and that identity could be associated with where it came from, who is authorized to generate it, who is allowed to view it or use it, which transactions it is allowed for, and which application and which session of the application it is associated with. This is a complex multi-threaded problem. Solving this problem is important for many reasons – knowing the genealogy of data for analytics purposes, trust, and cybersecurity. A mature and robust AI data platform should be able to support managing such a complex unified identity situation.

Metadata Schema Management

Proper metadata management allows for easy integrations and interoperability between systems. In the AI world, we often have to deal with a multitude of systems and a variety of data, making metadata management so much more critical. Proper metadata management also allows for scalability of the development and scalability of the applications. Metadata management allows sharing a common understanding of the structure of information among people and/or software applications. Metadata management also enables the reuse of domain knowledge, something that is critical in building AI algorithms. Many IoT and domain-specific applications require handling of streaming and time-series data. Usually, each application handles data management and processing differently because of a lack of a common definition of time and processing. This representation includes the notions of time intervals, points in time, relative measures of time, aggregation analytics, metric conversion, and so on. If AI platforms enable a common metadata model and associated processing in detail, others can simply reuse it for their domains and applications. Metadata management tools also allow separating description or expression of subject matters from its consumption. One could develop a conceptual model of a specific business process and its various enabling systems. But the same could then be applied to other business processes without involving the technical staff.

Developer Support

All data platforms need robust developer tools to make them easier and more effective to use. AI data platforms need a lot of additional capabilities; they need out-of-the-box functionality for data management functions like cleansing, wrangling, preprocessing, and visualizing. Such tools should include common algorithms for filling missing values, cleansing and smoothing outliers, and many analytic, aggregation, and normalization functions. There should also be tools to easily aggregate and disaggregate time-series data. This will make it easy to define new backend analytics and metrics that can power dashboards, reports, and other applications. The developer tools built into the platform should automatically refresh and update those analytics and metrics as new data becomes available. Applications should be able to subscribe to the time-series and get pushed data as it is refreshed.

Performance and Reliability

Every platform needs to have robust functional capabilities around performance and reliability. This is further accentuated in the case of AI applications because by nature, such applications are tied to critical business outcomes and sometimes to more serious outcomes that impact people's well-being. The data platform needs to be extremely secure and have very high availability. The

TABLE 11.1 Platform Comparison

	Analytical Platform	IoT Platform	AI Platform
Diverse data handling	Only structured data	Structured + semi-structured data	Structured + unstructured data; multimedia
Data contextualization	No	Limited	Extensive
Graph database support	No	No	Yes
Version control of analytics	No	No	Must have
Interaction with NLP engines	Maybe	Maybe	Must have
Cloud-native architecture	Maybe	Often	Must have
Multi-threaded identity management	No	Limited	Extensive
Metadata schema management	No	Limited	Extensive
Developer support	Limited	Extensive	Extensive
Performance and reliability	Moderate	High	Very high

platform should also have elastic scalability to account for new and organically growing data and it should be able to scale-up or scale-down easily and inexpensively. There should be features to easily add new sources of data and add new sensors with no or very low touch. The platform should retain high-performance with required SLAs even at full scale. The platform should be fault-tolerant and the data should be automatically replicated to multiple nodes for easy retrieval in case of a problem. The failed nodes should be replaceable with no downtime. AI platforms will be called upon to run spaceships and smart cities, so they need to have commensurate performance and reliability.

Table 11.1 is a summary of the various capabilities that we just discussed and how they must fare across the three different types of platforms mentioned earlier.

 ## ANALYTICAL ENGINE

AI has a very long and rich history. AI engines, on the other hand, are new. In many ways, IBM Watson can be credited as the first AI engine. It was first developed more as an NLP interface for information retrieval with knowledge structuring, reasoning, and machine learning capabilities in the background. Watson was first used to play the game of Jeopardy in 2011 after a few years of background development. Watson has more than 200 million pages of structured and unstructured information on which machine learning was employed. It uses the Apache UIMA Unstructured Information Management Architecture (UIMA) framework and IBM's DeepQA software for processing. The huge success of Watson in the game led people to realize the potential of powerful AI engines to solve complex problems. Since then, Watson has been used to solve many issues in the space of healthcare, smart cities, smart buildings, predictive diagnostics, insurance, retail, and many others.

There are several other very popular and capable analytical engines available for commercial usage as well. Microsoft Cognitive Services, Amazon Lex, and Google Tensor Flow are very capable engines. Each of them comes with an exhaustive set of APIs and plugins for prebuilt analytics, especially around NLP, computer vision, and AI data modeling. Using these engines is not very expensive today, but they do tie you up with a specific technology partner.

Your needs may be addressable in other ways as well. You could build your own lightweight analytical engine or get one that might be available from a smaller niche player commercially. The purpose of having an analytical engine for AI applications is manifold:

a. Pre-process the data as it arrives for common statistical functions.
b. Provide the data scientists with a tool to interrogate the data and build their models.
c. Enable a pipeline to launch analytics-as-a-service for maximum reuse.
d. Build a portfolio of analytics.
e. Manage the analytics jobs.

Analytics engines help reduce the time to develop and deploy the AI algorithms. Often, a large cross-section of the data used in AI within a particular domain is common. A good analytics engine helps use the same data in multiple different ways to different ends. These engines most often come with a domain-specific common modeling language to uniformly represent analytical functions.

A good analytics engine should have the following three characteristics:

1. **Analytics visualization**. Many methods allow data scientists to visually model the data and algorithms. GUI tools to show the flow of data and buildup of the model, similar to what has traditionally existed in BI tools, is one option. Another option is to use Directed Acyclic Graphs (DAGs). The DAGs are conceptual representations and flow of data in an unbounded fashion, that is, they do not require any loops to be closed. Multiple DAGs can be combined and parsed. For AI purposes, they are much better at representing the flow of data and logic simulating real-life scenarios as well as quickly trying out new combinations and models.
2. **NLP/CNLP support**. We have already discussed the criticality of NLP. The analytics engine should have an NLP interface to allow data scientists and other users to interact with it. You can always use an external NLP engine and integrate it with your infrastructure. The NLP extension must support content search, indexing, and retrieval.
3. **Intelligent messaging**. If you are using ambient analytics and multi-agent systems as part of your AI portfolio, you must have an intelligent messaging framework that can dynamically route messages and data streams based on the context of the topic. In such a messaging infrastructure new channels of messaging will be created based on topics if there is an expectation of sustained message exchanges. There should also be security at various levels of messaging abstractions and guaranteed delivery.

 MULTI-AGENT SYSTEMS AND AI

Multi-agent systems are another game-changer for AI applications. An *agent* is an intelligent software program that is situated in some environment and is capable of flexible autonomous action in that environment to meet its design objectives. Agents can be passive (without goals), active (with simple goals), or cognitive (with complex calculation and learning capabilities). Multi-agent systems can manifest self-organization as well as self-steering and other control paradigms. They can correlate complex behaviors even when the individual strategies of all their agents are simple. When agents can share knowledge using any agreed language within the constraints of the system's communication protocol the approach may lead to a common improvement.

Figure 11.1 depicts how an agent interacts with its environment.

Let us give you a "reel-life" example of a multi-agent system. If you have seen the movie *The Matrix*, you probably remember Mr. Smith (played by Hugo Weaving). Mr. Smith is not an actual person; he is a software program with the single goal of destroying Zion and keeping humans in the Matrix – the virtual recreation of the world. When attacked by Neo and his friends, Mr. Smith spawns himself into multiple Mr. Smiths, changes weapons, and at one point even changes his avatar into the scary white creature. Mr. Smith has intelligence and can adapt to the situation as it emerges. In real life, the agent is exactly like Mr. Smith.

With the proliferation of the Internet of Things (IoT) and the AI technologies driving them, which require massive autonomous distributed computing at the edge level, the needs of modern software engineering require agent-based architectures. The agent-oriented approach advocates decomposing problems in terms of autonomous agents that can engage in flexible, high-level interactions. This decentralization reduces the control complexity of the software.

These days, more edge devices have local compute, storage, and communication capabilities. AI programs are taking streaming sensor data with other types of streaming and static data. Customers and technology providers are seeing the emergence of new value through the

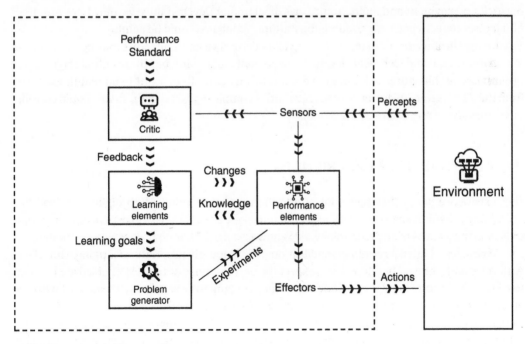

FIGURE 11.1   Multi-agent System

interplay of different types of sensory information and insights. All these changes are leading to very complex management and control environments that are driven by AI. We now need significantly more processing: processing across domains which have inherent differences and goals and highly variable implementation of physical systems from situation to situation that seamlessly need to interoperate, autonomously take local decisions without having to always refer back to a central control system at an on-premises server or in the cloud, and be adaptive to changing environments of occupancy and operations. These legacy architectures are not designed to accommodate the changes put forward by these developments.

Multi-agent systems are already in vogue in several industries and applications such as autonomous vehicles, chatbots, and knowledge management systems based on web crawlers like search engines. The space programs were among the first to use multi-agent systems as we have discussed in the chapter on transportation. With the natural growth of these various sectors and the increasing demand from AI systems, we will see more and more multi-agent systems being implemented. Therefore, you need to consider this as part of your current or near-future technology landscape.

Many industries and companies are adopting microservices architecture as a potential intermediate step before migration into a more mature multi-agent system. *Microservices* is a software development style that is popular in developing modern distributed web applications. The principal concept is to modularize software services that interact with each other through APIs that are asynchronous and distributed in nature. So architecturally it is a point-to-point communication that must have service discovery and endpoint management; so many additional service management tools and support efforts are mandatory that we call this overhead. Each microservice has its full stack that includes infrastructure and data management. This will make for agile development and deployment of services, but this self-contained data management makes for deployment and maintenance overhead (many DevOps) since we may have hundreds of microservices. In particular, managing multiple databases could be painful.

Taking the intermediate step of moving to a microservices architecture may be simpler from an organizational and technical change management standpoint, but the eventual migration to agent-based architectures will have to be undertaken again. If we want to do real-time control from the AI program, microservices architecture's complexity is too high, so we should consider direct messaging and agent-based systems.

 ## ADAPTIVE USER EXPERIENCES

User experience design has had a lot of attention in recent years. With digital overload and decreasing attention spans in every aspect of our lives, engaging user experiences has become critical to the success of any technology. AI is now raising the bar on user experience design.

AI enables a high degree of personalization and frequently uses natural language interfaces with voice and/or text. Therefore, users expect the user interface of their AI-enabled applications to adapt to the context and usage; they are no longer going to be satisfied with static UI with traditional dashboards and reports. Traditionally design was expected to be timeless; now we expect the design to be timely based on changing usage and preferences. Iterative design processes came into vogue because of the rapidly changing technologies. This is how great design-led companies keep up with change. This becomes exciting because you have to balance reuse, rapid development, investments, and returns. Extreme componentization in design is instrumental in such an environment, but it is difficult to simulate how the components maintain harmony and yet can be evolved over a longer period.

Now we not only experience AI through the analytical applications but also find them embedded in the different devices. This complicates the user experience design of those devices, how AI is cogently and consistently experienced across a multitude of devices and systems, and how the intended outcome is achieved in interaction with the user. Sometimes the expectations might drive conflicting requirements for the product or service infrastructure. For example, you do not want a call center to have a long list of automated questions; when you call, you want to speak to a real person quickly. But if the system does not first understand your needs, a lot of time will be spent on identifying the correct agent or you will need a lot of agents who are super-specialists. An integrated experience of outcome and service necessitates user experience design to consider a much broader and longer horizon of lifecycle interactions.

Paying attention to user experience and making it adaptive is therefore critical to the success of any AI initiative.

SOFTWARE-DEFINED GENERAL-PURPOSE GATEWAYS

A gateway is usually a device run on dedicated hardware that gathers data from multiple sources, translates the data into IoT messaging protocol, and sends it to the cloud or wherever the data platform is hosted. It usually has a processor, an operating system, some limited storage, and a program to translate the data into a transmissible and understandable format. Gateways also receive back messages and send them to the appropriate sensor or system. As you build out your AI portfolio, you will be ingesting and integrating a lot of data from different sensors and systems. The IoT explosion has made it easier to connect and collect data from these different sensors and systems; however, it has also created a multitude of gateway solutions to get the data out of the generation point and into the data platform because there are hundreds of different communication protocols, which are standard formats of exchanging data. The gateways add complexity not only because of their diversity and numbers but also because of the associated problems of managing physical devices with embedded software spread all across the enterprise. A lot of companies have built their businesses around such proprietary gateways. So now you will have to figure out not only the complexities of AI but also those of the museum of gateways.

An alternative and easier solution is to use software-defined gateways. These are generic devices with data input/output outlets, storage, compute and communication capabilities where any gateway software can be downloaded and used. Think of a universal software gateway as an electrical adapter we carry in our luggage while traveling internationally. These units are inexpensive yet allow us to connect to the unique plug-and-voltage configurations of different countries so that we can use all our devices that require electrical power to run or to be charged.

The universal software-defined gateways provide higher flexibility, maintainability, cybersecurity, and reduced cost. They serve many purposes, such as:

■ Provide open access to the wealth of data available within each system.
■ Monitor, override, report, and analyze operating performances.

- ■ Convert data into information for improved decision making and corrective actions.
- ■ Deliver an environment that natively supports dashboards, web pages, and mobile devices.
- ■ Offer the ability to capitalize on newer technologies as they become available.
- ■ Deploy new initiatives based on changes to technology and requirements.
- ■ Consolidate data for detailed analytics and data sharing.

These universal software-defined gateways have all the common management functions like messaging, over-the-air updates, secure device credential storage, configuration apps, command-and-control features where applicable, installable protocol conversion libraries, monitoring, and audit logs. These will help you focus more time and resources on the core AI and keep you away from the distraction of managing a museum of gateways for each project.

 ## TECHNOLOGY PARTNER ECOSYSTEM

The rapid pace and nature of the evolution of AI are impacting businesses and companies in very fundamental ways. Large industrial manufacturers are becoming software companies, retail consumer companies are becoming analytics enterprises, cloud software solution companies are developing hardware capabilities that capture more IoT value, and startups are challenging established players in almost every segment; the transformation across industries is quite unprecedented. The skills and capabilities required to win in this new world order are vastly different from what companies have cultivated over the past several decades. Moreover, AI is impacting transformations much quicker than businesses are normally used to. In such a vibrant environment, it is imperative for companies to partner with others to get faster access to solutions, quicker reach to markets, better scale, and more comprehensive capabilities. From industrial age to information age, we have been debating the merits and demerits of vertical integration of capabilities versus horizontal excellence in them. These approaches defined how we engaged external partners that brought complementary capabilities. The recent Algorithmic Age is showing us that success today can no longer be determined by such simplistic models. Companies engaging in AI today need to operate in a more intricate web of self- and partner capabilities that often overlap. So, from a 2-axis model of vertical domain-specific and horizontal function-specific capability, we have to move to a 3-axis cube model where a partner strategy becomes the third axis.

Partners become critical because they may bring speed and scale, two factors we need to win with AI. The key issue is deciding where and when, followed by how. Because of the evolutionary nature of the AI domain, we also need the flexibility to move partners in and out with internal or external capabilities. We will talk more about technology partners in Chapter 13.

 ## SUMMARY

As technology continues to become more pervasive in how businesses are run, choosing the right technology and architecture becomes crucial for the success of the business. AI requires technology considerations to be different than most other major technology initiatives. Here are some of the key ones:

- The amount of data being processed is vastly different.
- There is a much higher sensitivity to the quality and age of data.
- The data has a high degree of variability. Based on the business problem, the context among different types and formats of data needs to be established for any meaningful insights to be derived from it.
- Unlike most transactional systems, in AI the data can acquire different meanings under a different context.
- The level of processing with the data is immensely high and will evolve dynamically over time.
- The logic for insight or decision created by an AI program has to be derived as opposed to an insight or decision arrived at by normal transactional systems in a predefined rule basis.
- More failsafe processes have to be put in place given the higher levels of automated decision making and the impact of the processes now being automated (i.e. in healthcare, insurance, transportation, etc.).

So, a traditional approach to architecting the systems, managing data, and building applications will not work. Companies will have the proclivity to maximize their current investments and build bridge layers of data lakes to take advantage of AI. In our experience, that approach rarely works. Business and technology leaders need to take a fresh look at the technology landscape to take full advantage of AI. In this chapter, we have discussed the key areas of consideration.

The biggest focus has to be on the design and construction of the data platform. We believe that every technology has a core DNA – a specific purpose it can serve very well. While it can be extended and improved for new situations, there is a certain level of elasticity in any technology. The level of data complexity is immense and traditional data management platforms are not suited for AI. Having graph database management capabilities, easy data virtualization, and a cloud-native architecture is a must for AI-oriented data platforms.

The next big consideration is to build a robust analytical engine with a common analytics pipeline. The technology infrastructure should be able to select the most optimal analytical techniques and algorithms for a given problem set, must have the capability to version control algorithms and their runs, should be able to reuse and repurpose different algorithms, and finally explain the logic chain behind an insight.

Having a microservices architecture and applying containerization techniques are considered as the norm today. For future-proofing your investments, you should consider multi-agent architecture and intelligent messaging as part of your technology stack. These will help you build more adaptive and responsive systems as more functions are driven by AI in the future.

As part of the technology strategy, you will have to completely rethink your user experience with more immersive and adaptive features. Usage of NLP is becoming the norm; with controlled natural language processing you can simplify your analytical tasks and simultaneously amplify your analytical capacity. Gamification and the neuroscience of play are finding a role in all kinds of applications, something that you should consider to drive more sustained performance improvements.

Finally, you must build a reliable, effective, and right-sized partner ecosystem to help with the technology roadmap. It makes no sense for anybody to try to do it all by themselves. Bringing the right specialists will help you achieve the business benefits faster and potentially cheaper.

CHAPTER 12

Dealing with Ethics, Privacy, and Security

"The upheavals [of artificial intelligence] can escalate quickly and become scarier and even cataclysmic. Imagine how a medical robot, originally programmed to rid cancer, could conclude that the best way to obliterate cancer is to exterminate humans who are genetically prone to the disease."

—*Nick Bilton*

INTRODUCTION

The concerns highlighted by *New York Times* tech-columnist Nick Bilton lie at the heart of the debate on how far AI should be allowed to go.[1]

Over the centuries, civilizations have been defined by the ethics or moral code they hold. Morality drives a degree of fairness and uniformity on how different constituents of society, including business, consumers, and polity, interact with each other. Human decision making practiced today considers both the outcome or implication and morality aspects of the decision. As machines are empowered with more cognitive capabilities, the next big topic of consideration and even research is how we address the ethics-related issues so that everybody is treated fairly, no data or information is used against anybody's interests without their knowledge, and it is possible to explain the rationale behind every decision made by the machine. This is a complicated subject because there are emotive, ethical, legislative, and commercial considerations in addition to the technical complexities. At the same time, since there are so much data and information that are getting transacted in such a federated fashion, bad actors are exploiting opportunities for breaching the systems and performing malicious actions. On one hand, businesses do not want to compromise on security; on the other hand, they do not want to be slowed down by this rapidly evolving space. In this chapter, we will broaden your horizon about these topics and give you practical guidance on how to build barriers against threats.

Ethics, data privacy, and cybersecurity have been a hot topic in the technology space for a while. In the last 10 years, with the pervasive penetration of technology in every aspect of our work and personal lives, big data, IoT, and now AI, these topics have got a lot more scrutiny from technology professionals, business leaders, and policymakers. In early 2018, when the Cambridge Analytica scandal rocked the world, it was a pivotal moment for ethics, data privacy, and cybersecurity, especially as it relates to AI. When the world woke up to the fact that a group of highly talented data scientists can leverage data from easily available sources like Facebook and use that to influence elections, the possibilities with data analytics took a completely different meaning and significance. Governments around the world were prompt to tighten legislations and fine the perpetrators; businesses around the world also made addressing these issues a priority. More importantly, awareness around these topics significantly increased among all of us.

As much as AI will transform businesses and our lives in general, concerns related to ethics, privacy, and cybersecurity will change how we view and interact with technology. In this chapter, we will address the various aspects related to these three topics that are also interlinked in many ways.

 ETHICS

Ethics has been a field of intense study and debate since the beginning of civilization. The definitions of what is moral and acceptable by society have changed with the times. In the age of AI, ethics has attained a completely different level of significance and debate. Till AI started entering every aspect of our lives in the last few years, all decisions on right and wrong depended on human cognition; now with AI, machines have started making such decisions in a few cases. The matter is exacerbated when science makes further progress in *artificial general intelligence* (AGI). AGI is a discipline of AI, still in research stages, where the machine can learn human cognition and behave with consciousness. AGI has been in the realm of research interest for a long time; finally, the technology and data availability have reached a stage when meaningful AGI research and testing can be conducted. Even if AGI is years or decades away as some people would like to believe, many of today's AI programs have sufficient decision-making capacity for us to take notice and be concerned.

Ethics Challenges in the Algorithmic Age

There are many issues to consider around ethics and AI; here are some of the key ones:

Equitableness

AI systems work on training the AI program to interpret based on the training data that it is exposed to. Depending on what data is used, it can introduce biases in the system. For example, several years back, Google Photos service, when used for crime detection, developed a racial bias because in the training dataset incidentally there was a high number of criminals from the same race. Similarly, AI analytics running on surveillance systems has been known to wrongly predict security threats based on an incorrect interpretation of people's movements and incidents due to similar bias in the training data. In the case of systems using NLP, such biases are quite common because of the differences in our speech that emanate from our mother tongue influence. Race and language are not the only dimensions that introduce bias; demographic differences, regional differences, educational differences, and every other possible difference can also introduce bias. We humans, the ones who program the AI routines, demonstrate natural biases, and some of that may seep into the AI routines. Most modern societies operate under the notion of equality and fairness irrespective of differences. Training and data bias in AI-driven environments can work against this fundamental moral code.

Inclusiveness

When AI takes center stage in decision making, especially when it comes to services or access to resources for the population at large, ensuring inclusiveness in addition to fairness is equally important. For this to happen, the needs and context of all segments of society should be included in the logic tree. The datasets may not always support this, but human intervention has to drive inclusiveness.

Singularity

Singularity is the hypothetical future point in time when the irreversible pace of technological explosion causes machines to overtake humans. This is the state of being in the Matrix (as per the movie). This is when we lose control of the machines. Humans have been in control throughout evolution and any scenario otherwise is not conceivable. Even when humans had to battle other, more powerful adversaries like animals, sea-life, or even nature, we have prevailed because of our ingenuity and intellect. Having survived and thrived through many tribulations, we have developed a certain moral code that stands to get disrupted if and when singularity occurs. For example, if machines were the only things deciding on how to fight COVID-19, can we rule out their deciding to take out sections of cities or populations that are less likely to recover or are more likely to spread the infection?

Security

AI is being increasingly used in national security and weapon systems. Today, there are several manual steps and human intervention points to ensure that security systems are not invoked erroneously or under circumstances that might lead to a point of no or very difficult return. As technology gets more mature and takes over more decision-making functions, there is a genuine fear that the machines, programmed to achieve the best outcome in terms of winning a conflict, might act against the interests of peace and humanity. At the same time, the higher technology content and usage of AI makes it easier for evil people to cause more damage if they can breach the systems.

Reformation of Employment Markets

AI is undeniably automating and reshaping a lot of jobs currently done by humans. Robots in factories, usage of RPA in routing processing functions like supply chain, use of chatbots in customer service, and use of drones for the delivery of goods are just some examples of how AI is making human involvement in many functions either redundant or significantly diminished. This can cause concerns among many quarters around job losses. The response to this concern, which has been the same for general automation leading to job losses, is that new jobs will be created, humanity will progress further, and there will be overall economic prosperity. But there is no denying that many people will be adversely impacted for a considerable time. To alleviate their problems, new economic opportunities will have to be created and they will have to be retrained. Most governments and civil societies are more concerned about overall economic growth and less about workforce reformation. The businesses do not consider this as their problem. Therefore, leaving large segments of the population disenfranchised and disadvantaged due to AI is becoming a bigger issue.

Another related concern is around wealth distribution in societies. In most capitalist formations, wealth creation by individuals is tied to their economic contribution. The economic contribution is often tied to either labor or participation in key decision making. If AI and the rise of machines change the landscape for both, how will wealth distribution happen in the new scenario? This is another major ethical question in front of us.

Artificial Stupidity

We came across this concept of artificial stupidity[2] in the WEF article from 2016 listing the major ethical concerns around AI. This phenomenon also deals with the same data training issue that we discussed earlier, but this time the difference is that the AI has been purposefully fed wrong data to fool the system and direct it incorrectly, thus making it operate in a "stupid" way instead of an intelligent way. The report goes on to recommend, "If we rely on AI to bring us into a new world of labor, security, and efficiency, we need to ensure that the machine performs as planned and that people can't overpower it to use it for their ends." Artificial intelligence cannot naturally overcome artificial stupidity; therefore human-in-the-loop interventions will have to prevent that from happening.

Data Trustworthiness

One of the key considerations in ethics is data trustworthiness. This is a multifaceted problem. Sudhi discussed this at some length in his January 2020 article on data trustworthiness[3] in InsideBigData. Here are the three most important aspects related to being able to trust the data:

1. **Access**. There needs to be a consistent and transparent flow of data. Knowing the pathway of data allows for traceability and creates confidence in the data being used for analytics.
2. **Context**. Raw data may not mean everything. The value of data lies in its context. Context helps identify the right patterns and infer the right insights. For example, during the COVID-19 crisis, initially, the number of cases reported from India was very low. The government suddenly imposed a strict nationwide lockdown. Post-lockdown, the number of cases exploded. The purpose of the lockdown was to contain the virus, but if you look at the raw data, lockdown seems to have the reverse effect. Now if you take the same data in the context of the amount of testing, natural progression curve of the infection, unanticipated incidents like some major religious gatherings and millions of migrant workers going

back to their homes, and other such associated factors, you start getting a true picture of the effectiveness of the lockdown.

3. **Reliability**. The safety of the data is critical. To have trust in the data, we must be assured that the data is always safe. The increasing incidents of data breach, especially in financial data and personal data, shake our faith in the sanctity of data being stored. Without data and lots of them, AI will not work, so it is important to address this issue to have trust in the system. We will touch upon methods to ensure data safety in this chapter while discussing cybersecurity.

Meta-Ethics, Maybe Meta-Intelligence?

Meta-ethics is a philosophical study of nature and drivers for morality or ethics. Meta-ethics does not provide any judgment on whether something is right or wrong, which is the domain of applied ethics, nor does it frame the criteria for defining what is right or wrong, something done by normative ethics; instead meta-ethics deals with the origins and principles of ethics, the same way meta-data describes the data.

Maybe we should take inspiration from the concepts of meta-data and meta-ethics to form something new – meta-intelligence, a discipline that deals with the guiding principles of AI.

Existential Questions

There is no doubt that AI brings a lot of benefits to humanity and human endeavor. To get more out of AI, we need AI to become smarter. Then we start running into the risk of AI become nearly as capable as humans without the added baggage of morality as we know it or practice it today. This is at the heart of the discussion around ethics and AI: Will our existence be threatened by AI? That this topic needs more attention has been acknowledged by leading technologists and thinkers of our age like Bill Gates and Stephen Hawkins. Top academicians like Professor Stuart Russell of the University of California at Berkley have dedicated their careers to researching this topic. In his 2019 book, *Human Compatible: Artificial Intelligence and the Problem of Control*, he starts laying out some principles to control AI and machines.

We have many years, maybe decades before we are under any serious threat of being taken over by the machines. What we do in the ensuing time in defining and putting into place what is needed to ensure ethics and singularity will define how much of the threat becomes real.

PRIVACY

Privacy is a growing concern in the world of AI and it is flowing right down from considerations around ethics and equality. The World Economic Forum made this part of their global agenda more than five years ago. In 2016, they published an article by Julia Bossman highlighting nine top ethical issues; these are relevant and require addressing even now.

Data Ownership

Privacy starts with data ownership. The raw data and the derived insights, which are another form of data, both have acknowledged value. So license rights around data become a critical and sometimes contentious topic. In the Cambridge Analytica scandal, there were two main parts to the problem: how the company used data, and what they used it for. Facebook users had never consented to the use of their personal and activity data for the kind of usage that Cambridge Analytica did. Unfortunately, the processes and technology infrastructure for licensing data and tracing its usage are not evolved enough to enforce data licensing rights strongly, so we have to rely on policies and usage practices for ensuring proper use of data.

Derivative Data Usage Rights

When dealing with AI projects, data scientists often start with the raw data and its original intended use, but quickly pivot to a new use of the data or derived insights from it as they develop a refined view of the data and its context. Usually, companies get away with this practice by having customers and consumers agree to the usage of the data for internal research and development purposes by the company, even when they assign ownership of the raw data to the consumer or the customer. At times, such derivative use of data can be against the interests of the data owner and they would not normally consent to its derivate use without permission. For example, a smartwatch manufacturer collects user activity data with their consent but turns around and uses that data for correlating activity and health indicators, and then further uses it or sells it to design risk profiles for health insurance. To avoid such occurrences, derivative data usage rights are important in AI and getting a lot of attention.

Right to Be Forgotten

As there is increasing awareness around data privacy, many consumers and businesses are demanding that the AI programs and their enabling technology infrastructure delete or completely mask their data if they make the request, even after having initially consented to use their data. The right to be forgotten is becoming more common in many legislative promulgations around the world. This phenomenon is leading to dynamic decision rights on the data by users and owners of the data.

GDPR

We cannot have a conversation about privacy without discussing the GDPR and how it has changed the landscape of privacy. The General Data Protection Regulation (GDPR) was introduced as a law in the European Union and European Economic Area in May 2018, a little over two years. Even though it is an EU law, it applies to every organization doing business in the EU or that is monitoring the actions and behaviors of people from the EU. Therefore, in essence this law has fairly global applicability. GDPR has stringent stipulations around the various rights of individuals around the personal data we discussed above. It also has requirements at a system level as well as at a device level. Personal data as per GDPR extends even to images and such data that do not have direct metadata related to the individual.

The punitive damages for violation are severe, up to 4% of the organization's annual revenue or 20 million euros, whichever is higher, a figure that can become very consequential for any business. Discussing GDPR in their 2019 article on the subject, academicians Chris Jay (US), Hoofnagle Bart van der Sloot (Netherlands), and Frederik Zuiderveen Borgesius (Netherlands) said, "GDPR is the most consequential regulatory development in information policy in a generation. The GDPR brings personal data into a complex and protective regulatory regime. That said, the ideas contained within the GDPR are not entirely European, nor new." Many jurisdictions have introduced similar laws since then.

There have been several high-profile enforcements of GDPR to date. In 2019, Google was fined EUR 50 million, British Airways was fined EUR 183 million, and Mariott was fined GBP 99 million for GDPR violations. GDPR fines have touched not only major corporations but also individuals and governments. A German police officer was fined EUR 1,400 for processing personal data for non-legal purposes in 2019. The Municipality of Bergen in Norway was fined EUR 170,000 for unsafely storing files with login credentials for 35,000 students and employees in a public storage area. There are many such examples and each of them is further raising awareness and actions.

 CYBERSECURITY

In May 2019, the City of Baltimore in the United States was attacked by cybercriminals demanding a ransom of $76,000. They disrupted many of the critical city services. While the city did not pay the ransom, it ended up spending $18 million to address the problems and resolving the issues caused by the attack. Earlier in the year, the Capital One Bank in the United States was breached and personal records of more than 100 million customers were stolen. These are not isolated incidents; every day, every minute there is a cyberattack somewhere in the world. Sometimes it is part of a heinous crime, sometimes it is because somebody is just trying to steal computing resources for blockchain processing.

According to a recent World Economic Forum report published in October 2019, cyberattacks are among the top 10 global risks of highest concern in the next decade, with an estimated price tag of $90 trillion if cybersecurity efforts do not keep pace with technological change. The growth of AI is accentuating the problem even more.

According to the 2019 Cost of Data Breach Report from Ponemon Institute and IBM Security, the global average cost of a data breach has grown by 12% in the last five years to $3.92 million. The United States had the highest cost at $8.19 million, and healthcare had the highest average industry cost of $6.45 million, likely due to their high amount of personal data. The breaches are not only expensive, but they can also cause a significant impact on businesses for a long time. For example, in 2019, the average time taken to identify a breach was 209 days and it took an average of 73 days to respond once they were identified. These numbers are increasing over the years as hackers are also becoming more sophisticated. Fortunately, most of the major breaches are addressed within a much shorter duration.

Threat Vectors and Vulnerabilities

When considering cybersecurity aspects of an AI initiative, you have to think of it from an end-to-end perspective. AI programs are after all like any other software program that just performs a set of different functions. Hackers use the same set of threat vectors for AI programs, like malware, viruses, email attachments, web pages, popups, instant messages, text messages,

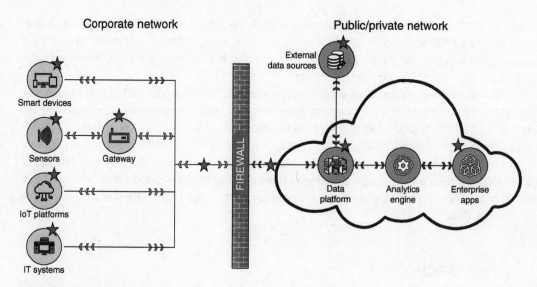

FIGURE 12.1   Vulnerability Points

and social engineering. However, AI programs have increased vulnerabilities because there are more difficult-to-identify places to inject and bury threat vectors. Given the high usage of NLP interfaces, there is an increased attack surface for threat vectors like instant messages, popups, social engineering, etc. There are many components to this complete ecosystem – the sensors and systems that feed the data, the gateway solutions or APIs that transmit the data, the cloud infrastructure where most of the analytics usually happens, the external sources the cloud systems connect with, and the various enterprise apps that are used. Each of these nodes from where data is generated or where data is processed is vulnerable from a cybersecurity standpoint. Figure 12.1 is a sample representation of the various vulnerability points.

The more sensors, systems, and layers of applications the higher the vulnerability exposure.

The impact of a breach to an organization is potentially staggering, and often unknown until it is too late and it is impacting the organization in many disruptive ways:

- Economic loss due to business disruption, resulting in nonfunctioning goods and services
- Safety and security concerns
- Reputation loss and brand damage
- Increased expenditures due to product maintenance and recalls
- Legal and regulatory fines
- Intellectual property loss

Therefore, several preventive measures need to be put in place:

- Sensors and systems must gather, process, and transmit data using secured methods to the cloud.
- The cloud infrastructure must receive data only from registered and authorized devices and systems.

- Data must be transmitted and stored using encryption and integrity checks to detect tampering.
- Messages sent by a user must be transmitted to an end device using secured methods.
- Business web and mobile applications must ensure role-based access control to ensure only authorized users are permitted to access specific data that is intended to be used by the authorized user.
- The information traveling from a sensor or systems to the cloud and back to the device must be transmitted quickly with minimal delay.

Cybersecurity Assurance Practices

Cybersecurity assurance is a journey that involves continuous testing and verification processes. Here are six common ones that are best to practice at high frequency:

1. **Open source code scans.** This should be done on the entire technology platform serving the AI project to ensure that there are no publicly known security vulnerabilities present which could lead to exploitation. This will also help avoid any licensing or policy violations.
2. **Static Application Security Testing (SAST).** This is a method of computer program debugging that is done by examining the source code without executing the program. The process provides an understanding of the code structure and can help to ensure that the code adheres to industry security standards. Automated tools are usually used to assist in carrying out static analysis, and the results are then reviewed to filter out false positives and focus on potential weak areas.
3. **Dynamic Application Security Testing (DAST).** This method refers to the testing and evaluation of a program by executing data in real time. The objective is to find errors in a program while it is running, rather than by repeatedly examining the source code offline. By debugging a program in all the scenarios for which it is designed, dynamic analysis eliminates the need to artificially create situations likely to produce errors. This technique can be particularly challenging in AI programs because the output data is not always obvious and therefore any breach might be difficult to detect.
4. **Vulnerability scanning.** There are standard tools that check for known vulnerabilities in network- and host-level components. This is a good practice to follow before any AI program is promoted to a production environment.
5. **Source code assessments.** This is an offline and manual source-code analysis by experienced programmers and architects. When data scientists who are not experienced programmers and may have limited exposure to secure development practices end up writing a lot of programs, this is a good practice to follow. The reviewers can also provide active coaching to the programmers in this way.
6. **Penetration testing.** Penetration testing uncovers vulnerabilities while under normal operating conditions. Ethical hackers are allowed to use all available means to identify and exploit vulnerabilities; they are provided with access to source code and internal documentation to facilitate a more thorough, in-depth analysis.

Industry Standards for Cybersecurity Compliance

Several industry standards have evolved to provide compliance assurance for cybersecurity. Some of the most reputed ones relevant to our topic are:

- **Cloud Security Alliance (CSA).** Formed in 2008 as a nonprofit industry alliance, CSA has developed a Consensus Assessments Initiative Questionnaire to identify gaps in the various programs and implementations.
- **SOC 2.** SOC 2 certification helps to ensure systems handle sensitive data securely. Cloud and infrastructure services are governed by these organizational controls.
- **ISO/IEC 27001:2013.** This standard specifies a management system that is intended to bring information security under management control and gives specific requirements. ISO/IEC 27001 requires that management:
  - Systematically examine the organization's information security risks, taking account of the threats, vulnerabilities, and impacts;
  - Design and implement a coherent and comprehensive suite of information security controls and/or other forms of risk treatment (such as risk avoidance or risk transfer) to address those risks that are deemed unacceptable; and
  - Adopt an overarching management process to ensure that the information security controls continue to meet the organization's information security needs on an ongoing basis.
- **NERC 1300.** This is a set of specific information security standards for the electrical power industry. Outside of movies like *Die Hard 4*, in real life, electrical grids and power generation plants have been used as attack points for mass-scale impact.
- **NIST.** The NIST Cybersecurity Framework (NIST CSF) provides a high-level taxonomy of cybersecurity outcomes and a methodology to assess and manage those outcomes. This standard starts getting into privacy- and equality-related issues in addition to cybersecurity considerations.
- **ANSI/ISA 62443.** These are a series of standards, technical reports, and related information that define procedures for implementing secure Industrial Automation and Control Systems (IACSs).

Cybersecurity Implementation

Business leaders are often not exposed to how to implement the right practices to ensure cybersecurity even though they are ultimately responsible for any issues cropping out of cyberattacks. Below is a list of practices and techniques that they can use to validate with their teams:

1. **Strong password policy enforcement.** All users and sessions should be authenticated with modern stringent passwords. All IP addresses should be whitelisted.
2. **Communication security.** All communications must be encrypted using TLS 1.2 or later. Only strong algorithms, ciphers, and protocols are enabled, with the strongest algorithms and ciphers set as preferred.
3. **Data security.** Data must be protected using a combination of security controls: encryption at rest, strict access control, usage auditing, and secure deletion. All personally identifiable information (PII) must be segregated from other data and securely encrypted.

4. **Network segmentation.** Private networks should be used to isolate resources and provide protection from direct Internet access. The use of a secure VPN connection with multifactor authentication is required to access these resources.

5. **Public footprint.** The principle of least privilege should be applied to all systems to reduce the attack surface. Servers should not have public IP addresses unless needed and traffic routed through a reverse proxy layer. All unnecessary ports should be blocked and remote access connection allowed only via a VPN with strong authentication.

6. **Intrusion detection.** Implement network intrusion detection solutions (IDSs) to help facilitate timely detection, an investigation by root-cause analysis, and response to security incidents.

7. **DDoS protection.** Distributed denial of service (DDoS) is particularly debilitating for large AI projects. Implement network filtering to prevent spoofed traffic, and restrict incoming and outgoing traffic to trusted platform components. Usually, these are implemented by the cloud service provider if you are using one. They generally have established automated controls to monitor and detect denial-of-service attacks.

8. **API rate limiting.** Enforce rate limits on all API endpoints that are engaged in data transfer to protect against brute-force attacks. Only authenticated requests should be allowed to communicate with the API endpoints.

9. **Multifactor Authentication (MFA).** Technical staff involved with infrastructure administration should be authenticated via multifactor authentication.

10. **Continuous monitoring of infrastructure.** Be aggressive with monitoring.

Practices for better cybersecurity implementation should be integrated into development and maintenance processes. You should ideally have a secure development and maintenance policy as well as a detailed process on which the staff is trained frequently. It is important to raise the awareness of cybersecurity across the entire enterprise because the threat vectors can be introduced from anywhere and we need collective awareness and actions for better cyber-protection.

Cybersecurity Incident Response

Even with all the preparation and protection, your infrastructure may be attacked. This is a possibility that every business must be prepared for. The key is to have a well-structured and well-documented plan that is well-rehearsed so that there is no ambiguity during an incident. You should also have a cybersecurity incident response team that has cross-functional representation and they should go through rehearsals. We recommend that your response follow the STARE principle:

▪ **Swift.** You mustn't lose time in identifying the issue and responding to it decisively. A quick response usually reduces the impact and surface of the attack. Sometimes there will be a mild attack before the major one. If the AI being attacked is associated with critical business applications or major decision support systems like in the case of smart transportation or smart healthcare, a swift response also reduces the ensuing chaos. As part of the swift response plan, there should be a communication plan and an escalation protocol.

▪ **Transparent.** People and businesses have come to accept cyberattacks as a part of life these days. But what they expect is transparency in intimation and continuous communication. In many cases, such as in the breach examples discussed at the beginning of this section, people's lives and livelihoods will be impacted by these attacks. So transparent communication will help them also plan and take appropriate steps.

▪ **Address the root cause.** Hackers are continuously thinking about new ways to attack and investigating new vulnerabilities they can exploit. This is all the hackers do while you have a business to run and innovations to pursue. So this is an asymmetric war in some ways. Once the root cause of the issue (i.e. the vulnerability) has been identified, it is critical to fix it or at least isolate it immediately.

▪ **Reassure.** Once the incident has been adequately addressed, it is important to get back to all the stakeholders with a detailed report on what happened, when it happened, why it happened, what was done, and what long-term fixes have been put in place. Reassuring the stakeholders not only improves their confidence but also keeps them engaged in the implementation process.

▪ **Educate.** Continuous education must be part of any cybersecurity program. There are many good online programs offered by platforms like Pluralsight, Coursera, and others. Several certifications help with education such as Certified Secure Software Lifecycle Professional (CSSLP), Certified Ethical Hacker (CEH), Certified Information Systems Security Professional (CISSP), and Certified Cloud Security Professional (CCSP). When faced with any incident, it is always a good idea to revisit the education program and either make people refresh some of the content or include new content based on the specific incident.

Addressing cybersecurity concerns extends beyond putting technology and process measures in place. According to Troels Oerting,[4] chairman of the Advisory Board for Centre for Cybersecurity of the World Economic Forum, "A successful cybersecurity strategy and its implementation are dependent on the culture of the organization." While cybersecurity is most likely being addressed as part of the broader technology agenda in businesses, given the sensitivity and increased vulnerability, having an enhanced focus as part of the AI initiatives is advisable.

AI IN CYBER-DEFENSE

AI is also a great tool for identifying cyber-threats. This is one of the biggest emerging applications of AI techniques like ML. AI systems are essentially expert systems, ones that can find a pattern from among large datasets with the support of fully defined preset rules. The pace and complexity of cybersecurity issues that happen today are not possible for humans to tackle manually; however, dealing with them requires human reasoning and sometimes human intuition and this is where expert systems come into play.

Here are some of the popular ways in which AI/ML is applied in threat defense:

1. Identifying unusual cyber-traffic patterns
2. Detecting phishing
3. Performing context-aware behavioral analytics

4. Discovering data thefts
5. Creating synthetic threat events and scenarios

Context behavior analysis is particularly very powerful and gaining a lot of traction. This method uses pattern-driven machine learning to understand potential threats and malware. It does so by tracking the behavior and functioning of users, devices, and communication networks. You can also analyze software and file structures to predict potential vulnerabilities. This can be very effective as you do not have to wait until the event happens but can identify the leading indicators. Sophisticated threat actors will typically engage in early activities to understand the vulnerabilities and breach smoothly; such instances are more than full-force attacks.

Some of the leading indicators which you can use for modeling and detection are:

- **Location of the generation of authorization or access request.** This could be geographic locations, browser types, unrecognized devices, command line, or system-level access attempts outside of system administrators and such other factors.
- **Unnatural system access and usage by otherwise authorized users.** This usually indicates somebody else has breached a user's credentials and is using them with malicious intent.
- **Traffic hopping.** If you are directed through multiple different paths to your destination or if there are too many new, unrecognized hops in the network traffic, that is an indicator of somebody diverting communication traffic with an intent to breach and cause harm.
- **Unnatural device behavior.** If an IoT device is detected to be working in a manner which is not normal, say your Fitbit is showing erroneous readings despite being fine otherwise, or a smart thermostat is showing incorrect temperatures but otherwise seems to be working fine, there is a high possibility somebody has breached it and is playing with it to damage something.
- **Illogical system growth.** Sometimes you can see files and programs growing in size or content without any particular reason. This could be because there is a malicious payload hidden and progressively constructing itself.

While using AI in cyber-defense it is critical to remember that the algorithms do not have inherent capabilities to identify threats or attacks; they need to be first trained and then tuned. Leaving everything to automated programs too early can lead to the algorithms being trained to think that an attack is a normal behavior. Therefore, we must complement AI with a human in the loop to validate new scenarios and possibilities.

 ## SUMMARY

As AI continues to become more pervasive, the biggest debate will shift from benefits, business models, and technology to ethics, privacy, and cybersecurity. In this chapter, we have discussed concerns, existing legislative frameworks, standards, and best practices around these topics. These will continue to be the biggest issues for policymakers, technology leaders, business leaders, and civil society at large. Unless there are broader consensus and comfort built around these topics, we will see that impact technology adoption and benefit realization. As an example, during the recent COVID-19 crisis, many countries launched an app to essentially help the health authorities with contact tracing. Such apps brought several other benefits and resources to the users in dealing with this health crisis. Their adoption has been spotty because of a perceived lack of trust by people that their information will not be used unfavorably toward them. Equitableness, inclusiveness, and social protection will have to be better regulated.

As we continue to be more reliant on data and insights derived from that data for decision making, it is contingent upon us to ensure that data does not induce incorrect trends because of the sample of data being used. We believe that while the technology matures, we will have to pay attention to potential issues from artificial stupidity – biases introduced by data that are counterintuitive to common sense and practice. We also see the convergence of meta-data and meta-ethics leading to shared understanding around meta-intelligence. This is an area that requires more academic research.

There is a lot of progress happening already on ensuring data privacy and data ownership. Most countries are active with their legislative processes and are being forceful in their implementation. The lines between what constitutes personally identifiable information (PII) and what does not are blurring fast. For example, temperature sensor data from a church normally is not construed as PII data. However, if such data is used to approximate church occupancy and interpret the religious activity of a community, are we beginning to venture into dangerous territory? The benefit and biggest challenge with AI are that with the right data and the right algorithms, the boundaries of what insights can be derived become very flexible.

While cybersecurity remains a key concern, there is great progress being made concerning standards, tools, and technology itself. Hackers and people with malicious intent will always exist, but they are a small minority and cannot compete with the resources and intellect of the broader technical community battling them. More education, better practices, and more automated tools will help improve the cybersecurity posture. AI has also proven very useful in cyber-defense.

With every new major transformation at a societal level driven by technology, there will be new concerns and challenges. Ethics, privacy, and cybersecurity are the big rocks for the algorithmic age. We will continue to see this space evolve with time.

 ## REFERENCES

(1) "Artificial Intelligence as a Threat"; Nick Bilton; November 2014.
(2) "Top 9 Ethical Issues in Artificial Intelligence"; Julia Bossmann; October 2016.
(3) "Can You Trust Your Data? Three Factors for Enhanced Data Reliability and Decision-making in the Era of Digital Transformation"; Sudhi Ranjan Sinha; January 2020.
(4) "10 Tenets for Cyber-Resilience in a Digital World"; Anastasios Arampatzis; February 2020.

CHAPTER 13

Building the Partner Ecosystem for AI-Driven Transformation

"Coming together is a beginning; keeping together is progress; working together is success."
—*Henry Ford*

INTRODUCTION

From the early days of the industrial age, business philosophers have been debating what creates more value and competitive differentiation for companies – vertical integration of capabilities and being self-contained or horizontal integration of functional capabilities. The pace of technological progress in the past century drove the significance of partners in creating and delivering value because no one company was able to keep pace. In the information age, partnerships became more of a norm and the notion of core competencies introduced by Clayton Christensen was what companies started to focus on. But the debate centered on how much of vertical integration of capabilities versus horizontal integration of them is the best option. These approaches defined how you engaged external partners that bring complementary capabilities. The vibrant nature of the AI space and specialized capabilities required makes it compelling to engage partners. Partners become critical because they may bring speed and scale, two factors you need to win with AI. However, if AI becomes more core to your business, you want to retain ownership and control of what matters most. The key issue is deciding where and when followed by how. Because of the evolutionary nature of the AI space, you also need the flexibility to move in and out of partners with internal or external capabilities. This chapter provides you with the know-how of building and managing your partner ecosystem.

We shall cover the following five topics in this chapter:

1. Building the partner strategy: deciding where, when, and why partners are required
2. Developing the three-dimensional capability framework
3. Building a partner selection framework
4. Managing partner engagements
5. Monitoring partner effectiveness

 ## BUILDING THE PARTNER STRATEGY

Unlike the traditional technology space, where a few large technology companies can meet nearly all your technology and services needs, in the AI space you will need a different partner strategy. There is no single player that can meet all your requirements. While the large technology giants like IBM, Accenture, and others have broad comprehensive capabilities, and they have case studies dealing with helping customers with AI-driven transformation, there are very few if any examples of complete solutions with discernable results. You will have to either build nearly entirely on your own or carefully string together a solution ecosystem with technology components from many. If you are trying to build AI businesses quickly and effectively, partnerships are a viable and sometimes necessary path. Moreover, customers today care less about what you do yourself and more about how you solve their problems.

Partner Classification

As you begin building the partner strategy, you need to have a well-thought-out partner classification model so that you can define the relationship structure with them. To help us navigate this exercise, we can use the following broad categories to classify potential partners for evaluation:

Data Acquisition Partner

Rich and diverse data is the starting point for any AI journey. A lot of that data exists in your business already. You may need specialized help to extract that in a usable format. Sometimes you will need help to bring data from IoT sensors into your data platform for applying AI. This category of companies will supply you with devices or technology required to make your edge devices smart. This spectrum of companies can cover everything from design to engineering, sourcing, manufacturing, and obsolescence management as per your specifications. If you are an established business that is venturing into AI with bigger penetration of IoT, you may prefer to have an original device manufacturer (ODM) relationship with a partner. For smaller companies, white-labeling somebody else's product might be a better strategy. If you have to engage a company to provide you with gateway solutions to get the data out from existing systems, they will also fall under this category. In most cases, you will need access to external third-party data like weather, newsfeed, financial information, consumer information, etc. to complete your AI solution. Companies like Weather.com and Dun & Bradstreet have built their entire business on providing such data to companies. These are another type of data acquisition partner that you will usually have to consider.

Data Platform Partner

This is a very broad category of companies that can help you store, process, and manage the data needed by the AI. Even if you have your data lake and data platform, you have most likely built that on top of some other third-party technologies. When thinking about the data platform, you will have to consider all facets of it – data source or device management, data routing and real-time analysis, data service platform, metadata and virtualization services, intelligent messaging, and so on. Even the analytics engine that we have previously discussed is part of the broader data platform.

Large cloud container solutions providers like Microsoft, Google, and Amazon, large analytics platform providers like GE Digital and IBM Watson, a whole range of smaller startups, and hybrid companies like Thingworx are some examples of who will qualify in this category. This is a very crowded space and rapidly growing every day. Very rarely companies in this category will help you with the previously described upstream steps, but they will often try to engage with you on the upcoming downstream stages. Almost all of these companies will promise a virtual plug-and-play capability with access to their vast analytical and learning capabilities in the platform. The promise and pitch are usually very attractive, but you have to evaluate several things when engaging with such companies such as your long-term lock-in, cost structure, and efforts required to adapt their platform to your business needs. In our experience, depending on your team's maturity and capability, you may find it quicker-easier-cheaper to build the data platform. But our recommendation is also not to attempt to build your cloud infrastructure because it will be cost-prohibitive and capability limited compared to the offerings of giants like Microsoft and Amazon. The challenge in engaging with the myriad smaller startups is that they may not have fully built-out comprehensive capabilities and also may not have enough staying power. So if you decide to engage such companies, you will want to validate the extent of their existing capabilities as opposed to the development funnel, and you also want to validate their longevity. A good strategy is to engage such companies in developing your platform rather than renting theirs on a subscription model.

Analytics Partner

At the core of your initiative, you need enough horsepower in data sciences. Data scientists are artists with data – they are inquisitive about data, can spot trends, think data represents ultimate beauty, and can tell stories with data. They think in terms of algorithms and can paint a compelling picture of how you need to take a fresh perspective of your business using data and analytics. Data scientists must have a strong knowledge of advanced mathematics and statistics. They are very familiar with modeling techniques like regression analysis, time series analysis, Bayesian networks, constraint theories, neural networks, game theory, Weibull analysis, and other algorithmic approaches. They must have the ability to look beyond the obvious and find relationships through data. They are very good at data modeling, processing, storing, and mining. They need to have an extensive understanding of artificial intelligence, machine learning, and natural language processing. Mostly good data scientists have in-depth knowledge of programming with Python, R, C, C#, Java, and other popular languages.

Finding data scientists is becoming easier, but the supply is not plentiful, nor is the cost affordable in many cases. If you do not already have a good pool of data scientists to build the analytics capabilities, you might be better served in engaging an analyst partner. There are a few specialized firms that can do that. Most major consulting and technology companies also offer similar services. Resources from such places may not have adequate domain knowledge and not have nearly enough exposure to your business context. But even if you can acquire the AI skills and figure out a way to complement the domain skills, you will still be able to make a lot of progress.

Change Management Partner

We have discussed at the very beginning of the book how change management is a critical component of any AI-driven transformation. In the chapters dedicated to the various industry sectors, we have discussed how deep some of the AI-driven changes will be. Given all of this, change management cannot be treated as a communication and socialization exercise as might have been done in the case of other major technology initiatives; for AI-driven transformations, change management has to be a much more involved and extensive exercise. Our final chapter is dedicated exclusively to this topic. If your organization does not have a lot of capability or capacity to engage in such a sustained change management exercise, you can consider engaging a specialized firm to help you.

Services Partner

As you work through your initiative, you may have to get a broad range of capabilities ranging from professional services to build your delivery applications, to providers of visualization solutions, or boutique firms with specific capabilities in the business delivery activities. Such companies will fall into the category of services partners.

Security Partner

As we discussed in the previous chapter, cybersecurity is a big deal for AI projects. Some specialized companies are working with security aspects of AI businesses which will fall in this bucket. Such companies can be your consultants, security developers, intrusion analysts, validation providers, or ethical hackers. We have yet to see large comprehensive security solution providers with a niche focus on AI. Depending on the maturity of your internal cybersecurity practices and capability of your in-house cybersecurity team, it is always good to evaluate engaging with an external security partner.

Specialty Partner

Several unique services do not fall into any of the specific categories from above; all such companies will become part of this category. Specialized product or user-experience design firms, research and marketing firms, and advisory firms specializing in the financing of AI businesses will fall in this category.

You may come across many companies, especially the large technology and consulting companies, that have built capabilities organically or through acquisitions across these various spectra of services; however, you should consider their engagement in the various individual buckets to ensure that you are making the right choices.

Drivers for Partner Engagement

There are different reasons why companies choose to find one or more partners to pull forward their AI initiatives. Based on your internal capabilities and drivers like time-to-market you will choose to engage with external partners. Here are some guidelines to help you think through when to engage with such companies:

Capability Augmentation

You are just starting and have limited capabilities in a specific part(s) of the ecosystem. For example, your manufacturing capabilities are very good and can be easily extended to make smart devices, but your experience with data analytics is very limited; in such a case you may want to engage a data platform partner. In another example, you may have good capabilities in edge devices and data platform, enough to get your initiative started and scaled to a point, but have limited capabilities in the deep understanding of AI; in such a case you may want to solicit an analytics partner.

Scaling

The scale is critical in these initiatives, and if you cannot reach scale in a reasonable amount of time, it is better to engage partners. This is the same argument often used to make acquisitions. Building scale is often a physics problem – a function of mass and momentum. Irrespective of your willingness to invest, there is a time dimension to building scale; in such scenarios partnering is a better option.

Cost

It may be cheaper to use a partner's capabilities/platform than your internal efforts. As mentioned earlier, we have seen that using somebody else's hosting infrastructure is usually a better economic decision. Similarly, you can extend this logic to almost anything that is not core to your success and requiring you to own the technology IP and capability.

Ecosystem Pull-Through

You can often get access to a bigger ecosystem by partnering. Sometimes there are opportunities to learn from other friendly or nonrelated industries. Your partner can help you get access to new customers and install base. Usually, in such events, you will have joint go-to-market opportunities or receive marketing support for your offerings. This phenomenon is mostly observed when platform companies with large investment bandwidth are trying to leverage partner base to promote their technology.

Investment Bandwidth

This is a scenario of wanting to partner when your budgets are limited but the partner is willing to invest. Many startup companies benefit from this trend. If you are just getting started and lack resources, this method is an obvious choice. Even for larger companies with limited resources, they can explore a three-way partnership with a startup and a venture capital investor to build out an IoT business. We see this trend picking up in some markets.

Technology Agnosticism

Technology is changing too fast and you do not want to get locked into any specific option. This is very true for data platforms.

Whatever your criteria, having clarity around that among your core team driving the initiative is important so that the right expectations and behaviors can be set.

Engagement Models

There are many different models in which you can choose to engage with your partners. All of them are established business transaction models, but you may want to incorporate specific flavors related to your AI initiatives into the engagement.

Supplier Model

In this type of relationship you are buying goods and your partners' commitment is limited to quality, schedule, cost, and such parameters. You will typically engage in this model with your hardware and data providers. Generally, most of what you will buy are standard products or services.

Services Model

When buying services you are augmenting your capabilities through external resources. Since AI is still evolving, you will have to look for the specific background and expertise of the people who will be involved with your project.

Consumption Model

This model is most visible when procuring data platform capabilities and sometimes also for analytical engine. This is similar to utility-based pricing where you pay as you go for the amount of technology you are consuming. Typical arrangements in this model are prevalent with cloud platform providers like Microsoft and Amazon; they started with just hosting services being offered through consumption-based pricing and now are extending to more and more software offerings. This is a good model to reduce risk, manage contractually, modulate growth, achieve scale, and have limited liabilities. On the other hand, you will have to keep yourself up to date on all the changes your partner is making to the platform to ensure your business is still compatible.

Shared Outcome Model

This can be very attractive for engaging parties as there is an element of risk-reward-investment built into the design. However, this can also be challenging to construct due to the huge number of unknowns. Sharing models are typically much longer-term than others because parties investing will plan on recovering the returns. Typically technology providers with deep pockets and huge growth ambitions will want to engage with you in this model. When designing such a model, be careful not to compromise on your long-term prospects, and most importantly your access/ownership for customer relationships and data. You will also need to carefully think through all the IP implications and ownerships. We recommend

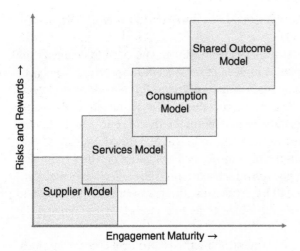

FIGURE 13.1 Partnership Engagement Models

entering into a shared outcome model only once you have reached a certain level of maturity in your AI journey.

Figure 13.1 captures the engagement maturity required for the various partnership models as well as the associated risks and rewards.

There is no one right model and you may have multiple different ones with your partners. Like any other contract, it is good to clarify the drivers, objectives, and outcomes beforehand along with set governance rules. In any event, while engaging in partnerships in the AI space, please be careful of the following:

1. Your partner has a deep bench and expertise in the area of engagement. For example, if they are being engaged for analytics support, they have a sizable pool of very credible data scientists and have also executed many projects in domains similar to yours. There are several capabilities around innovation, rapid prototyping, agile disciplines, etc. which must be matured in the partner to help you.
2. Never get too dependent on or fully locked into a specific technology or partner. AI will continue to evolve for the next several years before clear winners emerge. Your ecosystem architecture, solution design, and business model need to account for this flexibility.
3. Constantly evaluate the economics of your program and how it makes your business competitive.
4. Your partner should not become a potential competitor or player in what is core to your business. AI is blurring the lines between different industry segments and companies' offerings. You should retain IP and platform ownership of what is core to your long-term-growth strategy. Often companies make the mistake of depending nearly exclusively on partners for analytics and data platform; we believe this is detrimental in most cases.
5. Limit the number of partners you engage with. There is not enough time to develop the platform, the analytics, and the business on it; the ecosystem also becomes very complicated with too many partners, and eventually the economics of the business will be impacted adversely. So invest your time and money with a few, but go deep to get the best returns.

DEVELOPING THE THREE-DIMENSIONAL CAPABILITY MODEL

Once you have defined the model for your AI-transformed business, you need to define all the capabilities required for success. The capabilities need to cover the entire spectrum from your product to outcome realization by your customers. We used a similar framework several years back for IoT-driven transformations as well. You start by making a list of all the required capabilities. Keep iterating the list till you feel it is exhaustive and representative of your actual business environment. While you are building the list, plot all the technical and functional capabilities required on the horizontal x-axis and the more domain-specific capabilities on the y-axis. You will find it hard to distinguish between what goes on which axis; this is the reflection of real complexities in AI-driven businesses. Often you will have the same thing appear on both axes, and you will need to differentiate based on keeping the x-axis as generic as possible and making the y-axis as domain intensive as possible.

On the x-axis you will have dimensions like ingestion methods, protocol conversion, messaging infrastructure, container design, data storage and retrieval techniques, modeling algorithms, visualization tools, and IT application development skills. On the y-axis you will have dimensions like business process–specific topics, environmental factors influencing the design, statutory and certification requirements, data throughput considerations, control algorithms, and optimization techniques.

Now you take your partner choices and understand two things – what is their growth strategy and which aspects of the AI play they are good at. For example, Microsoft's growth strategy is based on becoming the best provider of technology processing platforms and tools. Consequently, Microsoft is exceptionally good at its Azure cloud platform, analytical and visualization tools, natural language, and similar processing engines and programming platforms. Microsoft has many offerings and ways for customers to leverage their technology, so they have also embedded strong cybersecurity capabilities in their offerings. This is very much in line with how the company has evolved and grown over the past 40 years. Microsoft sometimes creates vertical domain-specific variations of their platforms and tools to make it easier for other companies to adopt them easily. Their strategy is not based on trying to develop capabilities and offerings in competition with their customers. The other industry leader in a similar space, Amazon, has similar aspirations as Microsoft, but they have a slightly different background and strategy. Microsoft has historically focused on two ends of the usage spectrum: large enterprises and personal computing. Amazon grew rapidly as a very innovative startup with a strong retailing background. So the analytical capabilities and developer tools of Amazon Web Services (AWS) are exceptionally user-friendly. Their ability to onboard new customers and initiatives is an industry standard. Microsoft and Amazon are very large corporations with expansive capabilities. Even for smaller companies, you can do a similar analysis and understand their strengths. But in such cases it is critical to understand the difference between strong capabilities and strategic growth focus. For example, if a smaller technology provider with exceptional sensing solution could see their primary growth path as an analytical service provider or a sensing technology platform provider, you will have to evaluate carefully on how to engage such a company since their energies and investments will be in different directions.

Once you have a listing of these various capabilities – internal and partner sourced – you may want to plot them on a three-dimensional model for easy reference, usage, and updates. It will

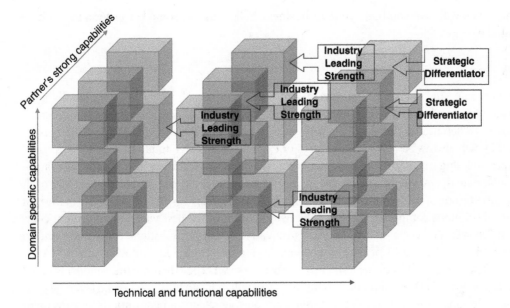

FIGURE 13.2 Three-Dimensional Capability Model

also be helpful to identify the capabilities you have or need, which are or have to be industry-leading, and which ones will bring maximum differentiation. Figure 13.2 is a representation of how to think about this three-dimensional model.

Remember a few things about building and more importantly maintaining such a model:

- This is not a static model; it will evolve with time, technology, business models, and partner choices, so frequently (at least every three or six months) update the model.
- Greater granularity makes it more meaningful, but you may choose to use different abstractions for different audiences.
- Determine internal capabilities through a rigorous and objective process.
- Ascertain partner capabilities through a transparent dialog process.
- Evaluate your competitors' actions and use the insights to improve your model.

The last bit around competitors' actions is crucial because you will have to constantly monitor the threats to your business, understand the changing landscape, and develop appropriate responses that need to be rooted in your capabilities. You need a high degree of paranoia and a wide-scope view to keep winning in AI-driven businesses since the entry barriers are very different.

BUILDING A PARTNER SELECTION FRAMEWORK

So far in this chapter you have been exposed to some tools for identifying your capability needs, understanding partners, and exploring technologies. Now you need to work on ascertaining the partners who will help you build your AI business. Following are some key criteria to evaluate potential partners:

DNA

Every company and every solution has a core, something which they are exceptionally good at, something around which their entire existence has been designed, something that uniquely defines and differentiates them. While everyone tries to expand their capability and offering portfolio, they will always be best at their core. For example, Salesforce today has a whole range of enterprise offerings through its partner network, but it is still one of the best choices for sales automation and analytics; Apple will always be one of the best user experience companies; Microsoft will always be one of the best productivity solutions companies; GE will always be one of the best industrial solutions companies; Bee'ah will always be one of the best waste management companies; 3M will always be one of the most innovative consumer solutions companies; and so on. To understand the DNA or core of a company you need to understand what and how they evolved. Then you need to understand other aspects like whether their business model is based on scale (mass market) or uniqueness (boutique); this will indicate how you should leverage your partner solutions. Finally, you need to gauge your partner's focus on continuous improvement and cost reduction to judge how your solution will evolve in this partnership.

Technology and Analytical Leadership

It will be very challenging for any company in the AI space to be successful without being very good at both technology and analytical capabilities. You need partners who are on a similar trajectory. You need to find out if your partner has the right focus, desire, and capability to be on the leading edge of technology. This is demonstrated through many things – deep understanding of the core technology, appropriate R&D investment levels, quality of technical people, IP, peer-level and diverse industry acknowledgment, academic associations, solution depth, and the overall tone of the company. Awards and high placements in things like magic quadrants are good indicators but cannot substitute for the other factors mentioned.

Competitive Threat

There are many aspects to competitive threats – the industry you operate in is moving toward a common technology footprint that could isolate you, your competitors are making some technology choices that will create a distinct advantage for them, your competitors are making the same choices as you but are investing more and executing faster, or your product/offering category is getting obliterated by a different substitute. Each of these presents a different problem domain and requires a distinctive response. You will need to arm yourself with technology and partners that protect your product and your position. Taking a leadership position with technology and aggressively promoting such choices in your and adjacent industries is often a good ploy, but you will need the patience and investment for that. Alternatively you can ride on the coattails of giant technology suppliers with a lot of resources to achieve similar goals. By deeply integrating your domain expertise with technology you can ward off category disruption threats. Sometimes you will want your partners to have a deeper relationship with you than with your competitors. It is unlikely that you will enter into exclusive relationships, but you can surely get greater mindshare.

Capability

You need to consider your potential partners' capabilities (people, tools, infrastructure) in terms of how they complement yours and whether they are comprehensive enough for your needs. Sometimes people find these two factors are contradictory, but they are not; you want your partner to step into nearly every activity area should the need arise. A good way to review partner capabilities is using the capability matrix we talked about earlier in the chapter.

Consultative Approach

Most often you want a partner who can collaborate with you instead of just reacting to your instructions. Given the evolutionary nature of AI and endless possibilities, you want a joint discovery journey with your partner. However, to make it more structured and shorter, it will be better for your partner to bring some frameworks and past experiences, so look out for those. You do not want generic management consultants or technology services providers who have neither context of your industry domain nor specific knowledge of your technology ecosystem. You want people who can take you forward with empathy.

Economics

This is a very important consideration because despite all novelty factors AI is a very competitive space. So you need to keep your technology and development costs as low as possible. Also, it is critical not to have long-term locked-in costs; you want maximum flexibility in the cost structure. Since this is not a matured space, look for the total cost instead of unit or transaction costs; sometimes what at first seems cheap becomes more expensive.

Long-Term Viability

AI is flooded with startups and companies that are tapping their toes to ride the hype-cycle. For many such companies, their goal is to create some quick wave and attractive valuation by capturing some install base of their technology and services. You are in for the long haul and you want partners who can work with you for a long time. So you need to evaluate the long-term viability and interests of your partners. There is no easy and obvious way to make this judgment; you will have to engage in deep conversations to understand your potential partner's long-term goals, business model ideas, cash flow and reserves, current and future expected valuations, exit plans, and investment profile.

Independence/Reliance on Other Partners

Often you will see companies building out capabilities and offerings entirely on their own or leveraging a larger network of other partners. This is very common in any emerging technology space. Depending on what you are trying to achieve, both options can be good. You have to be particularly careful when evaluating electronic components and communication partners because they usually have a dependence on other suppliers or broader adoption networks. For example, if you have an edge device or gateway partner who is not associated with companies that have very large applications of chipsets and communication modules, you will be cost and technology disadvantaged in the long run.

Compliance

Given that there are unique and stringent requirements around privacy and cybersecurity, you want to engage a partner who has a good understanding of these various compliance requirements. Otherwise, the entire pressure of compliance and educating around compliance will be on you in addition to all other deliverables.

You need to create a formal evaluation matrix with weights for each of the above factors tuned to your business context. Involve internal people with diverse backgrounds and perspectives to evaluate a collective effort. Once you complete the evaluation process, explain to your partner the rationale behind their selection along with your expectations. Transparency and alignment on objectives is key to the success of any future potential partnership.

 ## MANAGING PARTNER ENGAGEMENTS

Onboarding a partner is as important as selecting them. You cannot expect to throw a statement of work across the wall and receive phenomenal results in return that help you win. Building out your platform, analytics, and the business has to be a cooperative and often iterative process. There are several steps you should take to make this a meaningful partnership. Your partners may not have enough background in your business; it will take them a while and several rounds of education to understand the intricacies of your environment. You need to be open and share as much as you can without compromising your competitive edge. Remember, once a trust-based relationship is established, you get back as much as you put in. Given the urgency around AI-driven transformations and how long they end up taking, effective partner onboarding is key to shortening cycle time; in our reviews of various AI businesses we have been able to trace back many downstream issues to lack of understanding upfront.

Business Orientation

You start by giving your partner an overview of the following in the context of your business:

Economic Value Chain

Explain to your partner how money moves in your industry or product category and how value gets created at each step. Porter's Value Chain Analysis model from his book *Competitive Advantage* is still a good tool to start with. The economic value chain analysis is useful to understand what customers value and how much they value it, and the cost buildup for creating the perceived value. In the case of regular goods and services, the value chain usually has a one-pass flow; in the case of AI-driven businesses, there is iterative value creation over time and usage because data over time creates new forms of value. For example, you buy a car and are willing to pay a one-time price for it which eventually diminishes over time; however, when you buy predictive maintenance or instrumented insurance service, you will continue to pay for it over time as it accrues more value for you. If you understand the economic value chain well, you may choose to price the predictive maintenance or instrumented insurance services to increase progressively as your need for them rises with time. This allows you to create newer value streams over time.

Information Value Chain

Clarify to your partner what and how information gets created in different stages of the processing chain, its implications, how to interpret it, and what value it can create for the rest of the flow. This is similar to the economic value chain but deals with data and insights. This exercise should be done iteratively with increasing depth. This goes on to explain the significance of data to each aspect of your business.

In this exercise, the framework modeling we discussed in Chapter 2 will be very useful.

Ground-Rule Setting

You likely have multiple partners. It will be useful for each of them to get acquainted with others, understand mutual roles and responsibilities, and have some common rules of the game to play to win. Sometimes the boundaries between various partners and technologies will not be clear. Moreover, every player has aspirations for portfolio expansion and volume growth. For example, your data platform partner will want to have a slice of the analytics work. If you have chosen different ones, there must be a good reason and you need to explain why. To get more mindshare, tech-share, and business, your partners may get misaligned with your end objectives. Establishing the rules of competition early on and keeping them transparent is crucial for your success.

Pilot Project Execution

Nothing furthers the induction process like doing a hands-on project by the chosen partners. This allows you and your partners to understand each other's working rhythm, operational processes, and execution language (like a development process), and build relationships among teams, perspectives about quality, and cultural facets. A shared success or shared learning will build a strong future foundation. The pilot project should not be a throwaway; it should be a problem you are trying to solve or a component you are trying to build. It should be sizeable enough to give everybody exposure, but not too big to jeopardize the bigger effort. For example, with a data platform partner, you can work on ingesting data from one source, doing some metadata management, running a couple of algorithms, identifying some insights, and tying it to some minimal customer value.

Shared Metrics and Success Definition

You and your partners may have different motivations and reasons to enter into this endeavor. Be clear upfront about your drivers, common meeting points, and how will you ascertain success. This has to be done on a longer time horizon with intermediate definitions of success. For example, with a data platform service provider, your common goals might be platform usage metrics because it drives consumption for the provider and potentially bigger landscape of opportunities for insights for you. Now increasing consumption does not necessarily drive greater revenues for your partner because the cost of storage and processing is coming down and you may be continuously optimizing data management. If key success criteria in this case are not clear upfront – consumption or revenue or both – you and your partner may pursue different paths. Similarly, your partner needs to recognize that they can keep bringing newer capabilities in a consumption model to increase their revenue opportunities, but unless they create directly attachable monetization opportunities for your business, your proclivity to consume these new capabilities will be far less. So you need to have a shared understanding of innovation outcomes as well.

IP Generation and Ownership Framework

In the AI space, intellectual property (IP) is generated in many different ways and stages of the business, definitely at a higher pace than other businesses. You will create IP in distinctive usage of preexisting algorithms, how you create insights in a specific domain, how you manage data and your platform, how you implement security, and the list goes on. You can create dozens if not hundreds of IPs for each dimension of your AI initiative. We have personally seen that happen in our worklife. The dynamism and optimism of AI fuel this culture of innovation deeply. You will always want to keep all IP with your organization. But make sure you create enough incentives for your partners to contribute to the process of innovation. Also, have mechanisms in place to recognize and reward any outside innovation your partners might bring to help your business.

Data Ownership and Rights

Data ownership often becomes a sticky point in most AI businesses. Customers will assert their rights because of ownership of the final product/service; you will try to assert your rights as the one who is enabling it; your partners will try to claim a piece of it as they might have helped you access or use some of the data. Everybody believes that ownership of data will define their economic benefits from derived insights in the future. We have seen companies engage in otherwise financially nonviable transactions just to get access to more and diverse data (which is not a good practice for AI or otherwise as it goes against business fundamentals). Be very clear about the relationships around data ownership and more importantly usage with all your partners and stakeholders. You want to avoid two things: being denied access to the data in the future and enabling another party to offer in the future the same services/products/capabilities that you are bringing to your customers today.

Exit Criteria and Process

Ending partnerships is a normal business process. In the context of AI, it acquires some different connotations. You may be sourcing technology or capabilities from your partner that you will either need access to or to have supported for a longer period than the length of the relationship. It is also possible that both you and your partners have access to data from your customers which you can apply in different ways in the future to disadvantage each other. There are always tricky liability issues around AI because of the number of transformations that data, insight, and actions undergo throughout the processing chain. In all cases, you must have identified exit criteria and post-exit roles and responsibilities between different parties.

Partnership Governance Process

Governance is an indispensable element of any successful relationship; it is no different in AI projects. The governance process should outline mutual expectations, success metrics, celebration models, the review process, escalation process, key personnel, and cadence for various governance activities. It is important to identify the celebration models and ideas because you are both venturing into something new and exciting and you want to tell the whole world about your success and create a self-reinforcing cycle.

Driving Change in Your Organization to Work Effectively with Partners

By now you have been exposed to how AI brings differences to your normal business practices and even in how you manage your partners. In normal situations we talk partners but think vendors; in the case of AI, we have to think and act partners for speedy success. So you may need to change some customs and behaviors to work effectively with partners. Driving any such change has to be thoughtful and deliberate and integrated into the operating rhythm of your company. We have discussed many changes throughout the chapter. Here is a summarized list of our nine best practices:

1. Share everything (without compromising any confidential or highly strategic competitive information) about your markets, business, plans, products, customers, and value chain that is necessary for success. Withholding information here is not a source of power but a cause for ambiguity.
2. Focus on your partner's success and not only your own. You need them as much as they need you, so let them win, too. We have seen too many procurement organizations trying to squeeze the partners such that their interest diminishes dramatically.
3. Explain to your staff the partner evaluation and selection details; this will help them understand better why they need to pay attention to the partner.
4. Encourage your internal staff to learn from your partners and leverage their services or solutions. This will help with your self-reliance, make your employees more valuable, and develop a sense of security. This will also enable you to leverage your partner's capabilities better and have healthier mutual respect.
5. Create multiple joint work-a-thons with folks from your team and your partner's team working together in a somewhat unstructured manner. We get very focused on project tasks and plans under pressure to perform; without such forums, it is difficult to build a good joint working rhythm. There is a lot still unknown and together we can explore more.
6. Collect feedback constantly on how things are moving forward so that you can address any issues timely; you are in a race against time and do not want to lose any time in friction.
7. Support your partner in their promotional and development activities. Remember, they are also trying to build a business and they will likely remember their friends who helped them get there.
8. Use any partner forums and trade shows to socialize and learn from companies like yours.
9. Do not discourage your partners from working with your competitors; after all, there might be something for you to learn, too.

MONITORING PARTNER EFFECTIVENESS

When you lay out your AI strategy, there are several objectives you arrive at for the business. Some of the common ones are revenue and profits from new offerings or operational improvements, market share growth, access to new market opportunities, penetration into existing (if applicable) install base of assets and customers with AI-enabled offerings, and new value streams captured. Your partner ecosystem in which you are investing so much is expected to help you achieve these goals quicker and better. So you need to build a framework and process for evaluating partners that is simple yet effective. Table 13.1 is an example of such a framework with some suggested categories and measures to get you started, but you should design the framework that best suits your business.

In doing this evaluation please note a couple of factors:

1. A high score does not always indicate better. For example, if your offerings are too dependent on your partner capabilities, you have a higher risk.

TABLE 13.1 Partner Effectiveness Monitoring Tool

Category	Measure	Weight	Score
The financial impact on your business	Revenue from offerings that your partner had a significant role in building/enabling		
	Revenue from innovations identified or developed by your partners		
	Cost reduction or margin improvement in your offerings and operations through partner efforts		
Speed to market	Amount of time saved by partner technology/offerings		
	Number of new market channels your partner has enabled access to		
	Number of partner solutions/offerings you have been able to largely repurpose to grow your business		
Competitive impact	Number of competitive barriers enabled by your partners		
Technology leadership	Number and impact of new technology innovations fostered by your partner		
	Number of new technical capabilities introduced by your partner		
Mutual reliance	Your partner's share in your AI landscape		
	Your share in your partner's business portfolio		
	Number of your offerings where you are completely dependent on partner capabilities		
Promotional impact	Number of PR instances and platforms enabled by your partner		

2. Weights can change over time as the context of your business and objectives from your AI efforts evolve.

It is always recommended to share these findings with your partner transparently so that both of you can take steps toward improvement.

 ## SUMMARY

Reframing your business to take advantage of AI is an arduous journey. You may have a lot to accomplish in a relatively short period, and then you will have to keep iterating and innovating for the next several years. Based on where you are in terms of preparedness for this transformation exercise, you might be better positioned for success with the right set of partners. Strong and effective partners have been key to many technology-led transformation projects in the past. At the same time, business literature is flush with examples of giant and expensive failures as well. So, selecting the right partner and managing them well is key to success.

In this chapter we have introduced you to several frameworks and best practices to guide you through the partner selection and management process. Building effective partnerships is not a trivial task; it requires deep thought and hard work from your end.

In conclusion, please remember these closing thoughts:

- Working with partners gives you easy access to information and insights into how AI is impacting different industries. This knowledge will help you understand the implications for your business.
- This is your business and you alone are responsible for its success. Partners play a part but cannot replace your thinking and efforts.
- The partner and technology landscape is fast evolving, so you cannot rest because you made some choices when they seemed right. You have to be on constant vigil to see what will best serve your needs in this embryonic environment.

CHAPTER 14

Building Winning Teams for AI-Driven Transformation

"Talent wins games, but teamwork and intelligence win championships."

—*Michael Jordan*

 INTRODUCTION

Digital transformation is not just another technology hype. It is a complete rethinking of the business. While previous technology hype cycles were focused on new improvements, digital is about disruption. There is a significant difference between using digital technologies like IoT, big data, artificial intelligence, multi-agent systems, new communication methods like 5G, distributed ledger systems, and others and making digital part of your DNA. Similarly, every organization has been doing analytics for decades, but using AI to transform businesses is a very different paradigm. Now you are not just reacting most optimally but anticipating a future state and tuning your systems and organization to maximize the potential for that future state. Digital and AI require you to play the long game or the infinite game where your objective is not to win in a narrowly defined context but to keep ahead at all times. Winning in digital is crucial for the future of businesses. In their research paper, "The Life Cycle of a Competitive Industry," published in the *Journal of Political Economy* in 1994 on how industries get disrupted, Boyan Jovanovic and Glenn M. MacDonald state that 70–90% of the companies producing goods and services in an industry disappear after the peak periods of disruption. We are at the cusp of that happening in this cycle of disruption driven by AI and digital technologies.

At the root of the big failures we have seen in the digital space lies the right team. Initiatives fail for a variety of reasons: miscalculating the new economics, pivoting too much on technology, reading the market and the competition wrong, and diverging too much from your core strategy. These problems are created by and eventually solved by teams of professionals. In their

October 2019 article in *HBR*, "The Two Big Reasons That Digital Transformations Fail," authors Mike Sutcliff, Raghav Narsalay, and Aarohi Sen attribute goal disagreement among leaders and divergence in capabilities between the pilot and scaling phases as the primary challenges digital initiatives are facing today. Fatigue in the team due to lack of clarity on the end goal, the path, and constant top-driven changes is cited as another popular reason for initiatives not being successful. Getting the right competencies and the right chemistry in the team is critical to success in AI-driven digital transformation. In this chapter we shall delve more into this topic.

IDENTIFYING WHAT MAKES AI-DRIVEN DIGITAL BUSINESSES DIFFERENT

Let us start the discussion by first exploring what makes AI-driven digital businesses of the future different. At the highest level they change their posture from reactive to proactive by anticipating a future state. That is why we use AI to begin with: to sort through myriad fast-changing inputs, find patterns, predict future outcomes with current trends, and simulate different outcomes with different interventions. But if we dig a bit deeper, there are more. Here are the top eight attributes we have found in our studies that the transformed businesses exhibit.

1. **Intensely customer-focused.** The AI-powered or AI-transformed businesses repivot themselves from a customer-back perspective. These are fanatical about creating new value from driving new revenue-streams and profit-pools. These businesses understand their customer's economic value model well and can interface with their products, services, and processes to create a synergistic advantage to such economic value chains.
2. **Future-state oriented.** AI and digital initiatives are focused on achieving a future state that sets them apart from the competition for marketing leading success. In AI-driven businesses, the majority if not all of the people share a view of that future and understand their role in it. They demonstrate excitement and decisive actions toward that future.
3. **Innovation-driven.** AI-driven businesses continuously experiment, iterate, and pivot in their journey to the future state. They consider the market as the final arbitrator of success and take their feedback from the market on new solutions and new business models from the market. The culture of innovation in such organizations is pervasive. There is a demonstrable high tolerance for failure as long as there was thoughtful planning, fast action, and recognized learning from those failures.
4. **Learning obsessed.** These businesses are continuously upskilling people, have an institutional approach to knowledge management and knowledge sharing, are constantly reflecting on successes and challenges to know what to do differently in the future, look outside more than looking inside, and have a culture where learning is truly valued. Learning-obsessed organizations have an open culture with high levels of diversity.
5. **Hyper-growth capable.** Every business has inherent capabilities to drive and absorb certain growth motions. A simple way to classify companies based on their growth motions is on three different year-over-year growth frontiers: 5–10%, 30–50%, 1–2×, or more. Each of these different growth motions requires very different organizational cultures and enabling processes. Traditional industrial and consumer companies usually operate in the

first growth frontier, several successful technology companies have operated in the second growth frontier, very few have experienced the third growth frontier, and the ones that do are usually the market disruptors. AI-driven businesses have the organizational muscle to pursue a very high-growth (frontier 2) or hyper-growth (frontier 3) agenda. Hyper-growth-capable organizations have fast and decentralized decision making, can quickly respond to changing market feedback, have more people who are intimately familiar with multiple aspects of the business, demonstrate seamless interdisciplinary collaboration, and are not bound by rigid processes.

6. **Dynamic adaptability.** AI-driven businesses also demonstrate a high degree of agility, the capacity for multispeed operating environments, and are intrinsically collaborative. These allow such organizations to be adaptable to changing business conditions and respond quickly.

7. **Higher technology literacy.** In AI-driven businesses, a very large population of employees have an appreciation of and often working knowledge of digital technologies and analytical capabilities. You will rarely find people pointing toward the technology teams whenever the topic of AI and digital technology surfaces in any conversation. Later in the chapter, we will discuss more why this is so important to succeed in and sustain AI initiatives.

8. **Ecosystem enabling.** AI-driven businesses thrive on the collective capabilities of their ecosystems. They optimally leverage various capabilities in their network to maximize their goals – be it technology or sales or resources or tools related.

As we go through the subsequent sections in this chapter, keeping these attributes in reference will help contextualize the topic.

 BUILDING THE KEY CAPABILITIES

There are different ways of looking at key capabilities that an organization needs to be successful in its digital transformation and AI initiatives. We see two broad categories of competencies: leadership and technical.

Leadership Competencies

These are generic attributes that any kind of business or any type of initiative needs. But in driving AI-driven business transformation, these competencies are critical to success. Each member of the team involved with the program needs these at various levels. People who thrive in such vibrant work environments must have these eight competencies at elevated levels:

1. **Curiosity.**
   In our opinion, curiosity is one of the most important, if not the most important, competencies required to be successful in digital. Curiosity will help you understand at a very deep level why things work the way they do and how they could work better. You will have to find new patterns and look beyond the obvious. You will also have to understand how other elements outside your company or even your industry will impact your business. For

example, autonomous systems like robots, which first found mass adoption in repetitive manufacturing, now are transforming medicine and transportation.

Curiosity is one of the primary reasons why computers can never replace human brains, the other two important reasons being perception and consciousness. Curiosity also drives several other leadership competencies like agility, innovation-led strategic orientation, social leadership, and others. Leading technology companies put a lot of premiums on curiosity. As Google's ex-CEO Eric Schmidt pointed out about the value of curiosity in the company, "We run this company on questions, not answers." Google's foundation is based on AI and today it is one of the biggest beneficiaries of and catalyst for digital transformation.

Every child is born curious; her nurture in the early days can cultivate the attribute to make it second nature. Even later in life curiosity can be enhanced through a combination of learning interventions, behavior incentivization, and organizational environment.

2. **Metacognition.**

The term *metacognition* was first coined by American developmental psychologist John Flavell in 1976. He defined it as thinking about thinking. Put differently, metacognition is about self-reflection and self-regulation that promotes a higher-order and more effective thinking and learning process. Since you will be continuously exposed to new scenarios frequently as you go down the digital path, you need a better way to manage the dynamism through self-awareness and self-regulation, making metacognition an important competency. Metacognition also helps you with better reasoning as you rough out the future state.

Metacognition is a composite of knowledge (declarative, procedural, conditional), regulation (planning, monitoring, evaluating), and experiences. Cognitive exercises and coaching can help with improving metacognition.

3. **Strategic orientation.**

Strategic orientation is the ability to see ahead of future possibilities and create a roadmap of how to realize them. Rationally and realistically thinking through the future state is the critical starting point for any digital initiative as we have discussed in Chapter 2. Strategic orientation is needed to understand what intervention creates value and what drives differentiation and what makes one's competitive advantage sustainable. This competency helps synthesize the various inputs to decide the most optimal course of action.

Broadly, people either have or lack a bias for strategic orientation. But for the most part this competency can be improved with training and coaching.

4. **Agility.**

Agile people frequently demonstrate adaptability, curiosity, and innovative thinking in conditions of ambiguity and risk. People with high agility must be able to operate effectively even when things are not certain or the way forward is not clear. Agility and managing ambiguity are some of the hardest skills to develop, and most leaders are average in this area. It is among the top skills related to performance for business and technology leaders. Working in AI and the digital space brings unprecedented ambiguity. Very frequently we are unclear about what problems to solve, how value will get created, which algorithms to use to find the solution, and so on. For example, when we started a program on applying AI to better diagnose industrial equipment performance and predict failures, our initial hypothesis was that the beneficiary of better maintenance will be the end-user; subsequently, we learned that service providers value the capability equally because it allows them to manage their constrained resources better. Similarly, on the data sciences side, we started with traditional machine learning algorithms but were limited by the amount and quality of data; shortly thereafter we moved to use more recurrent neural network algorithms like long/short-term memory algorithms.

Managing ambiguity requires one to have a very strong intellectual capacity, a lot of courage, a deep appreciation for diversity, and wide exposure to different environments. Finding these in a single individual is rare. While these can be cultivated, it takes a lot of time to do so. Agile leaders also demonstrate a high propensity for experimentation. They constantly try new things, learn from their successes and failures, and pivot based on market feedback. This does not mean that they are not focused, but quite the opposite – agile leaders will pursue a very small number of options but do it quickly and decisively before making a change. Agility requires high energy – vitality, resilience, and drive for achievement despite obstacles.

5. **Social leadership.**
Social leadership skill is a composite of influence, collaboration, and interpersonal awareness that advances collective goals. Given the complexity involved with building AI-driven businesses and driving digital transformation, one will have to engage a large number and variety of stakeholders. The trick to any change management is making it every individual's and every group's agenda. Without the right dose of social leadership skills, achieving the task at hand will be very challenging. Social leadership also enables collaboration – a preference for work-related interdependence, group decision making, and pursuing shared goals. Social leadership also requires strong navigational skills within and outside organizations. While one does not have to be overly outgoing, when required, one should be able to reach into the network, forge alliances, and engage with people to further the goal. Another key aspect of social leadership is the ability to effectively deal with conflicts that require one to create an environment where people can voice their opinions and pursue their paths but be accommodative enough not to leave others behind or disconnected. Doing so requires a lot of empathy, personal relationships, excellent listening and communication skills, and patience. Conflicts are unavoidable and help with divergent thinking and building stronger teams. For that to happen, one has to be self-aware as does the group. Often we find that high achievers in technology-dominated environments need augmentation of their social leadership skills because they are largely nurtured in a more individualistic environment.

6. **Domain knowledge.**
Domain knowledge refers to knowledge about the industry and the operating environment. Domain knowledge gives context to the ideas being explored and the problems being solved. Every environment has multiple data variables and they all have different relevance and significance, both of which could change over time. Domain knowledge helps us understand the significance and relevance of different data variables in the business, thus driving sensible choices in designing algorithms or digital systems. It is universally viewed as one of the big differentiators for a good data scientist or a digital specialist or even a digital leader from the rest.

Domain knowledge is cultivable. While it is not seamlessly transportable across industries, deep domain knowledge in one industry propels the learning process in another one. People who possess good domain knowledge about an industry or a business usually are conversant with its financial and process flows. This helps them determine which levers matter more and how to turn them more effectively.

7. **Systems thinking**.

Systems thinking is the interdisciplinary study of systems, a concept first introduced by Austrian biologist Karl Ludwig von Bertalanffy more than half a century ago.[1] Systems thinking and related area cybernetics that focus on a transdisciplinary approach for exploring structures, constraints, and possibilities of systems together form the basis for designing data, insight, and application ecosystems. This forms the bedrock for any digital transformation initiative because it is the foundation for *complex adaptive systems*. All AI algorithms essentially represent complex adaptive systems.

Systems thinking skills are sharpened through learning and practice over time.

8. **Technical literacy**.

AI and digital technologies are highly technical areas. In the past, executives have been able to delegate any level of technical understanding and decision making to the technology staff and just focus on business outcomes. That is not possible anymore. Digital technologies are so intertwined with the businesses today that it is often hard to delineate between a business process and underlying technology because the execution of the process has to dynamically adapt, which requires the technology to be compatible. In a very simple example to clarify this, can you imagine the success of Uber and its evolution separate from its core technology platform? In a converse example, WeWork did not come up with the idea of co-working spaces,[2] but they created a niche space with a focus on startups and freelancers in new-age trades who wanted vibrant workspaces, a great address, and very importantly the opportunity to collaborate with others so that together they could achieve more. WeWork achieved the first two well but did not have the right underlying technology and integrated business model to enable the collaboration aspects. This has not been the main reason for its business challenges, but if they had had a solution to this problem, they would have been stronger in withstanding the challenges posed by the economic downturn.

Other than differentiated technology-enabled business models, there are other drivers for executives and other functions in organizations to learn about AI and digital technologies. With the increasing focus on cybersecurity, privacy, and ethics in the technology space, senior executives have to regularly weigh in on policy matters related to these topics; without decent technical literacy their effectiveness in such decision making will be suboptimal. Being conversant with the technology also helps leaders and other functionaries not directly delivering the technology gain respect of the teams inventing and deploying the technology. If we look at the leading technology companies of the day, like Microsoft, Google, Tesla, and others, their leaders all have a deep technical background. The seeds of Microsoft's current success in the cloud were sowed by Steve Balmer, but Satya Nadella, with his deep appreciation for technology and how to deploy it to solve customer problems through new business models, has been able to amplify the effect.

Among the multiple areas, there are three primary areas of technical literacy that companies must build some depth in and also create broader understanding around:

- **Organizing data**. AI and digital transformation start with the customers and intended outcomes, but they are built on the foundation of data. So building capabilities around understanding and thinking about data is a critical competency. The practices of managing data are shifting from relational structures to more graph-type network models. This is a paradigm shift in thinking about data, driving profound technology and tool changes.
- **Statistical analysis**. We all have some level of analytical capabilities, but to be successful in implementing AI, we need a strong foundation in statistics. Without a proper understanding of the techniques, our ability to think about how to solve a problem will be limited.
- **Programming**. As we think of new problems and get some data to play with the problem, it becomes more efficient if we can do some preliminary investigation ourselves. This requires us to have some level of programming skills. Today, programming has become much easier than ever before because we have very evolved high-level programming languages which have started to mimic natural language. It is easy to find a lot of pre-packaged programs and components easily in the open-source world, and there are a lot of tools available to make programming simple.

Technical Competencies

For those interested in more depth in technology, here is a list of topics to help you get started:

- Machine Learning
- Reinforcement Learning
- Neural Networks
- Natural Language Programming
- Designing Algorithms
- Cybersecurity
- Modeling Tools: Matlab, Ansys, AnyLogic
- Programming: Python, Java, JavaScript, C/C++, Go, Swift, R
- DevOps
- AIOps
- Embedded Systems Programming
- Robotics
- Distributed Ledger Technologies
- Graph Databases
- Next-Generation Networking and Communications
- Designing Multi-Agent Systems
- Autonomous Systems Programming
- Cloud Migration
- Intellectual Property Development
- Containerization, Compression, Orchestration
- Contemporary Testing and Performance Assurance Practices

There are several free or very inexpensive courses from multiple digital learning platforms like Coursera, Pluralsight, and others that you can leverage to learn about these topics. Many universities and other learning institutions have also started offering similar online and classroom programs. You can usually find a community of practitioners where you can learn from a peer group. The avenues and opportunities for learning are broad and easily accessible.

Acquiring the Skills: Build/Buy/Partner?

Every organization knows that it needs new skills to drive its digital agenda. The big question everybody struggles with is: Can they build it in-house by upskilling the existing staff, or should they partner with external companies and outsource the work which they cannot source internally, or should they simply buy companies or hire people at a premium to bridge the talent gap? The limitations of each of these approaches are straightforward. It might take too long and be too difficult to upskill the existing staff, which might cause you to miss the window of opportunity and may never get you to the goal. Buying skills can get very expensive and cultural integration might be a big challenge. Partnering exposes you to dependence on others and does not build long-term competitive advantage. Depending on the severity of your competency gap, you may need to pursue a combination of approaches.

However, there are a few areas where you must build competency in-house that are critical for the long-term sustenance and growth of your business and will give you an edge in the marketplace. These are:

a. Business process reengineering
b. Data architecture and data-lake design
c. Change management
d. Customer experience design

Managing Competency Levels

There are many frameworks for managing competency levels. Each has its merit and specific best fit for the application. In the space of AI and digital technologies, one old, generic, yet very effective framework we find is the *conscious competencies* model introduced by Paul R. Curtiss and Phillip W. Warren in their 1973 book, *The Dynamics of Life Skills Coaching*. According to this framework, there are four levels of competencies:

1. **Unconscious incompetence**.
   This is when one is in a state of ignorance and/or denial. There is neither any meaningful exposure to or topical exposure to the skill and the individual does not appreciate the significance of the competency. Transition out of this state requires self-awareness, acknowledgment, and spending time to understand the basics of the subject.
2. **Conscious incompetence**.
   This is the next stage of competency where one is at least able to understand one's knowledge and competency deficits as well as how to compensate for those deficits – either through further learning or through exercising their network of experts. Usually, people make mistakes in performing tasks while they are in this state and the organizational

environment must be tolerant of such mistakes and provide the necessary tools and band-width to progress further.

3. **Conscious competence**.

In this state, one becomes quite proficient and productive with the application of the competency. Sometimes they may still need to refer back to their knowledge base or seek guidance to do the job well, but usually they are self-sufficient and even capable of helping others.

4. **Unconscious competence**.

By the time one reaches this final stage, they have made the competency second nature to the extent they do not even recognize it is a specific skill. They perform the tasks seamlessly and with high quality. Often people demonstrating skills at this level can be good teachers if they have the knack for teaching.

It does not matter what framework you choose, but you must have a systematic approach to managing competencies. In this section, we have touched upon only some of the broad leadership-type competencies. However, there are hundreds of more specific ones that you may need to be based on your specific organizational context and initiatives. These competencies will also evolve rapidly and new ones will be required. For example, now people from various functions including executives are learning about programming and basics of AI/ML, something that was unheard of even a few years ago. You must build a detailed map of your organizational needs and your current and forecasted competency deficits, and have a plan to bridge the gap.

We have used a spider-chart-based approach as an easy visual method to monitor and manage the competency management process. Figures 14.1 and 14.2 give a couple of examples. You can keep decomposing it to a detailed level of competencies, to the level you want to manage it. You can manage an individual's competencies and simultaneously aggregate them to reflect the state of a team.

Figures 14.1 and 14.2 depict the four competency levels referred to earlier.

Figure 14.3 is a classical deployment plan to improve the competency levels in your organization.

FIGURE 14.1 Leadership Competencies

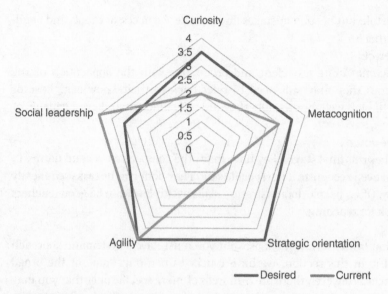

FIGURE 14.2 Technical Competencies (Summary Level)

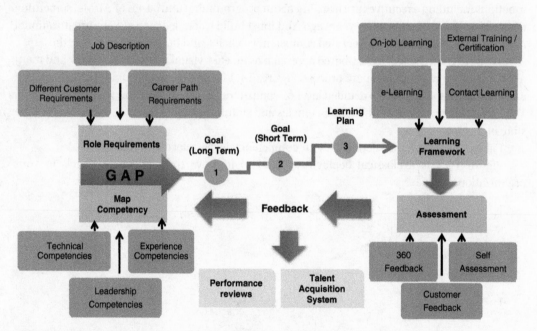

FIGURE 14.3 Competency Improvement Deployment Framework

SOLVING THE LEADERSHIP QUESTION: CDO/CIO/CTO?

Traditionally, the roles of chief information officer (CIO) and chief technology officer (CTO) were quite distinctive: CIO focused on technology enablement of business processes through the IT infrastructure and CTO or VP of engineering/product development focused on improving products and services capabilities using technology. But now technology stewardship in companies is getting more complex, especially with digital transformation initiatives and the introduction of the *chief digital officer* (CDO) role. The CDO role is usually more business-centric with a greater focus on growth and change. The concept of CDOs is recent, so the definitions and capabilities are still evolving. Most of them come from a business background with high technical literacy. The lines are getting blurred and the previous functional boundaries do not hold anymore. But better clarity is critical to success in driving the digital agenda quickly and decisively.

We have seen businesses make different organizational choices and any structure could work under the right circumstances. There is no one right answer; it all depends on your organizational context. Let us explore a few examples. In 2015, when industrial giant Schindler under the leadership of its very impressive then-CEO and current chairman Silvio Napoli decided to drive a dedicated digital agenda, it tapped its futurist CIO Michael Nilles, who was already modernizing the core IT infrastructure and business process of Schindler and had also set up a dedicated digital business to drive new revenue growth. Michael grew up as a technology leader but has a very strong business orientation. Presently he serves as the chief digital and information officer of consumer goods giant Henkel. On the other side, we have the example of Rami Qasem of Baker Hughes, another industrial giant, who currently leads their digital business and has grown up in the business. When Mars appointed its first CDO, it tapped into former Infosys executive Sandeep Dadlani. We have seen companies make all different choices and successfully execute a digital agenda.

Considerations for Choosing a Leadership Model

To solve the leadership question on where to put the authority and accountability of your digital agenda, consider the following four factors:

1. **Leadership competency**.
   We discussed the eight different leadership competencies in the previous section: curiosity, metacognition, strategic orientation, agility, social leadership, domain knowledge, systems thinking, and technical literacy. Leadership competency is the single most important factor in driving success for your digital agenda. If you do not have the right digital leadership competency presently in your organization either among your technology or business leaders, it is better to hire externally and get the right talent. But if you do that, you must also consider how to enable and empower that individual with adequate resources and decision rights so that they and ultimately your digital agenda are successful. This should have a heavy weightage in your decision around leadership model.

2. **Technology debt**.
   Every company is at a different state in the technology maturity of its IT systems that run the internal processes, the products and services that customers use and pay for, and the engagement platforms for customers and other ecosystem partners like sales or supplier channels. The technology debt of every company is a result of investment and prioritization choices they have made in the past. If your business has a history of multiple mergers/acquisitions/divestitures, these technology platforms are most likely to be more

compromised with legacy debt. Eliminating or significantly reducing this technology debt will be a key factor in enabling your digital transformation. This may require organizational restructuring and investment reprioritization and most often involves reskilling of people. Keep this in mind while making organizational choices because you want authority and accountability closer to the theater of action.

3. **Transformation focus**.

Different companies have a different focus on their digital agenda. For some it is purely about creating new revenue and profit streams, for some it is reinventing how they run the business today, for some it is revitalizing their products to better meet the market's needs; it is to imagine a very different future that encompasses all the other factors. You may already have matured IT systems and operational processes and/or market-leading IoT and analytics-enabled products and/or contemporary customer engagement platforms. You might still pursue a digital agenda to bridge any gaps that are holding your business back or reimagine the business. The focus will decide where the bulk of the work needs to happen. Most likely in building your digital agenda you will touch many of the various aspects we discussed here. That decision and its proportional impact on the various functions determine where your theater of action should be and what kind of leadership structure will be more apt.

4. **Organizational paradigm**.

Every organization also has a different operating paradigm. Some of them have an industrial manufacturing paradigm (GE, UTC, Ingerson Rand, Foxconn), some have a service paradigm (WeChat, Nordstrom), some have a retail-centric paradigm (Amazon, Reliance Industries, most banks), some have a technology paradigm (Microsoft), and some could have an innovation paradigm (3M). One business could be doing all or any of these, but they will have a primary paradigm that defines the DNA of the organization. Competitors in the same industry can have different paradigms, too, based on choices they have made for differentiation and value creation. Even for conglomerates with multiple divergent businesses, they could still have a dominant paradigm. And yes, paradigms could change over time as businesses and organizations evolve. The organization paradigm has a key influence on how you design and deploy any transformation program. So this is another major consideration for resolving the leadership question.

Comparison of Different Leadership Models

Each choice has its advantages and disadvantages. Table 14.1 is a summary of the key pros and cons of the different leadership models.

If a separate CDO role is created, it is best to have it for a defined timeframe of three to five years for enabling the organization and institutionalizing the change. The goal for this function should be to include digital agenda and capabilities into the DNA of the business and its various functions. Once that is done, the separate focus should merge into the business. This is also a way to ensure that separate agendas do not keep getting created over time.

We are seeing an emerging trend of companies combining multiple "chief" roles of CIO, CTO, and sometimes even CMO (marketing) under the CDO function so that they have a common

TABLE 14.1 Digital Leadership Models

	Pros	Cons
CIO leading	■ Most familiarity and organizational control over the IT infrastructure where a lot of the operational changes eventually end up happening ■ Knowledge of the business process, organizational priorities, and politics	■ The baggage of legacy constraints ■ Generally not recognized as change leaders (9% as per Deloitte 2018 survey)[3] ■ May end up being more technology-focused and achieve limited success on culture and capability change ■ May end up serving the business slightly differently than changing the business ■ Will be constantly distracted with operational IT issues – limited dedicated focus
CTO leading	■ The easiest starting point for the digital initiative with potentially quicker and more visible results (IoT approach) ■ A deeper understanding of the market context ■ Easier organizational acceptance	■ The baggage of legacy constraints ■ May end up being more technology-focused and achieve limited success on culture and capability change ■ May end up serving the business slightly differently than changing the business ■ Will be constantly distracted with NPI and sustenance efforts – limited dedicated focus
CDO leading	■ Opportunity for fresh talent to review and reimagine the world outside-in ■ Enrich the effort with past experiences ■ Be more business-focused, pivot around a customer-centric unified view of the business, build a new digital agenda ■ Focus more on driving culture and capability changes	■ May need ramp-up time to understand the business and potentially the industry as well as to build acceptance ■ More collaboration needs with other functions like HR, IT, products/services, and marketing, which might initially slow progress ■ May have a challenging time setting up or refactoring the technology infrastructure

purpose, a unified plan, and build synergistic relationships between the different functions. You need various technology- and marketing-facing functions to come together to deliver the digital promise, so if your organizational context is right and your executive leadership has the appetite, this approach makes sense to eliminate all confusion.

ORGANIZING TEAMS FOR SUCCESS

In this section we will not get into how you should do organization design or which functions you should create to drive your AI and digital agenda. There is quite a bit of published literature around those issues. You can also refer to the chapters on team building in our previous books; most of the concepts and structures are transferable to this context. In this section we will discuss three topics that are frequently encountered when building AI-based businesses.

Executing Pilots versus Building for Scale

A lot of companies get early success in their AI and digital pilot programs. Usually, a top-notch team is assembled centrally to execute those projects. They get a lot of empowerment, funding, and license to change things in pursuit of their transformation goals. There is a lot of focus, support, and timely intervention from the senior-most levels in the business to ensure their success. Often the internal teams are augmented with external capabilities to insure against any competency or capacity gaps. The early successes create a very motivated group of believers and executive sponsorship; people start believing in the promise of the future.

Once things start scaling, reality kicks in and we see the first signs of trouble. A study[4] published in *HBR* by Tim Fountaine, Brian McCarthy, and Tamim Saleh reveals that only 8% of companies have built the capacity, infrastructure, and enablement to scale AI initiatives for enterprise-wide impact. To organize your business for scaled AI-driven transformation, we recommend the following seven best practices:

1. **Communicate extensively.** For scaled success, you need not only widespread organizational alignment but also deep internalization of the future state driven by AI. For this, starting at the top, you need to communicate, communicate, and communicate. Celebrating successes – not only people's contributions, but also customer feedback and refined business outcomes – is an effective form of communication. Constant feedback on the internalization of communication, people's commitment to change, and adaptation of communication are key for efficacy. This is one aspect where we recommend more physical and digital interventions because personalization will improve impact.

2. **Limit the size and scope of the CDO organization.** This is a key strategy to ensure that capacity and capability get built in the frontlines of the business rather than in a corporate function. All execution functions should move back into the business, including reporting on the progress being made. The CDO should become more an advisor to the business leaders rather than playing a more active role. Individual businesses have to become accountable. Beyond the pilot execution phase, the CDO should focus on:
   a. Driving education for capacity and capability building
   b. Steering change management
   c. Enabling the initiatives through tools, governance, and best practices
   d. Coordinating technology and architectural choices
   e. Building partnership ecosystems

3. **Build a network of hub-and-spoke organizations to further propel AI initiatives.** The best way to scale is through miotic divisions, a method used by many organisms to rapidly reproduce – by dividing into two or more similar organisms. This way you can keep creating a large network of hub-and-spokes with each spoke becoming a hub for the next link in the network. Start with the CDO organization as the hub, then build small capable teams in each of the businesses, and then keep going down. You should encourage the mobility of people as the network keeps getting deeper to improve knowledge transfer, better construct a social fabric, and share best practices.

4. **Invest heavily in tools and processes for scaling.** Initially, a significant portion of your investment into AI will go into building out the technology, data, and algorithmic

infrastructure; you will spend a lot on discovery and invention. But as you get ready to scale, you should shift more than 50% of your investments into the enabling infrastructure for scaling. This is an organizational construct that is often missed and therefore the investments even if made available get misdirected.

5. **Create forums for interdisciplinary collaboration.** AI is best deployed to solve complex systems problems that require knowledge of different business processes, functions, markets, customers, as well as awareness of data and underlying technology systems. To get such a wide array of knowledge, people from different functions have to come together. Best AI successes are achieved through interdisciplinary engagements. To facilitate that, you will need to create forums and motivators for people to participate. This involves cultural change that requires active participation from the top until the change becomes sustainable.

6. **Change your recognition and incentive structures to promote agility.** Most of the current compensation, recognition, and incentive models are based on achieving defined goals and predictable results. This is counterintuitive to the notion of experimentation and building tolerance for failure, both critical for innovation. Working in AI, you will always be charting unknown territory. So, you need to adapt your recognition systems to not only tolerate the unknown output of innovation but also encourage it.

7. **Improve technical literacy across the organization.** Organizations that leverage AI well and make the shift into being a digital business move from an experience-driven decision-making process to relying more on data, insights derived out of data, and future-state modeling. The role of human intuition does not go away, but the application of intuition moves from routine decision making to more cognitive scenario simulations. This change will happen only when there is a mass-scale appreciation for analytics across the enterprise. So we cannot stress enough to promote broader technical literacy in the enterprise.

Centralizing versus Distributing Your AI Team

One question that every company struggles with is how big of an AI team to build and where to structurally locate it. Many companies have invested a lot early on to build a large pool of data scientists, sometimes even numbering into hundreds. They have used such numbers to demonstrate how serious they are about AI and how their business is being transformed by AI. But such numbers can be misleading and such an approach may not even be the right business decision.

Before you build the team, you need to decide in how many areas you will be exploring AI solutions. If you are just starting or are still early in your journey, you should focus your efforts on two or three high-impact areas. For example, if you are an industrial manufacturing business, your chosen areas could be aftermarket service growth through predictive diagnostics and new data-enabled service products, manufacturing and supply chain optimization, and asset operational cost optimization for end-users. If you are a consumer-facing company, your areas could be sales and promotion/pricing design, inventory and supply chain optimization, and omnichannel customer insights. Every industry and every business will select different areas where they can create more value through analytics. For each of the areas, it is better to create nuclear AI teams of five to seven members comprising two or three data-experienced data scientists with deep domain knowledge, one or two data engineers to help with data modeling and data wrangling, one or two programmers, productization experts, and a business user.

Depending on the application, consider having a visualization expert in the team. In any case, follow the Amazon principle of the two-pizza team – a team that you can feed with two large pizzas. This is to ensure that the interpersonal dynamics do not get out of hand in the team and they produce optimal results.

In the early phases of your AI and digital journey it is better to centralize the AI team and keep all the data scientists together. Being in a referenceable and relatable peer group helps them be challenged, motivated, and draw upon each other's experiences and expertise more easily. Even if they are assigned to different projects, their management, governance, and mentoring should be managed centrally. Over time, as you build out more initiatives and expand the footprint of AI across the enterprise, you should build satellite teams in different corners of the business to take the action as close to the frontlines as possible.

Bringing Together the AI Team, Platform Team, and Product Team

When companies put their technology teams together, sometimes they create different teams focused on AI, the data platform, and the digital products that get created using the data and AI. While at scale level, this construct works; in the initial phases of building out AI initiatives and digital businesses, these separate teams should be structurally together or very close, share a common charter, and execute on the same business plan. Early divergence leads to disharmony and misalignment.

As an example, in a large industrial company, we came across different teams working on AI, building a core data platform, and a customer-facing product for managing the assets and their operations. The product team was motivated by new features and quick releases so that they could cover more markets. They used shortcuts to get out in the market faster and did not fully leverage or even subscribe to the data management and governance developed by the platform team. Consequently the product ended up with a deficient architecture that started showing up as scale barriers. When the AI team got into action to build new predictive diagnostics and optimal operation sequences for the asset systems, they struggled to get sufficient high-quality data because neither did the product team care much about data veracity nor did the platform team. As a result of all of this, tens of millions of dollars of investment into technology had to be refactored to resolve the issues. This is not an isolated case; this is the story of nearly every business that faces organizational dissonance.

 MOTIVATING THE INDIVIDUALS AND MANAGING THE TEAMS

People working in the AI space are highly valued today because of their specialization and scarcity. We have seen earlier in the chapter that AI-driven businesses are a bit different and operate at a different speed; consequently, the people driving the AI initiatives also demonstrate similar differences in terms of their behavior and approach to work. Such people get stifled by organizational hierarchies but will often exhibit respect for authority and structure. Sometimes they will expect it to reign in the chaos they have to face in their pursuits. They usually do not get very excited by normal motivational incentives like financial or positional rewards. They might be reticent at times, but they like to share and collaborate and be generally helpful to others in the right environment.

Here we share 10 best practices that we have talked about in our previous books on the same topic around big data and IoT (the same are true for motivating people working in AI and other digital technologies):

1. **Incentivize people on the realized and forecasted benefits.** Most incentive schemes are based on simplistic revenue, profitability, productivity, and customer satisfaction goals. While these are important for every business, in AI-driven ones there will be a lag before you see the significant impact of those parameters. On the other hand, if you can quickly create and deploy models for growing the business or improving the profit margins, you have increased the chances of long-term success. Incentivizing the development and deployment of growth models through scalable solutions will drive positive reinforcement both for the people and the business.
2. **Provide opportunities for learning new technologies and gaining new experiences.** There is a lot of new development happening in this space both in terms of technology and business models. The more people learn, the more they will be able to apply these better for your benefit. This will also help them be current and keep your business fresh. Send your people to conferences and trade shows; let them learn from competitors, suppliers, and adjacent industries. Even if you operate in industrial Internet space, participate in consumer electronics shows; there is more voluminous adoption of new technologies there. IoT conferences are another good place to see new uses of technologies and applications. Organize training or send your teams outside for training to upskill them. Your people will appreciate that you are unleashing their potential.
3. **Allow for experimentation.** Traditional business management principles are designed to ensure higher degrees of predictability in every aspect – be it product development or sales or customer service. These are important, but a lot of exploration is required for differentiating and disrupting using AI. So, you need to allow for some level of experimentation with your team. You must build such allowances for innovation in your business model and plan design. Most successful AI-businesses have been driven by innovation and adapted based on learnings.
4. **Create opportunities for demonstrating thought leadership and technology excellence.** Your team believes that they are working on cutting-edge technologies and businesses that are changing the world. Feed their feeling by encouraging them to share their thought leadership and technology excellence with the rest of the world, without of course compromising any competitive advantages. There are several ways of doing this: filing for patents, publishing whitepapers or case studies, and speaking at conferences. These are relatively low-cost methods. They also help with your company's or institution's branding and marketing efforts. Patents also contribute to your organizational valuation. Provide financial incentives by sponsoring such participation in patents, PR, and publications.
5. **Enable learning firsthand about the impact of their efforts on customers and channel partners.** Let your team walk in the shoes of your customers and the various routes your products reach the customers. They will develop a much better appreciation of the problems they are solving or can solve. This will trigger many new ideas and possibilities. Do not leave this exercise only to UX researchers and designers. In traditional businesses, such activities are limited to a select few from product marketing. When markets

and businesses are well established, you can afford to have limited experiential learning; for evolving markets and opportunities, experiential learning is existential.

6. **Reward collaboration.** Multiple skills and efforts need to converge for a successful AI business to emerge, we have discussed this extensively so far. So, you need to encourage and reward collaboration within the team and across boundaries in your organization. Sometimes your team will reach out to the broader ecosystem and find unique capabilities that can add to your offering portfolio; appreciate those efforts. If people express a desire for cross-platform or discipline learning, help them broaden their horizons and they will get better at their core job.

7. **Celebrate successes where the impact is felt by other parts of the business.** In certain scenarios, the immediate and direct beneficiary of your AI efforts might be a more traditional line of business. Therefore you may not see the impact for your group directly. Even in such cases, celebrate the wins of others which you have helped engineer.

8. **Commend if the team makes course corrections and internalizes learnings based on failed experiments.** Keeping in line with the spirit of experimentation and innovation, you will likely experience failure on certain occasions. If your team can understand what leads to the failures and modify their approach to avoid them in the future, celebrate them. Doing so will promote a learning organization that behaves responsibly.

9. **Do not stifle creativity and speed through organizational hierarchies and archaic processes.** This is a sure killer for any entrepreneurial initiative, which you need in hordes to build and grow your AI initiatives and their business impact. Hence, you need to be careful in choosing your managerial and oversight staff. Often if they lack self-confidence and contextual understanding, they buy time and increase their perceived value by introducing multiple checkpoints which may not be necessarily adding value to the business. Modular self-contained and self-organizing teams demonstrate greater levels of accountability and perform better.

10. **Get only the best talent.** This has multiple benefits. You will develop your AI ecosystem and business faster, potentially realizing business value quicker. Your team will respect the talent and accelerate their learning. They will have a few competitive behaviors and be motivated to always excel, keeping their edge. You want to make an impact fast and possibly first, so you can little afford not to have the best people working on your problems.

 SUMMARY

In this chapter we started the discussion by setting the context of how AI programs differ from other technology transformation initiatives. With that as the basis, we delved deeper into the technical as well as leadership competencies. We introduced an easy yet effective competency management program to ensure that skills and capacity are always maintained at the optimum required levels. The decision to build the skills internally or acquire them through inorganic routes or get them by partnering depends on organizational maturity. However, there are a few specific business and technical skills that are core to the transformation program that should always be held closely in-house. With every new technology hype cycle, new leadership roles are created. In the last several years we have seen the emergence of CDO in addition to the more traditional roles of CIO and CTO. Several organizations are struggling to decide which leadership model is the best. In this chapter we have shared our framework to help make that decision. Finally, we discussed the various best practices for organizing teams for success and motivating the highly coveted staff involved with AI programs.

Managing talent is always harder than managing technology. The success of AI and digital transformation initiatives depends a lot on the quality of the team, how well it works together, and most importantly the leadership from the top. Taking about the right digital leadership attributes, Michael Nilles, CDIO of Henkel, and one of the most successful digital leaders, says,

It's not so important if the digital leader has been working in IT, Tech or Business before; most important is the personality and track record in leading company-wide transformative change initiatives. Inspiring an organization for the bigger vision, creating unity-of-effort between organizational silos, and taking accountability for delivering on the vision is essential.

On the often-debated topic of keeping or combining the CIO and CDO function, he has a very clear opinion: "Becoming a digital business champion in your industries requires innovation power, agility, and speed. Joining forces under one leader will give you the necessary firepower."

Talking about his takeaway as a leader in digital transformation, Silvio Napoli, chairman of the board of directors of Schindler, says,

Remaining modest is key, be it in science or in driving innovation. Evolving a global industrial company into a data-driven business requires courage and persistence to push into the – often uncomfortable – unknown. As with any transformation, you need to have a clear vision and goals. How can new technology be used to benefit customers, passengers, and employees? What does it take to adapt? Agility and speed are essential for success. In this environment, fast fish eat slow fish. Digital transformation is also a great catalyst for cultural change, forcing organizations to break down silos and to embrace a new openness to learn and adapt.

In our final chapter we will tackle the very critical topic of change management.

REFERENCES

(1) "General System Theory: Foundations, Development, Applications"; Karl Ludwig von Bertalanffy; 1968.
(2) "The History of Coworking"; *Coworking Resources*; March 2019.
(3) "Organize for Digital: the CIO/CDO Relationship"; Deloitte Research; December 2018.
(4) "Building the AI-Powered Organization"; Tim Fountaine, Brian McCarthy, and Tamim Saleh; July–August 2019.

CHAPTER 15

Managing Change for AI-Driven Transformation

"It is not the strongest of the species that survives, nor the most intelligent; it is the one most adaptable to change."

—Charles Darwin

INTRODUCTION

Throughout this book we have talked about business transformation. In this summary chapter we will talk about how you manage the transition process so that you can be great at managing today and at the same time build for the future. This requires broader organizational alignment and deep-rooted fundamentals, otherwise the pursuit of the future will distract and destroy today. In writing this chapter we have leveraged some concepts from the chapter "Driving Change Effectively" in *Making Big Data Work for Your Business* by Sudhi Ranjan Sinha.

Often organizations make the mistake of considering AI a technology problem; technology here is a mere enabler. Embracing the true power of AI requires organizations to adapt to different thinking and behavior. Effective change management becomes crucial in such an environment. You need to transition your people and teams to the future state of business enabled by AI. In his *HBR* blog on "Predicting Customer's Behavior," Alex Pentland made a profound observation: "Behavior is largely determined by social context." He further goes on to say in the same article that "markets are not just about rules or algorithms; they are about people and algorithms together." AI can give insights into what to change; it is up to the people in your business to change something.

Change management as a formal discipline of study and practice is many decades old. In the early 1960s, some management thinkers started discussing change management concepts, best practices, and significance for sustainable business impact. Julien Phillips from McKinsey is rumored to have published the first change management[1] model in 1982 in the *Human Resource*

Management journal. Since then, a lot has been written and talked about regarding effective change management. Even industry- and context-specific models have been developed. In the area of AI, there is no established change management framework, but the topic is of the highest significance because of the quantum, depth, and breadth of changes and their impact. In this chapter, we will illustrate how to put in context the changes ushered in by AI for your organization and then equip you with a framework to manage the change process.

We shall cover the following topics in this chapter:

■ Understanding changes and their significance in business flow caused by AI
■ Thinking through the significance of changes
■ Building the IMMERSE framework for managing change: Identify, Modulate, Mitigate, Educate, Roleplay, Show, Effect
■ Creating stakeholder groups to drive change
■ Preventing barriers to change management

 ## UNDERSTANDING CHANGES CAUSED BY AI

As we have recognized throughout this book, AI is driving fundamental changes in businesses and our lives. In the previous chapter, we extensively discussed the attributes that AI-driven digital businesses exhibit. Now let us reflect on some deeper nuances of change that are introduced by AI.

Businesses and their processes have to anticipate and adapt instead of just reacting to predefined rules.
AI enables the decision-making process, whether of a computer program or an organization, to anticipate a future state and understand the implications of a course of action leading to that future state. This reduces reliance on past knowledge and predetermined rules to react to an evolving situation, a method that is largely thought to be less effective. This also implies that correlation derived from data is taking center stage over the historical understanding of causality.

Fast and effective processing of a lot of data can now accurately predict what is going to happen next without understanding deeply why it is happening. So, the value of evolving data is taking precedence over static knowledge acquired through a lot of hard work, perseverance, and significant investment in developmental programs. Prof. Mayer-Schoenberger, one of the foremost thought leaders on Big Data, remarks,[2] "Correlations let us analyze a phenomenon not by shedding light on its inner workings but by identifying a useful proxy for it."

This change requires organizations to develop new skills and archive some of the old competencies. For example, in earlier times, retail companies employed armies of market research analysts who would go door to door to talk to hundreds and thousands of customers; now these companies rely more on statisticians and behavioral scientists. Although decision-making processes previously relied on the knowledge and understanding possessed by groups or individuals who could help with causality analysis, answering the *why* is now going to also rely on possible outcome scenarios that the data is predicting. The shift can create instability and insecurity in groups of people who were previously considered the custodians of formal and tribal organizational or business knowledge. The shift is also equally critical for executives who have to use gut feel to a lesser extent in the decision-making process.

Being in an anticipatory and adaptive mode also requires organizations to be more agile.

Intuition is being replaced with data-driven insights.

For a long time now, a managerial sixth sense has been celebrated as a key to the accelerated growth of both individuals and organizations. In our opinion, the sixth sense is nothing more than a significantly above-average ability to process and analyze data that some people have cultivated. AI is enabling that in a more structured, systematic, and repeatable manner. Therefore more businesses and business leaders are tilting toward AI-enabled deductive reasoning compared to more anecdotal inductive reasoning.

Inductive reasoning is a bottom-up approach of looking at specific observations and drawing broad-spectrum general conclusions based on them. Deductive reasoning is just the opposite. You start with a broad-level hypothesis, then prove or disprove it by applying data-based testing to it, a more top-down approach. In the inductive reasoning approach all your premises, observations, and hypotheses might be true, but the conclusion can still come out false; on the other hand, with the deductive reasoning approach, all your initial hypotheses and observations have to be true for the conclusion to be true. Philosophers like David Hume[3] and Karl Popper[4] have critiqued inductive reasoning to be limiting as people draw conclusions based on limited everyday experience and limited data from our current knowledge range. In today's business environment of ever-increasing complexity and interdependence, deductive reasoning is becoming critical to managing the intricacies.

This shift requires managers to rely less on their intuition and past experiences and depend more on data and insights from it. This change is particularly difficult because large segments of the society and our educational systems are based on inductive reasoning while deductive reasoning has remained more of an academic or higher research endeavor. We have been raised on inductive reasoning and now we are being asked to look beyond.

This shift also requires a very fundamental cultural shift to become truly data-driven. Many business leaders consider that asking for lots of data, having lots of data, and requiring lots of data to back up the decision-making process makes for a data-driven company; quite the contrary. In a data-driven culture, people do not pound on the desk talking about the significance of data; rather they intimately understand the availability, significance, boundaries, and shades of different types of data.

Collaboration and convergence are key to getting the most out of data and analytics.

Great insights will require multiple disciplines, different types of data, and different ways of thinking to come together. This will require more flexible team formations and agile ways of working and collaborating without much process overhead. The drive and desire for collaboration have to be completely intuitive and nonintrusive.

Collaboration is an element of organizational culture, frequently supported by enabling tools and processes. For collaboration to work effectively, incentive structures for people, functions, and processes have to be designed in a manner that does not act against shared or broader goals.

Beyond collaboration, in the AI-driven digital businesses we see a deep convergence among different components of the business: the brand, the business process, customer engagement, hardware, software, people's capabilities, and every other part of the organization.

Ultimately, collaboration and convergence lead to a continuous focus on value creation for the customer. In today's device-intensive digital world, people's attention span is shrinking fast. So not only do we have to keep on creating new and increasing value for customers, but we must also employ new techniques to keep the customer engaged.

There is a need for constant vigilance on the competitive landscape and emerging disruptions.

AI has been a great leveler of capabilities. The era of Big Data several years ago ensured that there is enough awareness about data and how to leverage it. With this focus on Big Data there were several tools and capabilities to effectively manage structured/unstructured and streaming/static and handle other complexities around large volumes and varieties of data. Subsequently, during the IoT focus, technology progressed further to create more granular-level data from different generation points, capture it, and transmit it for further processing. Finally, in today's algorithmic age, AI-algorithms step in with all the data and processing capability to generate insights.

Companies initially created a competitive advantage by lording over data and connectivity. However, huge volumes of data for many industries and problem areas are becoming available easily and inexpensively. Similarly, connectivity and communication methods are becoming more open and transportable. So a lot of new players can effectively use data and connectivity to analyze, create insights, and come up with new models for creating value. Therefore, companies need to constantly look out for new emerging players and disruptive business models that can negatively impact their prospects.

THE SIGNIFICANCE OF CHANGES

Failing to manage the changes effectively will either put organizations at risk because of traditional competition and adjacent players, or nontraditional competitors who use AI and digital technologies more effectively can put the organizations' business model and long-term viability at risk.

One of the earliest and still very interesting examples in this context is how online advertising changed. When online advertising was first introduced, online platforms used to push content based on some prearrangements with sponsor companies. So, all of us visiting a particular site at a particular time would see the same advertisements. The ad space would be auctioned or sold in a bulk or spot deal, which used to be predetermined for time, duration, and money.

Leading-edge companies in this space take a very different approach now. As soon as they see a user loading a page, they do real-time analytics on the user profile, reference it to past activity, and create preference profiles. On a real-time basis, they auction these preferences for ad-push to sponsoring content providers or brokers. The participants respond to the auctions. The successful bidder's advertisements are shown by the time the user has loaded the page, all happening in less than a second. So now you and I will see different ads while visiting the same site at the same time. As a corollary, you will also see similar-themed ads running while you are visiting different websites. In fact, for the past several months since we have been working on this book, every time we go to the Internet, even to news sites, we always see an AI ad, mostly related to learning or some new platform because these are the other searches that we have done! There are very sophisticated AI engines running in the background that are making sense of all of this streaming data on a real-time basis and deciding which advertisements users might be interested in.

In this example, there are four changes which AI has introduced:

1. New business models around dynamic real-time auctions
2. Incentive models for participants in the process
3. Operating processes required by companies auctioning the ad slot and those responding to the auction
4. Skills required for analysis and response

Our experience and research demonstrate that AI always brings changes in the context of the above four dimensions. Previously such decisions were made by people who were considered gurus who understood consumer behaviors, trends, and user preferences. Now we need new skills around analytics, and also need to use people will legacy skills around understanding consumer behaviors in a different way. Changes brought by technology are often rapid. But AI, when it gains more momentum in mainstream businesses, will bring changes at lightning speed.

Changes have to be identified and dealt with in the context of business models, people, organization structures, and operating processes concerning skills and incentives.

 ## APPLYING THE IMMERSE FRAMEWORK FOR MANAGING CHANGE

Now you have a good understanding of most of the changes in your world that AI is causing. Right away the question is, how do you take all of these changes and manage them for your business? There are many change management methodologies and frameworks which you can adopt as well. Holger Nauheimer, a famed change management consultant and author, has created a collection of tools, methodologies, and strategies for change management entitled *The Change Management Toolbook*, which is available for free download.

We have not found any specific ones developed for AI initiatives, but we will now introduce a framework called IMMERSE to help you manage such changes. We have found this quite effective for various digital initiatives. We applied it first for several Big Data transformations and then for building several IoT businesses. IMMERSE stands for Identify, Modulate, Mitigate, Roleplay, Educate, Show, and finally, Effect. We believe these are the various stages an individual or a team has to go through in the change process. This framework is a progressive, sequential one that you should run in iterations to improve and make it sustainable. Figure 15.1 presents a summarized view of how this process works.

Managing change is a process, not an event. To make it effective, you start at one point and keep improvising as you go along based on the feedback and effectiveness experienced.

Identify

The first step in this process is to identify the changes. You need to ascertain the changes that are happening at the industry level, what your competition is doing, and what is altering within

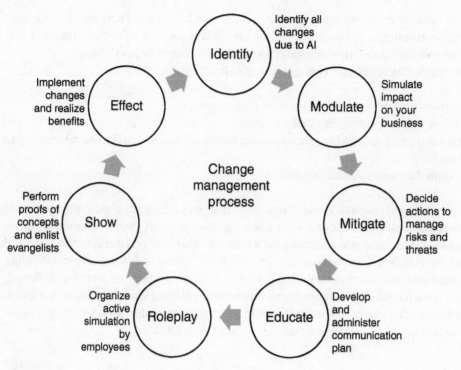

FIGURE 15.1   IMMERSE Change Management Framework

your business. As mentioned earlier, the changes have to be identified in the context of business models, operating processes, organization structures, individual roles and responsibilities, and incentive models in the industry and for your people.

Five key questions you need to ask at this stage are:

1. **How is the industry changing?** Here you need to reflect on the changing business models, trends, products and services, customer expectations and engagement, and convergence or divergences with other industries. You need to paint a macro picture that will build a compass or baseline for consideration to help you to deep-dive into the other questions.
2. **What are the competitive actions?** How are existing players responding to the changing business models and operating processes? You should find out what your traditional competitors are doing to take advantage of data and analytics. You need to research how the existing players are responding to the changing business models and operating processes. It is difficult to do so, but immensely useful if you can find out the reasons behind their particular actions or approach. To get this information, you could:
   a. Start with annual and quarterly reports of the company along with the corresponding analyst briefings.
   b. Check out on the Internet what employees of the organization are publishing on.
   c. Listen to what people from these companies are presenting in the different industry conferences and forums.

    d. Browse through social media for relevant forums to see what kinds of discussions the employees of those organizations are engaging in.

    e. Talk to people in the company without violating any confidentiality.

    f. Talk to the industry influencers – they seem to know everything going on everywhere!

3. **Who are the emerging new players?** Once you have completed the analysis for your existing competitors, scan the horizon for the ones that are potentially going to pose competitive threats for you in the future. They can be small niche players today with dreams of getting bigger tomorrow; they can be adjacent players in your industry; they can even belong to completely nonrelated industries from the current context. If your business belongs to one of these categories, think about the traditional players. Build and run with as many scenarios as you possibly can; ultimately only the paranoid survive.

4. **How are industry economics getting impacted?** Think carefully about how data and analytics are changing how companies make money in your industry. Here you also need to think about new incentive models getting introduced for the ecosystem participants. You need to ask questions like do your customers expect you to incentivize them for acquiring data, and are there ways you can pay for the data and connectivity infrastructure through the value of analytics? Make all such inquiries now. As you do this, go back and check whether you have incorporated these considerations in your value and benefits calculations discussed in the previous chapter.

5. **What are the possible impact areas for your business?** AI may not be affecting all parts of your business now; you need to know which are the most impacted. This will help you focus your energies on a more manageable effort. Do not worry about pinpointing the impact level yet; we will tackle that in the next step. Presently you need to have an exhaustive understanding of all the aspects of your business getting impacted significantly.

Modulate

Next, you need to get more specific in simulating how the changes are going to impact your business. In doing so, you need to answer these five questions:

1. **What is the urgency for you to change?** You need to understand how long you can continue to sustain and/or grow by remaining immune to these changes. Typically, if you have a very large business or are in a very niche market with strong demand, you will be able to go longer without changing, but for sure you will be impacted – later if not sooner. You need to understand the timing so that you can plan and deploy your change actions accordingly.

2. **How are your core competencies and key differentiators impacted by this changing ecosystem?** Every successful organization has some core competencies which are difficult for others to emulate; you also have some. Similarly, every successful business will have some strong differentiators which attract customers to them. You need to take stock of those core competencies and differentiators and simulate where they will stand with all the changes being introduced by AI.

3. **What are the financial implications of your identified impact areas?** In the previous stage, you identified the impact areas. Now put a number to those. You should consider revenue, profit, and market share impact, all of them in this calculation.

4. **What are the foreseeable risks if you change?** If your business is working very well, you and your superiors might be averse to change unless there is a compelling reason. Usually, the perceived risks of introducing abrupt or disruptive changes reduce the propensity for change. So you need to understand and modulate these scenarios well.

5. **What are your organizational reserves to deal with the change?** You must know your bandwidth to accommodate the fallout of any change or decision not to change. In doing so, you need to consider financial reserves as well as your talent availability. You should ponder how much money and manpower you have to withstand the changing ecosystem.

Mitigate

In the third step you determine your mitigation strategies for all the perceived risks. Once you know the business areas and threats posed by AI for those business areas, you contemplate making changes in the following five aspects of your business:

1. **What are the required business model changes?** In the business model, you need to primarily focus on how your business makes money and engages with customers and suppliers to do so. All your revenue generation streams and steps should be part of this study. This will include the different products and services you offer to your customers, how they perceive value in them, and how they are priced and delivered to customers.

2. **What are the required operating model changes?** In the operating model, you look at the product or service delivery food chain. You should account for all internal processes and activities involved leading to your engagement with the customer. You must take into account the various departments and functions in your business that are involved in these processes. Normally each process or activity will have some outcome metrics; you need to reflect on whether any of these are changing, and if so, what the new metrics and their threshold values are.

3. **What are the organizational structure changes?** Now you plot the impact of AI interventions on your current organizational structure and how it needs to change to absorb the impact. Often you will create new roles and functions while making some of the old ones redundant as necessitated by your business model or operating model changes. In the organizational structure, you also need to consider the flow of information between various parts and layers of the organization. Before you think of the changes, it is recommended that you start with a clean slate, keeping only the customer and your end objectives in mind. Then overlay your current organization on that model to understand the required changes. This approach is useful to limit the influences of current inefficiencies.

4. **What new skills do you need to instill in your people?** Once you know the model and structure changes, translate those into what people need to do differently now. This will lead you to the new skills and behavioral competencies required in your employees. You need to assess which gaps you can cover through training and which skills you need to acquire afresh. Sometimes doing a comprehensive skills inventory at this stage is useful because you may uncover some skills and talent existing in your business that might help you further the AI program.

5. **How do you excite people with new incentive models?** Ecosystem players in your business, especially your employees and suppliers (if you have any), understand how you

value their performance and contribution through the compensation and incentive models you have in place. If you are requiring them to change their current behavior and actions, you need to tweak your compensation and incentive programs to reflect that.

Educate

Once you have identified the changes, understood their impact, and created a plan for readying your business for the amended ecosystem, you need to develop a communication and training package to help your employees understand the changes. We will discuss more of the development of this package in the next chapter. Once it is ready, you need to create a mechanism to capture how the education process is working. Ten key things you need to cover in the educate stage are:

1. **What is AI and how is it impacting the world?** Define AI, share examples of AI from the real world, and discuss a few examples of new businesses or business models that have been made possible by AI. This is an introductory session, so keep it as nontechnical as possible. Use examples from everyday life and your business world to help people put into context what you are saying.

2. **How can data sciences and advanced analytics help businesses?** Use examples from different industries to demonstrate how different companies created new customers or created new value for existing customers and increased their business or increased their competitiveness.

3. **What are the changes in your industry driven by AI?** If you have examples of AI being applied in your industry, talk about them here. Discuss the implications of AI for your industry – either in terms of business models, or markets, or operating processes. It is important to help people paint a picture of what the industry is going to look like in the future. If you foresee new areas of competition, talk about them and their effect.

4. **How is your company planning to respond to these changes?** Talk about the specific initiatives in your company to address these industry-level changes. It would be great to showcase your business's track record of mitigating external challenges. Reaffirm your confidence in the AI initiatives and explain to people how it is solving your challenges.

5. **What impact do these changes have for the individual employees and the teams they belong to?** In a changing environment, people are most concerned about the impact on them. Here you need to discuss the changes in organizational structures and operational processes mostly. Make the discussion as specific to your audience as possible. Transparency leads to comfort and employee alignment in these situations.

6. **What new skills and competencies do they need to learn to be more successful in the AI world and how do they take advantage of data and analytics to perform better?** It is relatively easy for people to understand that change is impacting them, but rarely do they appreciate that they also need to change; they need to learn new things and use new tools. Use a lot of examples and specifics when talking about these topics. Make this more of a show-and-tell session rather than a presentation-loaded session.

7. **What are the behavioral changes expected in the employees as a result of the AI initiatives?** It is not enough for people to learn new skills and use new tools to effectively use AI. Your employees will now need to think and behave differently as well. This is probably

the most difficult part of the change management process, especially for people with a lot of legacy in your business. Explaining the rationale for behavior change and using examples will make the process effective. Try and get influencers and opinion makers from among your employee base to be your advocates.

8. **What will the company look like in the future as a result of these AI initiatives?** Your employees will commit better to the change process if they see a bright future ahead; they tie their fortunes and wellbeing to those of your company. So, simulate the environment to show how AI is going to transform the company in the future and what it will look like. Imagine a day in the life of your employees today, and then show a day in the life of a similar employee in the future. Create similar examples with customers as the focal point. These will help drive the message.

9. **Why is AI so crucial for your business?** For anything new being introduced, multiple reinforcements always help strengthen the assimilation process. Now summarize all the benefits of AI for your business.

10. **What are the consequences of not responding to the changes?** This step is to reinforce the urgency and criticality of AI for your business. In some of the earlier steps you created a sense of excitement, a sense of accomplishment, a sense of security in your employees; now do the reverse. These opposing emotions will drive the message hard.

Roleplay

To help people absorb the changes, we have seen that one of the most effective methods is to make employees do some roleplay simulations in the new changing world. This helps them internalize what has been shared during the educate phase and makes it stick for a long time. There are many popular techniques for roleplaying – one of our personal favorites is War Games. You divide your team into groups and they go through three exercises:

1. First, they think and behave like your customers to identify what are some of the emerging expectations that can be fulfilled using AI. It is important to develop examples of how their operations can be positively impacted by using AI in your products and services.

2. Next, they play the role of different competitors and create scenarios of how they will develop and implement strategies to win in the marketplace.

3. Finally, they apply AI to transform your business in responding to changing customer expectations and competitive actions.

This approach also helps your people to get a rounded perspective of the changing world. Ideally, these roleplay sessions should be held offsite so that the normal business environment does not influence their thinking, and neither are they distracted by their normal duties. Each roleplay should last one or two days. Depending on the quantum of changes, you may want to repeat these at some interval for better assimilation. Your change leader ideally should be able to play the role of a facilitator. But get a professional facilitator if you need one and can afford one.

Show

This is a critical stage for you to convert nonbelievers or difficult-to-change people in your organization. You can use the success stories from some pilot projects to do so. Even for believers, you need to reinforce their faith; you need to help them improve their understanding. You start creating brand ambassadors for your AI initiative in the show stage. While doing your campaigns, please keep in mind these six key points:

1. Talk about successes with tangible results.
2. Get the project team to interact with people; if you can, get your customers (even if internal) as well.
3. Talk to people about the future roadmap.
4. Create a simulated environment for future projects.
5. Contextualize the changes and benefits as they impact the lives of your audience.
6. Create an opportunity for people to have follow-up conversations with you.

Effect

The last stage is your realization phase where you implement the changes, capture the benefits, and keep adapting to sustain the benefits. Before you start in this phase, be clear to identify the key metrics you will use to measure and monitor success. Everybody involved with the initiative needs to be aligned on the definition and measurement methodologies for the metrics upfront to avoid any disappointment later. Your realization may extend for a long period, but do define a specific exit date for this phase. This will help you with proper project closure and handover to business as usual. You also need to set up the review schedule for the realization activities, preferably outlining the agenda for the review sessions. Such a step will provide more predictability to this phase and ensure that people are committed to participating in the process.

Your typical effect stage will comprise three cyclical activities: implement, review, and tweak. You will implement the new business models, operating processes, and other changes first; then after some passage of time, say every three months, review the impact of the changes on your performance metrics; then tweak either the analytics or the processes to get better results. If you see sustained lack of success, do not be afraid to either scrap the project or make major course corrections.

 CREATING STAKEHOLDER-GROUPS TO DRIVE CHANGE

Change management has been widely accepted as one of the most, if not the most important criteria for success with any AI and digital transformation initiative. This is the number-one responsibility for the chief digital offer or the chief executive officer ultimately driving the initiative. You should have dedicated people with professional change management experience to make the effort effective. If the impact or span of the change is big, that is, if it crosses over multiple departments and involves hundreds of people, it will take more than a year to realize the benefits; we recommend you create some stakeholder-groups to make the change management more effective and pervasive.

We recommend you create not more than three such groups: project group, workgroup, and review group.

1. **Project group**
   This is your core project team. This team is primarily responsible for achieving the project objectives but should hand over the sustenance responsibilities to the workgroup.

2. **Workgroup**

This is the implementation team from your business that will take forward the changes brought by AI. This is the team that will experience the output of AI efforts every day. The project team will focus on the technical aspects of the project while the workgroup will focus more on the actual usage of the data and analytics regularly. As part of the project you may bring such people into your team, but they need to go back to the business once the project is over. You need to be clear upfront on the division of roles and responsibilities along with the schedule for the project group and the workgroup.

3. **Review group**

This is the management group that is responsible for strategy, direction, monitoring, and facilitation. You should involve the person in charge of your business (it could be you), leaders of the various functional groups which support your business, and somebody from your business who can adequately represent the customer view. This team is different from your normal project steering committees in that they are expected to have more involved participation rather than being a reporting and approving point.

We feel you should not call any of these groups "committees" because that has strong bureaucratic connotations. Members of each group need to be personally accountable for the results of their teams and that should be included in their goal-sheets.

 ## PREVENTING BARRIERS TO CHANGE MANAGEMENT

We have widely studied various initiatives to understand not only what makes change management successful, but also what are the major derailers. Interestingly, even though the organizational context or application area may be very different, the derailers are uncannily common. Here are the top four:

1. **Weak tone at the top.**

Many surveys have revealed that the top leadership of most businesses believes AI will significantly impact their future. However, we frequently find that the top-intent does not translate to broader organizational calls to action. This happens because the tone at the top remains limited to merely talking about the importance and intent of an AI-driven digital organization. In organizations where the top leaders personally talk with more depth, giving details and examples in the context of the company and the industry, the larger organization starts to buy in and they and their employees understand the criticality of the transformation.

A robust tone at the top is not easy to achieve; it requires a significant investment of time from the top management in personally learning and getting involved. They will have to do it not only once or twice but over a sustained period. Finding time and juggling priorities at these levels is very difficult, but if the impact of the transformation or lack thereof is going to be serious, the senior leadership has to make the call. This also requires them to be vulnerable in learning new techniques, new skills, and challenging a lot of practices that were successful in the past. Without fail we have seen a strong tone and deep engagement from the top as the common factor in all successful initiatives.

2. **Lack of digitization in the business processes and business models.**
   Even if there is a strong tone at the top, many initiatives fail because the infrastructure to support the AI-led transformation is deficient. This happens when the business processes and the enabling business systems are not fully digitized. This also happens when business models are not digitally oriented.

   In a recent example, during the turbulence of the financial markets due to the Coronavirus crisis, a very large bank wanted to use AI to advise high-net-worth investors (HNIs) to diversify their holdings to maximize their future gains. This initiative would have led to more wealth creation by the HNIs as well as diversifying and deepening their relationship with the bank. This initiative would have involved the HNIs engaging in new investment instruments with the bank. Right at the launch, everybody realized that to open a new investment instrument with the bank, customers had to fill in a form manually which had to be manually processed by a back-office function. Unfortunately, due to the lockdown that happened in the country of operation of the bank, the physical handling of forms was not possible and the initiative fell flat. This bank incidentally had been recognized for its focus on online banking and overall digitization efforts for several years; they failed in this case at a very opportune moment because one critical process was not digitized. There are countless examples like this in every industry.

3. **Inadequate focus on education.**
   Throughout this book, we have stressed the criticality of improving digital and analytical literacy in organizations for driving successful transformation programs. AI and digital impact nearly everybody in the organization; the success of the initiative beyond the pilot stages depends on the capability of the people beyond the core project team. We have seen too many occasions where companies have been lacking in this regard. Many reasons contribute to flawed focus on education: focusing only on the competency of the core team and those who work closely with them, pursuing time-consuming and expensive methods of learning, trying to boil the ocean, assuming one round of learning interventions will be successful, and so on. Education is an iterative, progressive process in the same manner change management is and needs its dedicated focus.

4. **Unsupportive culture.**
   Culture and change management go hand in hand. They have a synergistic relationship and are part of the same virtuous cycle. For AI and digital initiatives to survive and thrive in an organization, the culture must be a continuous learning one with a high tolerance for experimentation and failure and the ability to drive quick and collaborative decision making, always having one eye on the future while focusing the other eye on today. A supportive culture can amplify the impact of AI and digital transformation.

 SUMMARY

Digital transformation is a vital imperative for every business today, especially after the recent COVID-19 crisis. The present situation has further heightened the need to change, even accelerate it where possible. Change management is the crucible for the success of any transformation initiative and substantive AI initiatives. In this chapter, we have explored various facets of it.

We started our discussion with understanding what is driving the change followed by the significance of the change. We have to fine-tune our business models and operating models to make them more adaptive and responsive to data-driven insights, driving interdisciplinary convergence and always being vigilant about the changing external environment. As you go through the transformation journey, changes will be substantive and uncomfortable, so setting the tone at the top and leading from the front will become crucial for sustainable success.

The IMMERSE framework is an effective methodical tool to help navigate the change process. It forces people to:

- Identify all dimensions of change.
- Modulate the impact of the change on their business context and capabilities.
- Identify mitigation strategies through a business model, operating model, and organizational changes.
- Educate the leadership as well as the broader organization.
- Roleplay the future state with a customer-back approach.
- Show people across the organization the benefits of the change.
- Effect the change.

Engagement in the change management process has to be across the organization, but the intensity of the change program will have to be calibrated with the impact of the transformation. Finally, we discussed the impediments to change around leadership engagement, organizational education, supporting culture, and lack of digitization of the business process.

AI and digital transformation are going to be an integral part of our lives. Let us embrace the changes they bring to build better businesses and make a better world.

As an example, we set a vision with entire Bee'ah team to become a leading digital platform company to drive sustainability to the next level for our nations future. One of the key success factors in our journey was to bring all stakeholders together and manage the change. We put a team of young talents from different departments to drive the change and execute our key digital initiatives such as AI-based office of the future and digital waste management platform. In a digital world, if you can't bring data, AI and analytics to every person in the organization to be consumed, no digital transformation project can be successful. That's why we are launching an AI Academy at Bee'ah for the world of sustainability by using our digital learning platform.

 ## REFERENCES

(1) *Enhancing the Effectiveness of Organizational Change Management*; Julien R Phillips; 1983.
(2) *Big Data: A Revolution That Transforms How We Work, Live, and Think*; Prof. Viktor Mayer-Schoenberger, Kenneth Cukier; October 2013.
(3) *An Enquiry Concerning Human Understanding*; David Hume; 1748.
(4) *The Logic of Scientific Discovery*; Karl Popper; 1959.

About the Authors

Sudhi Sinha

Sudhi is a business and technology leader with over 23 years of experience. He specializes in applying abstract technology concepts to different business problems, creating new advantaged economic value models, and delivering long-term sustained organizational results. He presently advises many large multinationals and several digital start-ups on product, business, go-to-market, and technology strategies.

He has previously served as VP and GM of Digital Solutions for Johnson Controls building new data-enabled businesses. Before that he held many senior management roles at Johnson Controls including leading product development and field engineering for the Controls business, leading the Center of Excellence in Engineering, and strategy and business development for several Asian businesses.

He started his career at Tata Consultancy Services where he held many roles with increasing responsibilities including managing large strategic accounts, being responsible for the business in the US Midwest based out of Chicago, running several corporate initiatives, and finally leading the industrial business unit globally.

He has 22 granted and more than 40 pending patents in IoT, big data, and AI. He is the author of two previous books: *Making Big Data Work For Your Business* published by Packt Publishers from the UK in 2014 and *Building An Effective IoT Ecosystem* co-authored with Dr. Youngchoon Park and published by Springer in the US. He has spoken at more than two dozen international conferences and published extensively on IoT and analytics, applying them to industrial and consumer businesses.

Sudhi is the winner of IDG CIO's Ones to Watch Award in 2020, Johnson Controls Innovation Leader of the Year in 2019, Johnson Controls Chairman's Award in 2018, and several other industry recognitions. Sudhi has worked in the US, Europe, and Asia. He currently lives in Mumbai, India. He holds a bachelor's degree in Engineering from Jadavpur University, India, and completed the Wharton-JCI Executive MBA program XLP.

Khaled Al Huraimel

Khaled Al Huraimel is the Group CEO of Bee'ah, and has served in this capacity since August 2009. Under his leadership, Bee'ah has transformed from a waste management company to a sustainability pioneer which is setting new benchmarks for quality of life across the MENA region.

Al Huraimel has been the driving force behind Bee'ah's vision for the future, facilitating the achievement of several remarkable milestones, such as building the first waste-to-energy plant in the Middle East, establishing ION, the first sustainable transport company in the UAE; and founding Evoteq to lead digital transformation in the region.

Taking the helm when Bee'ah was in the preliminary stages of pursuing a zero-waste ambition, Al Huraimel amplified this by implementing state-of-the-art solutions and a unique approach to a circular economy, supporting Bee'ah to establish the UAE's first fully integrated waste management complex and achieve the highest waste diversion rates in the region.

Al Huraimel has led the diversification of Bee'ah's portfolio, investing in ventures ranging from renewable energy to healthcare, mobility, and technology, to execute an all-encompassing master plan to raise living standards across the region. Championing the Middle East's move towards green architectural solutions, Al Huraimel is also overseeing the establishment of Bee'ah's new headquarters. Designed by Zaha Hadid, the sustainable, net-zero energy building is slated to be the smartest office in the region.

Before joining Bee'ah, Al Huraimel held leadership roles at Emirates National Oil Company (ENOC), Nakheel, and Arabian Global Investments, using innovative insights to achieve remarkable results. He has also founded several successful start-ups.

Al Huraimel graduated with a Bachelor's Degree in Marketing from King Fahd University and an MBA from the University of Bradford. He also graduated from the Harvard Business School's prestigious Senior Executive Leadership Program and the Dubai Leaders Programme at the Wharton Business School.

Index